Springer Texts in Business and Economics

More information about this series at http://www.springer.com/series/10099

Ashish Malik
Editor

Strategic Human Resource Management and Employment Relations

An International Perspective

Springer

Editor
Ashish Malik
Faculty of Business and Law, Central Coast Business School
The University of Newcastle
Ourimbah, Central Coast, NSW, Australia

ISSN 2192-4333　　　　　　　ISSN 2192-4341　(electronic)
Springer Texts in Business and Economics
ISBN 978-981-13-4406-0　　　ISBN 978-981-13-0399-9　(eBook)
https://doi.org/10.1007/978-981-13-0399-9

© Springer Nature Singapore Pte Ltd. 2018
Softcover re-print of the Hardcover 1st edition 2018
This work is subject to copyright. All rights are reserved by the Publisher, whether the whole or part of the material is concerned, specifically the rights of translation, reprinting, reuse of illustrations, recitation, broadcasting, reproduction on microfilms or in any other physical way, and transmission or information storage and retrieval, electronic adaptation, computer software, or by similar or dissimilar methodology now known or hereafter developed.
The use of general descriptive names, registered names, trademarks, service marks, etc. in this publication does not imply, even in the absence of a specific statement, that such names are exempt from the relevant protective laws and regulations and therefore free for general use.
The publisher, the authors and the editors are safe to assume that the advice and information in this book are believed to be true and accurate at the date of publication. Neither the publisher nor the authors or the editors give a warranty, express or implied, with respect to the material contained herein or for any errors or omissions that may have been made. The publisher remains neutral with regard to jurisdictional claims in published maps and institutional affiliations.

Printed on acid-free paper

This Springer imprint is published by the registered company Springer Nature Singapore Pte Ltd.
The registered company address is: 152 Beach Road, #21-01/04 Gateway East, Singapore 189721, Singapore

This book is dedicated to all my family members and friends

Foreword

I am pleased to present this timely book by Dr. Ashish Malik for a variety of reasons. First, the content covered and approach adopted by the book is important and germane to managing people from a strategic perspective especially in present uncertain and complex business environment. Second, the book is written by a scholar who is well-informed and well-versed in the field. Dr. Malik's continued focus on strategic human resource management (SHRM) research in an international context, covering high technology and knowledge intensive services industries such as IT, Telecom, Healthcare, and Business Process Outsourcing, has been interwoven in the content and its application in this research-based book. Third, the breadth of SHRM and employment relations (ER) issues covered in the book and the in-depth cases carefully curated from select countries provide critical insights useful for students, academics, and practitioners. It integrates the key learnings of how change and strategic thinking and HRM strategies can have a major impact on people, businesses, and the societies in which we operate.

The book presents a collection of key SHRM and ER topics and focuses extensively on applying research and analysis using a case-study-based learning approach. This blend of problem-based learning and participant-centered learning approaches from a wide range of global SHRM and ER issues is examined using a diverse collection of international case studies. The book has three parts. Part I consists of seven chapters and lays out the key theoretical foundations and underpinnings of SHRM and ER. This part offers a focused research review of the key theoretical approaches in HRM and ER. Part II also comprises of seven chapters and focuses on how from a strategic perspective, leaders and managers may exercise strategic choices in their design and implementation of several HRM practices for achieving the desired goals of their business enterprise. Part III highlights complex SHRM and ER issues using real-life cases studies focusing on content covered in the first two parts of the book. This part features a selection of contemporary research-based case studies from several developed, transitioning, and emerging markets, wherein each country's contextual environment adds to the complexity in undertaking analysis and problem-solving of the issues at hand. The book's unique problem- and case-based learning approach is ideal for engaging in higher-order learning suited for final year or capstone courses in HRM programs. For the less prepared, the book offers the learners advice on how they can use these approaches. Overall, this book presents a well-positioned and exciting view of the businesses of managing people from a strategic perspective incorporating a breadth of examples from the author's own research as well as contributors from a number of countries. I commend this effort and have no doubts that it will find a ready and receptive readership around the world.

50th Anniversary Professor of International HRM   Pawan Budhwar, PhD
Associate Pro Vice Chancellor International (India)
Co-Editor-in-Chief, British Journal of Management
Aston Business School, Aston University, UK

Preface

The theoretical roots for the study of human resource management (HRM) in organisations have existed in the Western contexts for over a century when seminal ideas of influential management thinkers such as Taylor, Drucker and McGregor were in prevalence. Earlier conceptualisations of work and employment adopted a different (pluralist) emphases and focused on terms such as labour welfare, labour relations, personnel management and industrial relations to name a few. One could argue, this view reflected contemporary developments in the field of HRM, albeit with different ideological and philosophical focus that have been in operation for several centuries. For example, in India, work practices were influenced by the ancient ideas of *Chanakya* (also referred to as *Kautilya*), whose pioneering work on *Arthashastra* was regarded as a treatise in the field of economics, politics, military strategy and governance. This seminal work had also developed ideas of organisation and administration in the fourth century BC. Indeed, one only needs to turn back and look at the practices of one of the world's oldest multinational corporation–the erstwhile *East India Company*, which was founded in the early 1600 in India by the British to pursue trade with the East Indies. Even though it ended up trading, in the main, in the Indian subcontinent, its operations spanned across several borders.

Managing people in the colonial era was quite different from how we manage people today. Some might even ask, has the nature of capitalism or business goals changed in principle? If so, what might have caused the change? Were these changes triggered by changes in people's aspirations of seeking better and humane conditions of work and employment? Or, due to changing political agendas, new legislation for protecting workers, change in ideologies and other influences such as religion and industrial revolution? These questions bring to our mind the importance of changes in context and its distinctive and highly variable character.

While the immediate focus of HRM and employment relations (ER) is on managing people and work within an agreed framework of the employer–employee relationship and setting the rules for engaging people and governing their conditions of employment, HRM and ER is also influenced by multiple, direct and indirect factors. These include a range of factors such as different: stakeholders state, regulation, customers and institutions. It is by learning the multiple and specific instances from different contexts that we may be able to generate some generic guidelines for understanding how we manage people and work.

My motivation to write a book that balances theoretical elegance with rich contextual insights of problems HR managers face is partly informed by a belief that is captured in Kurt Lewin's maxim 'there is nothing so practical as good theory' and George Box's aphorism in the study of statistics that 'all models are wrong but some are useful'. Acknowledging the above challenges, the choice of case-based learning is rightly situated for developing skills necessary for the complex nature of what the field of HRM and ER represents.

This book requires some introductory understanding or experience of the core concepts in the study and practice of HRM and ER as well as applying the common principles employed in the use of case-based teaching and learning. The book takes the view that an important source of learning HRM and ER is using a practice-based approach wherein cases from real world can simulate thinking and action on complex HRM and ER problems. By using discussion and participant focused learning approaches, which are essentially a higher order pedagogies, the book offers a distinctive learning opportunity for embedding learning from a range of cases on various aspects of strategic HRM and ER, from local and global contexts, to develop deeper understanding and refining of HR skills.

I hope the learners enjoy the cases from a number of cultural and industry contexts

Ourimbah, Central Coast, NSW, Australia   Ashish Malik

Contents

Part I Theoretical Foundations of SHRM & ER

Introduction... 3
Ashish Malik

HRM and ER: A Strategic Perspective............................. 13
Ashish Malik

Strategic HRM & ER: Best-Practice Versus Best Fit............. 23
Ashish Malik

SHRM & ER: The Resource-Based View........................... 35
Ashish Malik

Institutional Theory and SHRM.................................... 43
Ashish Malik

Strategic Choice and SHRM & ER.................................. 53
Ashish Malik

Professionalism and Ethics... 63
Ashish Malik

Part II HR Profession and Design and Implementation of Strategic HRM and ER Practices

Work Design and HR Planning: A Strategic Perspective........ 75
Ashish Malik

Strategic Performance and Commitment Management.......... 85
Ashish Malik

Strategic Learning and Development.............................. 93
Ashish Malik

Managing Employee Voice... 105
Ashish Malik

Managing Change and HRM 119
Ashish Malik

Strategic Compensation and Benefits Management 133
Ashish Malik

Special Topics in SHRM & ER 141
Ashish Malik

Part III Cases

Case 1: To Cyber-Vet or Not to Cyber-Vet: An Ethics Question for HRM 157
Peter Holland and Debora Jeske

Case 2: Work-Life Balance in an MNE Context 163
Anne Bardoel

Case 3: Crisis and IHRM 169
Konstantinos Tasoulis and Maria Progoulaki

Case 4: Japanese Cross Border M&A and German Target Employee Alienation Issues 175
Ralf Bebenroth and Roman Bartnik

Case 5: Dorian LPG's Rapid Fleet Growth: A Story of Maritime HR Planning and People Management 181
Maria Progoulaki and Konstantinos Tasoulis

Case 6: Appraisal at Systel Technologies 195
Mathew J. Manimala, Malavika Desai, and Divisha Agrawal

Case 7: Patanjali: The Black Swan 209
Shashwat Shukla

Case 8: Recontextualizing Diversity: The German Case 223
Jasmin Mahadevan and Iuliana Ancuţa Ilie

Case 9: Stressed and Demotivated Public Servants… Looking for a (Motivational) Miracle at Paywell Agency 235
S. De Simone, L. Giustiniano, and R. Pinna

Case 10: Managing Change and Employee Well-being in an Italian School: Psychosocial Training Intervention as a Possible Solution 243
S. De Simone, R. Pinna, and L. Giustiniano

Case 11: Gender Inclusive Leadership for Innovation and Change: An HR Head's Reflections 255
Payyazhi Jayashree, Therese Sevaldsen, and Valerie Lindsay

Part I
Theoretical Foundations of SHRM & ER

Introduction

Ashish Malik

Human Resource Management in Context

There are several learnings one can assimilate by studying how changes and differences in an organisation's macro-economic, legal, political, social, cultural and technological context has an impact on managing people, or what we commonly refer to as human resource management and employment relations (HRM & ER). A major case in point from the twenty-first century is the catastrophic impacts of the 2008 global financial crisis (GFC) on managing people in the organisations directly affected by it. Recent research on the topic suggests that in a post-GFC era, multiple HRM approaches were adopted by firms even within one industry (Malik 2013) and in different industry and national contexts (Malik 2017). Some have argued that most of the responses in dealing with the pressures imposed by the GFC had led to long-term negative impacts on employees, wherein these impacts can be largely explained by neoliberal orientation of people who were responsible for causing this crisis (Bolton and Houlihan 2007; Marchington and Kynighou 2012). The approach taken by this book is to embed learning using theoretical insights balanced with learning from case studies from different contexts. I believe a case-based approach is critical in providing insights in applied disciplines such as HRM and ER to allow the learner to engage in higher order learning skills. To this end, this chapter begins with an overview of the case-based approach to learning, highlighting the conditions where such an approach is most effective. The skills of a facilitator of learning are also acknowledged as important in bringing the most out of the specific cases.

A. Malik (✉)
Faculty of Business and Law, Central Coast Business School, The University of Newcastle, Ourimbah, Central Coast, NSW, Australia
e-mail: ashish.malik@newcastle.edu.au

© Springer Nature Singapore Pte Ltd. 2018
A. Malik (ed.), *Strategic Human Resource Management and Employment Relations*, Springer Texts in Business and Economics,
https://doi.org/10.1007/978-981-13-0399-9_1

A Case-Based Approach to Learning Strategic HRM and ER

The use of case studies in teaching has historically been prevalent in Law schools, however, a number of applied disciplines such as business studies, medicine and education have since adopted the use of case studies in their teaching (Merseth 1991). The case-based teaching method though popularised by the Harvard Business and Law school is now used as a common pedagogical (or rather an andragogical) approach in most business programs. There are a number of prescriptions in the way this approach has evolved and how this should be applied to different geographical settings to accommodate the contextual demands of a given program or unit. Implementing a pure "Harvard style" participant-centered learning (PCL) approach using case studies is not always possible or practicable in all contexts because of the contextual factors such as class size, cohort characteristics, resources and other institutional and curriculum-based constraints that often come into play. A variation to the theme is not only necessary but also a pragmatic choice to suit the contextual factors.

Applications of Case Studies

Case studies are typically used to develop students' higher order learning skills of analysis, synthesis, problem-solving and decision-making. This is often done using limited, messy, and sometimes even conflicting information in a case to arrive at a conclusion. One of the key advantages of case-based teaching is that it is useful in developing insights of broader principles for dealing with a given problem, using specific scenarios and facts from 'real life' organisations. A case study without an issue, problem, rule-based analysis or key decision to be resolved does not serve any real purpose from an educational and learning standpoint (Ellet 2007). A well-developed teaching case study is different from a short, end-of-chapter caselet or a half-a-page textbook case, as these latter categories often have little or too simplistic information and generally do not advance multiple skills for higher order learning. This does not mean that short cases should not be used. They have a place and are illustrative. Short cases are also good to embed in adopting this pedagogical approach before learners are introduced to longer and more complex cases. They can and do develop relevant skills as per above, though to a limited extent. A good case study should have enough detail for the learner to make an informed decision but at the same time it should not be too long or easy and straightforward that the learner loses interest because of the limited challenge or excessive information that it offers. A good case study must provide a hook to engage the learner to continue to read and provides sufficient information to undertake problem-solving, analysis and evaluation or, as the case may direct, but without making obvious, what the conclusions are (Ellet 2007).

As noted above, there are many issues to keep in mind before choosing the use of case-based teaching. Briefly these include:

- *Level of the course*- typically well-developed cases work better in post-graduate courses or in the final year courses of undergraduate degrees.
- *Curriculum goals of the unit/program*- the learning goals of a course must support the need for higher order learning, failing which, there might be issues of (mis-)alignment to be dealt with.
- *Culture of case-based teaching at the institution*- this is an important consideration for instructors to bear in mind, especially if there is little or no culture of use of case studies at an institution. In such scenarios, case-based teaching is unlikely to deliver best results. The suggested path is to gradually introduce its application at a program level and have shorter and easier cases in the early stages of the program.
- *Profile of learners*-an understanding of the profile of the adult learners is vital as these profiles vary in each cohort. Typically, a same case can be taught differently to two very dissimilar (with no work experience versus extensive work experience) cohorts of students. The discussion leadership skills, for each cohort required of the facilitator of learning, is vital in striking the right balance. Highly experienced cohort of learners can bring in their depth and breadth of learning for solving the same problem, than learners with little or no experience.
- *Formative versus summative assessment of cases*- it is a good idea to have a balance of formative and summative cases in a course as the former serves as a dry run for what is in store. The former also builds skills and confidence for use of cases across a program or in a unit. Use of case studies in summative assessments is known to increase the learner's motivation. It is also recommended that there be a balance in terms of the mix of cases in a course. For example, the number of summative cases in a module and their levels of complexity. Ideally, the learning should progress from simple to more complex cases, however, this may not be necessary if there is already an established culture of case-based learning at the institution.

Undertaking Case Analysis

Deciding on the adoption of case-based teaching is a key decision and its implementation needs careful consideration. Depending on the purpose of adopting this pedagogical approach, which is usually driven by a course's requirements, its implementation can be adapted to suit the specific learning requirements of a course. As such, this may mean that the skills of the learners, facilitators and assessment strategies will need to be developed accordingly. There are number of commonly used resources available to learners regarding 'how to' analyse cases. Thinking clearly what is the stated or implied in the learning from a given case and its ordering by the instructor can set the tone really well. On a first reading of the case, the reader must identify and develop a description of the common situations and occurrences in a case study (e.g. problems, decisions, evaluations, rules etc) keeping in mind that there are many ways of dealing with each situation. Additionally, in analysing the case, attempts should be made to (1) characterise the situation or task at hand; (2) note the key tasks/questions to be answered, while keeping in mind that there may not necessarily be a single right answer to the posed question. Common tasks and situations in a case include: problem-solving, decision-making, evaluation, rules application and so on. These require undertaking hypothesis generation or problem identification, establishing a decision criteria, evaluation, building a chain of evidence, developing actionable plans and reviewing possible alternatives to the original hypothesis (Ellet 2007: p.28).

Leading the Case Discussion

This is perhaps the most challenging part of the overall approach as its success depends on a number of institutional factors and skills of the learner and facilitator. Implementing case-based learning is not easy especially if there is no established culture of case-based teaching in an institution. Additionally, depending on the intended use of the case study, the facilitator can create an expansive or a restrictive learning experience for the participants. The key guiding principles in most case-based approaches are: preparedness of the learner and the facilitator, participation by all in the class discussions (at an individual and where necessary, by design, at collaborative levels), having patience and avoid jumping to conclusions too prematurely, fostering collaborative discussions and developing an appreciation that there may not always be a single right answer. Such assumptions will facilitate free flow of information, improve listening skills, allows participant contributions and maintain a balance of opposing and sometimes competing views. It goes without saying that such an approach requires facilitator and leaners' attention to micro skills of questioning and responding. The facilitator must also restrain from over participation and must not be biased or prompted by extensive self-participation. Keeping in mind the content covered in Part I and Part II of the book, Part III offers several long case studies from the real world organisations focusing on a range of HRM & ER. Although Parts I and II have a few end-of-chapter cases, the cases in Part III of the book presents an opportunity for learners to explore in greater detail the applied, complex and diverse nature of the field. Christensen and Raynor's (2003) account of why hard-nosed managers should care of management theory in practice is a good read to get convinced of the value-add such an approach might offer.

Overview of the Book

The rest of the book is structured as follows. Chapter "HRM and ER: A Strategic Perspective" begins by explaining the key terms of strategy, HRM and strategic HR. It begins by highlighting that the study of strategic management offers numerous conceptualizations of the term *strategy* and that the study of strategic human resource management and employment relations (SHRM & ER) must seek differentiation and adopt a pluralist approach. This chapter places heavy emphasis on developing a contextual understanding of how people management, strategy and context interact to shape the multiple goals of SHRM&ER.

Chapter "Strategic HRM & ER: Best-Practice Versus Best Fit" builds on the strategic management processes introduced in Chapter "HRM and ER: A Strategic Perspective". In this chapter, a firm's competitive environment is analysed. Managers make informed choices with regard to the nature and extent of their work and employment practices in line with a firm's competitive positioning. The choices that managers exercise in the design and implementation of HR practices need to be grounded in a firm's strategic business environment. While this may sound logical, but there are some schools of thought, such as the best-practice school, which offer a much more prescriptive view. In contrast to the best-practice school, the best-fit school adopts an 'it depends' or a contingency-based approach. The best-fit approach has a number of variants outlining a range of contingency factors on which the design and implementation of HR practices depend. This chapter considers each of these two approaches and its popular variants and its impact on SHRM and ER theory and practice.

Chapter "SHRM & ER: The Resource-Based View" shifts the discussion from an 'outside-in' approach to strategy and HRM to an inside-out approach through the theoretical lens of the resource-based view of the firm (Barney 1991). In this approach, a firm's resources and capabilities form the centre of attention in deciding how firms achieve sustained competitive advantage. Employing the VRIO (valuable, rare, inimitable and organisation) framework, this chapter discusses not just which capabilities matter most, but also how organisations can develop capabilities that are valuable, rare, inimitable and organized in a way that prevents other firms from shaving away the value it has created.

Chapter "Institutional Theory and SHRM" provides an overview of institutional theory and how it applies to the study and practice of SHRM &ER. This chapter explores in detail the contextual environment of a firm with a particular emphasis on the impact of institutional mechanisms in shaping the nature and extent of SHRM practices in an organization. Having explored the major contributors of SHRM schools of thought, this chapter offers a theoretical analysis of institutional theory. Boselie (2010) suggests that firms are affected by a number of circumstances –internal and external to its environment and that is what creates its unique context. In short, Boselie (2010) notes that a firm's internal context, which includes aspects such as its history, socio-technical systems, structure and set of administrative policies that govern its daily workings. The unique ways of conducting its business or its cultural influences is also considered. DiMaggio and Powell (1983) noted two aspects of an organisation's external context. Based on Pauwee (2004) and Boselie (2010: 23), they noted: "a firm's market mechanisms and institutional mechanisms collectively shape its external context." This chapter explores how, through human agency, strategic choices and degree of leeway can be changed and challenged through active and passive developmental approaches to bring about differentiation through HRM & ER practices.

Building on the above idea of strategic choices, Chapter "Strategic Choices Theory and SHRM & ER" explores through the lens of strategic choice theory, how managers implement HRM & ER strategies in a given institutional environment. The key theoretical insights from strategic choice theory are used to analyse the pluralist nature of ER strategies and how choice making occurs in organisations. This chapter highlights that there are several stakeholders that influence choice. We mustn't forget that strategy is not just the exclusive domain of management; even unions have strategies that can have a profound impact in shaping the nature of employment relationships and a range of employment outcomes. A strategic approach to employment relations (ER) describes a pluralist approach taken by managers, which is a longer-term, more thoughtful and consistent approach to the management of its workforce and employment relationships. In other words, ER strategy for managers in business, public sector and most other types of organisations is that part of a firm's strategy that is related to industrial/employment/ employee relations. Depending on the context, it may be a subset of an organization's HR strategy, or separate to and in some cases may even dominate the HR strategy. While this may sound highly analytical, its development and implementation is also fraught with challenges. Also in this chapter, as part of a firm's growth strategies of which internationalization, mergers and acquisitions (M&A) or some form of network of inter-organisational collaboration, we look at how these forms may impact on a firm's international HRM (IHRM) practices. The chapter highlights the differences between an IHRM approach as compared to domestic HRM. M&A as a strategic choice option and its impact in a cross-border context is briefly examined in this chapter.

Chapter "SHRM & ER: Professionalism and Ethics" examines whether a core set of HR competencies are necessary for HR practitioners to successfully design and implement HR policy and practice choices. The literature on this topic shares significant overlaps with the nature of key HR roles and competencies required by HR professionals in a number of countries. This module examines some of these dominant professional HRM and ER competency models. Related to professional competencies is the adherence to a set of ethical standards and professional code of conduct that HR practitioners and managers must demonstrate in their day-to-day decisions about managing people. This chapter highlights the challenges associated with the ethical dilemmas that HR practitioners are confronted with in dealing with the differences in their personal, professional and organizational values and ethical frames.

Chapter "Work Design and HR Planning: A Strategic Perspective" highlights the importance and limits of operational and strategic approaches to HR planning. Following a careful and strategic approach to HR planning, organisations must focus on the design and implementation of work systems that allow firms to manage the duality of organisational flexibility on one hand and employee commitment on the other. Maintaining a strategic approach to HR planning, this chapter also explores strategic issues in recruitment and selection of employees and considers what happens to HRM practices when some firms adopt an internal versus an external orientation to attract and select people.

Chapter "Strategic Performance and Commitment Management" focuses on an important but controversial theme of relationship between performance (at an individual or systems level) and HR practices. While there are several guidelines for motivating people and groups for achieving high performance in an organisational setting, the literature on this topic is voluminous due to the multifaceted nature of performance. At a micro (individual) level performance, there is an established body of literature which highlights the importance of ability, motivation and opportunity enhancing factors as key predictors of high levels of individual performance. Boxall and Purcell (2011), for example, remind us of the classic performance rubric [$P = f(AMO)$], wherein 'A' or ability, 'M', motivation and 'O', opportunity are vital factors in understanding how ability and motivation increases an individual's performance. Line managers and supervisors play an important part in providing the 'opportunity' for their staff to willingly apply their skills in the workplace environment. At a systems or group level, managing performance requires a much more sophisticated approach given the multitude of 'system-level' internal and external factors that come into play. In this latter stream of research, several models of high performance and high involvement work systems of HRM practices have been proposed in the literature. Some of these approaches assume the guise of universalistic prescriptions while others fall under best-fit and other strategic HRM&ER approaches.

Chapter "Strategic Learning and Development" focuses on a key aspect of an individual's performance–the ability of employees. The role learning and skill development play in building individual, organisational and dynamic capabilities is examined here. Beginning with the theoretical foundations of why firms invest in individual-level training, the chapter explores the theoretical foundations of the human capital and neo-human capital theories. At an organisational systems level, studies of high performance work practices (HPWPs) also highlight the importance of training and a presence of a learning culture in improving the performance of organisational processes and outputs. The RBV approach also highlights the importance of investing in certain types of skills, resources and capabilities that align with its VRIO prescriptions in order to generate value and deliver high performance. Other theoretical influences are also covered in this chapter focus on how HRD connects with organisational performance. Finally, a brief discussion on retaining talent through career planning and employee counselling is also offered.

Chapter "Managing Employee Voice" looks at the 'O' in the AMO framework by reviewing the emerging terrain of direct and indirect forms of employee voice in dealing with routine and strategic work-related decisions (Boxall and Purcell 2011). From a strategic HRM & ER perspective, moving the discussion on an either or approach to employee voice—i.e. direct or indirect voice—this chapter focuses on the extent to which employees have the space for a *genuine* say over the decisions that affect their conditions of work. Employees' and managers' ability to influence and bring about positive change, a key HRM competency covered in Chapter "SHRM & ER: Professionalism and Ethics" is further examined in the next chapter.

Chapter "Strategic HRM & ER and Managing Change" looks at all three aspects of the AMO framework in dealing with one of the most important HRM functions–managing change. Despite change being a natural process, why do most organisational change management initiatives fail is the focus of discussion of this chapter. Building on the extensive work undertaken by Nilakant and Ramnarayan, this chapter presents a framework for understanding and managing the key tasks of change and highlights the role of HRM in successfully managing and supporting change. Nilakant and Ramnarayan's framework of four common tasks of change and what an HR champion must do to successfully design and execute change is covered here. Finally, attendant to the topic of managing change, and taking a holistic and systems level view of development as an outcome of change, this chapter briefly touches upon the importance of organisational development interventions in implementing change.

Chapter "Strategic Compensation and Benefits Management" focuses on the 'M' or motivation in the AMO framework. HR managers, in determining the nature and extent of rewards and benefits must determine the basis for designing and implementing schemes for motivating employees. Although compensation and benefits are significant HRM practices but to deliver on these practices from a strategic HRM perspective, there are several key considerations. These include: the wider organisational context, the operant business model of the firm as well as some intra-firm dependencies such as culture, style and orientation of senior leaders towards the employees as well as the strategic goals of the firm. It is for this reason that compensation and benefits are considered a controversial and contested function. As such, HR practitioners should balance numerous tensions of equity and equality in administering pay and benefits. The decisions surrounding pay and benefits often trigger emotions of perceived inequity, injustice, nepotism and invokes power and political behaviour in organisations.

Chapter "Special Topics in SHRM & ER" the final chapter deals with some topical issues and trends in the field of strategic HRM. This chapter focuses on developments in the wider meso-level environment that causes firms to explore new ways of working. In times of such change, the HR practitioner has to perform a balancing act and at times, restore the lost faith and credibility of the function. This is especially true in times of change and organisational crisis. To this end, a selection of the topical issues will be explored in brief. Analysing the relationship between innovation and SHRM&ER relationship focusing especially on work, product, process and business model innovations and how these might transform business and individual outcomes, is briefly covered in this chapter. A discussion of the related concept of organisational ambidexterity (OA) and its relationship with HRM and innovation outcomes, wherein the ability to firms to manage the duality of simultaneously balancing exploration and exploitation of learning for growth is also provided. Increasing interest in Public Sector HRM provides an overview of how the neoliberal pressures in public service are increasingly challenging public service motivation ethos and the desire of public service people to commit their careers to this important part of society. What are the key pressures leadership in the public service is facing in managing what has essentially been a professional bureaucracy will be explored. This chapter also deals with the emerging topic of Green HRM, employee well-being and HR offshoring. Despite the growing importance of HRM& ER function in organisations, there has been an increasing offshoring and outsourcing of a number of routine and non-routine HR functions. What might be the cause and can this replace local and context-specific delivery that HR & ER offers is also explored. Poor employee well-being, its incidence, causes and how it affects the credibility of HR is explored in this concluding chapter.

Conclusion

The range of topics covered in the book will be a constant source of challenge and engage the learners to achieve higher order learning. The narrative is deliberately kept brief to allow learners to engage with the literature independently as well as based on their interest in a particular topic. Through this book, it is hoped that the reader and participants in the case discussions will appreciate why context and choices matter and the important role human agency plays in the design and implementation of SHRM&ER practices in shaping performance and achieving a balance with the goals of social legitimacy and welfare.

Bibliography

Barney, J. B. (1991). Firm resources and sustained competitive advantage. *Journal of Management, 17*(1), 99–120.

Bolton, S. C., & Houlihan, M. (Eds.). (2007). *Searching for the human in human resource management: Theory, practice and workplace contexts*. Basingstoke: Palgrave Macmillan.

Boxall, P., & Purcell, J. (2011). *Strategy and human resource management*. Basingstoke: Palgrave Macmillan.

Boselie, P. (2010). *Strategic human resource management: A balanced approach*. Berkshire: McGraw Hill Higher Education.

Christensen, C., & Raynor, M. (2003). Why hard-nosed executives should care about management theory. *Harvard Business Review, 81*(9, September), 66–75.

DiMaggio, P. J., & Powell, W. W. (1983). *The new institutionalism in organizational analysis*. Chicago: University of Chicago Press.

Ellet, W. (2007). *The case study handbook: How to read, discuss and write persuasively about cases*. Boston: Harvard Business School Press.

Malik, A. (2013). Post-GFC people management challenges: A study of India's information technology sector. *Asia Pacific Business Review, 19*(2), 230–246. https://doi.org/10.1080/13602381.2013.767638.

Malik, A. (2017). *Human Resource Management and the Global Financial Crisis: Evidence from India's IT/BPO industry*. Abingdon: Routledge. https://doi.org/10.1039/c7sc04083k.

Marchington, M., & Kynighou, A. (2012). The dynamics of employee involvement and participation during turbulent times. *The International Journal of Human Resource Management, 23*(16), 3336–3354. https://doi.org/10.1080/09585192.2012.689161.

Merseth, K. K. (1991). The early history of case-based instruction: Insights for teacher education today. *Journal of Teacher Education, 42*(4), 243–249.

Paauwe, J. (2004). *HRM and performance: Achieving long-term viability*. Oxford: Oxford University Press.

HRM and ER: A Strategic Perspective

Ashish Malik

Key Learning Outcomes
At the end of this chapter, you should be able to:

- *Define the terms strategy, HRM and strategic HRM*
- *Describe the dominant approaches to strategy*
- *Identify the key goals of HRM*
- *Examine and analyse the relationship between strategy and HRM*
- *Analyse the key forces impacting an industry*

Introduction

This chapter begins by explaining the key terms of strategy, HRM and strategic HR. It highlights that the study of strategic management offers numerous conceptualizations of the term *strategy* and that the study of strategic human resource management and employment relations (SHRM & ER) must adopt a pluralist approach and place heavy emphasis on developing a contextual understanding of how people management, strategy and context interact to shape the multiple goals of SHRM&ER. This is followed by the commonly understood goals of HRM. As noted earlier, a descriptive understanding is a precondition to analyzing how to manage people and work in organisations. Based on description, we can seek to generate guiding principles from specific learnings. This approach requires collective learning experiences from a diverse set of circumstances and involves developing a thick description of what people and managers do at a workplace. Based on

A. Malik (✉)
Faculty of Business and Law, Central Coast Business School, The University of Newcastle, Ourimbah, Central Coast, NSW, Australia
e-mail: ashish.malik@newcastle.edu.au

such an approach we can seek some answers into the *what*, *why* and *how* of managing people in organisations.

Strategy

To begin with, a commonsense understanding of strategy in a business context, according to Cascio and Boudreau (2012: 2) is when a business can answer the following questions: "Why should customers buy from your company, as opposed to others? What do you do better than anyone else? What do you offer that is valuable, rare and difficult to imitate?" Adopting a more conventional planning approach, De Wit and Meyer (1998), note strategy is a firm's intention to achieve its objectives through well-defined plans in a way that firms are able to achieve alignment or fit between its goals, resources and the wider business environment. Quite apart from the design and planning schools of strategy, Leopold and Harris (2009: 27) suggest "Strategies are outcomes of human interpretations, conflicts, confusions, guesses, and rationalisations rather than clear pictures unambiguously traced out on a corporate engineer's drawing board." Others (Grant 2010: 58) note "My key assumption is that the firm operates in the interests of the owners through maximising their returns (profits), which implies maximising the value of the firm." Whereas, Leopold and Harris (2009: 15) also state: "To see work organisations as negotiated orders is to recognise that they involve continuously emergent patterns of activity and understanding that arise from the interplay of individual and group interests, ideas, initiatives and reactions – these interests and differences reflecting patterns of power and inequality applying in the society and the economy of which the organisation is a part."

Key Approaches

What does the above tell us about strategy? One thing is clear that there are several conceptualisations and each serves the theoretical emphasis it takes. For instance, Grant's view is more unitarist than the latter statement by Leopold and Harris, which is consistent with a pluralist ideology. For instance, if one were to use a Marxist frame, then organisations are purposive entities and they exist for generating a surplus through efficient allocation of resources. Boxall and Purcell (2011) bring an important consideration that organisations do not exist in a vacuum–they are embedded in the wider business, social and institutional environment in which they compete with other organisations to sell their products and services. This applies both to for-profit and not-for-profit firms, who in today's free market environment compete for all types of resources—financial and non-financial. Hence, they have to differentiate and offer a customer value proposition that helps fill a market gap or indeed creates, a thus far unexplored market. While this may ensure survival in the short to medium term, the journey for achieving sustained competitive advantage is often hard and requires a viable business model. By achieving financial viability, firms can begin to embark on achieving sustained competitive advantage through continued refining of their business model and strengthening their core value proposition, especially if they see competitive rivalry and intensity is beginning to offer similar or better value proposition in the same strategic milieu (Boxall and Purcell 2011; Malik and Rowley 2015).

Reviewing the voluminous terrain of strategy literature is not the focus here, instead, a flavour of common classifications of strategy literature that are evident in the literature on HRM& ER is offered. Briefly, one popular classification of strategic management offered by Whittington (1993) classifies strategy approaches into two groups: an outside-in approach, under which, strategy is largely determined by external environment; and the second, an inside-out approach challenges the underlying assumptions and the dominance of external environment and industry structure. This latter view focuses on the human, technological, social and managerial characteristics of organisations, or what some scholars have termed as 'core competences' of a firm (popularised by Prahalad and Hamel 1990) for achieving competitive advantage. The focus is on acquiring competencies, capabilities and resources that are *valuable, rare, inimitable,* and *organized* in such a way that creates barriers for competitors to replicate a firm's customer/core value proposition (Barney 1991), as per this approach. This approach is also referred to as 'resource-based view' (RBV) of the firm or the 'stretch' view of strategy. This school of thought is covered in detail in chapter "SHRM&ER: The Resource-Based View".

Within the outside-in approach, the structure–conduct–performance (SCP) paradigm is a dominant school of thought, wherein, in a given industry structure, the performance of a firm is depends on how the buyers and sellers in an industry behave. This view that led to the popularization and development of the industry dynamics approach and Porter's competitive forces model (Porter 1985, 1996). Institutions too, have a significant influence on strategy. This approach to strategy is often labelled as the 'market-based' view of strategy and sometimes also referred to as the external-fit view of strategy. In line with this approach to strategy, the role of managers is to develop a better understanding the competitive dynamics of the product markets that their firm wishes to operate in, analyze and understand the industry structure, and the internal and external environmental factors that are affecting it. The logic in this approach is premised on the quality of rationality and analysis undertaken by managers in informing its strategic choices for achieving competitive advantage.

One of the key contributors of the *outside-in* approach, Michael Porter, who developed the *Five Forces* model, offers a useful framework for analysing industry structure and dynamics. In analysing the wider environment, this framework is often used in conjunction with some of the popular environmental analysis tools such as the PESTL (political, economic, social, technological and legal) framework. A further understanding of the internal and external factors affecting an organisation can utilize the SWOT (strengths, weaknesses, opportunities and threats) analysis tool. Porter, in his *Five Forces* model (1985) highlights the influence of five forces on competitive dynamics in any industry. These forces are: the bargaining power of buyers, bargaining power of suppliers, threat of new entrants, threat of substitutes and rivalry among existing players. The impact of environmental forces on a firm's business cannot be understated.

Application Examples

Take the case of the global movie rentals industry, where Netflix changed the competitive dynamics through its investment in disruptive technologies. This affected, in a relatively short period of time, the structure, conduct and performance of the movie rental industry. One of the applications from the above set of analytical frameworks is that firms exercise choices based on their analysis and then as Porter suggests, determine their basis for competing in an industry e.g. whether they compete on the basis of *cost leadership* or *differentiation*. These two generic decision points define the *competitive strategy* a firm may generally pursue. Because of the chosen competitive strategy, the allocation of resources and the way these resources are organized is a major decision and is difficult to reverse such decisions without cost implications. Applying the concept of generic competitive strategies to the Australian retail shopping experience, one can see discernible differences in the way the shopping experience is organized for example in Big W and Kmart versus David Jones and Myers. While the former appears to follow a cost-leadership strategy, the latter group is clearly focusing on differentiation in the products as well as the personalized service that one receives at David Jones and Myers. There are likely to be distinctive differences in the hiring and rewarding approaches in each of the above two retail outlet examples. It is likely that the latter group will employ a variable pay structure with some team-based rewards for staff to provide effective customer solutions than a standard industry award for rewarding them.

A related next step is the supporting functional activities that follow from the choice of a firm's business and competitive strategies. Boxall and Purcell (2011) note three distinctive levels of strategy: business strategy- which determine the business an organisation wishes to be in; competitive strategy- which determines the basis of competing in the chosen sphere of business; and finally the entire value chain of functional strategies–such as human resources, marketing, finance, technology and so on and how these functional strategies need to achieve fit with the chosen business and competitive strategy. This latter focus on functional strategies is a key focus of strategic HRM and ER. Before engaging with this issue further, it is pertinent to define HRM and map its relationship with strategy.

Defining HRM

In line with the above observation, Boxall et al. (2007) classified the wider study of HRM into three sub-fields. The first sub-field of *micro-HRM* focuses on the functional aspects of HRM (e.g. the employment lifecycle such as on HR practices of HR planning, recruitment and selection, induction and socialisation, training and development, performance management, rewards and remuneration, managing employment relationships). *International HRM* sub-field deals with the management of people in global and multinational enterprises. Issues of local responsiveness or integration of the parent firm's global best-practices at its subsidiary locations, better coordination and control are among the key areas of emphasis in managing people globally. Finally, the last sub-field of HRM research adopts a strategic approach to HRM (or SHRM for short). This approach focuses on linkages between HRM practices with business strategy by designing an integrated set of high performance work practices or systems (HPWP/Ss) for creating and realising value through an organisation's human capital pool and human capital management processes. Although the above three sub-fields are quite distinct in their emphasis at a practice level, the overarching goals which they aim to serve bears significant overlaps. Boxall and Purcell (2011) for example, identified several goals of HRM: economic goals, which focus on achieving a cost-effective HR resource model, one which offers enough organisational flexibility and creates human resource advantage through appropriate investment in skills and practices; socio-political goals, which focuses on maintaining social legitimacy in its actions especially as organisations operate in a social context; and the managerial prerogative in the form of power managers can exercise over labour. The above set of goals can be thought to exist on a continuum from a unitarist to a pluralist approach. Legge (1995), for instance noted the distinction between 'hard' HRM approaches focusing on the efficiency goals versus 'soft' HRM approaches, focusing on the humane side of managing human resources. Strategic approaches to HRM should attempt to balance the needs of diverse set of stakeholders and not focus on one stakeholder i.e. the shareholders.

HRM and Strategy

The literature on SHRM focuses on linking a firm's business and competitive strategy with its HRM practices. While this may seem like a logical step to achieve alignment and fit, an organisation's decision to pursue a given competitive strategy or the process of strategy making is far from simple; it involves exercising choices by managers. In most cases, these choices have constraints, as resources are limited and organisations being political entities, have to balance the multiple and often competing interests of its internal and external stakeholders. It is in this backdrop of strategic decision-making and negotiation that strategies are shaped at different levels. This presents challenges for some of the more prescriptive schools of strategic HRM thought.

Depending on the strategic choices (Child 1972, 1997) that managers exercise, the paths which a firm may embark upon may vary. Typically, managers collect information about the environment and its structural conditions. They then evaluate and learn from it and further use such learning to inform their ability to refine choices (Child 1997). These choices then need to be actioned and subsequently the outcomes, at some stage, needs to be evaluated (Child 1997). For example, some firms may choose to grow organically whereas others may decide to take a growth path of diversification through mergers and acquisitions or enter in joint-venture partnerships and so on. Depending on the choices made, the implications for SHRM will also vary. To be strategic, HRM has to embrace both a bottom-up and top-down communication approach: or in other words, inform and be informed by strategy. While former assumes a much more proactive role HR leaders, wherein HR receives membership at the executive table, the latter, however assumes a more reactive role for the HRM function, wherein it is more of an implementer of the choices made by the senior management or what some refer to as, *the dominant coalition*. Of importance is maintaining a right balance between proactive and reactive approaches to achieve strategic integration and fit. Broadly, in terms of strategic choices that traverse the field of strategic HRM are covered in the chapters on *best-practice versus best-fit view of SHRM, resource-based view of firm as applied to SHRM, strategic employment relations* and the impact of *institutional perspectives in shaping SHRM*.

Critical Reflections

What appears from the preceding discussion is that the nature of conceptualization varies based on the theoretical background and worldviews that are examined. While consensus may not always be possible or desirable, what is critical to remember is that organizations are purposive entities and they must organize work and activities in ways that are productive and sustainable. Overtime, we have seen some prescriptions regarding the optimal ways of organizing work and motivating people to carry out the productive tasks on a sustainable basis. The approaches will vary depending on the nature of product and labour markets and where such goods and services are produced and consumed. There are some guiding principles and tested approaches that seem to work in certain contexts more effectively than others. Often firms that are more successful organize their production function and work that is different to their competitors. This idea reinforces the notion of a differentiation view of strategy in a manager's decision choice menu.

Illustrations and Skills Sandpit–Industry Analysis and Market Concentration

Several examples from the low-cost and legacy airline carries that can be seen as variants of a cost-leadership or differentiation strategy. The key point for managers is to make a choice based on their analysis of the competitive forces affecting a particular industry. By virtue of industry evolution, technological changes and the market positioning in some industries is more attractive than others. This was borne out in the consulting firm, AT Kearney's CR3 curve. AT Kearny studied the combined market share of three largest companies (CR3) in an industry. In their analysis, they found that an 'S' curve (typical of organizational life cycle curve, which goes through the stages of growth, fragmentation and shakeout, plateau and decline) could be plotted for all industries that are especially in the maturity and/or decline stage. Industries such as defence, beauty care, beverages and tobacco industries, for example, had a CR3 of as high as 70% whereas the banks and airline industry had a CR3 of between 20–30%. This analysis simply highlights the intensity of competition and rivalry that is present in the latter group of industries and that the profitability in the latter group as a result, is very low.

Concept Integration with Cases and Learning Activities

There is evidence of application of the *Competitive Forces* model in the *HR Planning at Dorian LPG* case study. The dominant focus of the case is HR planning in times of an organization witnessing high growth in an industry that is highly capital intensive. Like the airlines industry, the case aptly illustrates how such an analysis can inform managerial thinking and decisions. To further explore the concept, attempt the learning activity at the end of the chapter entitled *Analysing the Fast-Food Industry*.

Conclusion

Although subject matter expertise and underpinning theories are important for informing practice, such knowledge can be developed by contextualizing the learning through use of real life examples and case studies from the real world. In line with our pedagogical choice of case-based learning stated earlier, the application of various strategic HRM & ER concepts and how they apply to a number of industry and national contexts, this book offers a wide selection of case studies from the manufacturing to services sectors, from both domestic and international settings. Further, the level of analysis varies from an industry through organisational to group and individual levels. Attention has also been paid to include cases from industry sectors that implement a range of HRM practices in service sector from the lower end of the service complexity continuum to high-end complex services. Such differentiation in the choice of case studies included in this collection allows us to understand the complexities at play in shaping strategic HRM & ER decisions and practices in diverse settings.

Glossary

HRM focuses on making decisions that relate to developing and implementing policies and practices for managing work and employment relationships for effectively and efficiently achieving the goals of an organisation while also keeping in mind the needs of the employees.

Pluralist approach acknowledges there is conflict in a workplace context and that both actors in the employment relationship- the employer and employee are seen as seeking to maximise their interests. The overarching ideology of this approach is to engage and progressively manage and deal with conflict rather than ignoring or avoiding it.

Strategy can be defined as an organisation's concerted effort to align the achievement of its goals in a given environment, often through differentiation.

Strategic choice is the extent to which a firm has leeway in making decisions from a strategic perspective

Strategic HRM is a sub-field of HRM that adopts an integrated and holistic approach to developing differentiated HRM policy choices and practices that can provide a firm with a distinctive source of sustained competitive advantage

Strategic ER is a strategic approach to employment relations (ER) that adopts a pluralist approach over a longer-term in a more thoughtful and consistent manner to manage the key workforce and employment relationship demands placed by a range of stakeholders.

Unitary approach focuses on promoting a common and unified set of values and ways of behaving in an organisational context for achieving its business goals. The overarching ideology of this approach is that goals can and must be achieved through employee commitment and there is little or no scope for challenging this line of thinking. Often those who challenge are offered learning interventions or are considered exhibiting inappropriate values and behaviours and may face disciplinary action.

Key Questions and Learning Activities

Question. 1 Discuss how an organisation's competitive strategy might impact its functional HR strategy?

Question. 2 What are the key challenges in adopting a strategic approach to HRM?

Question. 3 Is Porter's industry analysis sufficient for exercising strategic choices? Why? Why not?

Learning Activity 1: Analysing the Fast-Food Industry

At some stage of our life, we would have bought a burger from McDonalds, KFC or a pizza from Dominos or Pizza Hutt. As Michael Porter noted, "The essence of formulating competitive strategy is relating a company to its environment. Though the relevant environment is very broad, encompassing social as well as economic forces, the key aspect of the firm's environment is the industry or industries in which it competes. Industry structure has a strong influence in defining the competitive rules of the game as well as strategies potentially available to the firm."

Based on the above example, your task is analyse the fast-food industry in a country of your choice. You may find it useful to read the short summary of the five forces model by Porter (2008) in analysing the industry dynamics that are critical to your understanding of the intensity of competition, overall profitability in a given industry, and thus crucial in formulating and implementing strategic choices. Using the above framework and based on your own personal knowledge and experience, the task is to:

1. Begin by a specific definition of the fast-food industry in a geography of your choice.Explain the rationale of your choice.

2. Evaluate the strength of the five forces individually for the fast-food industry.
3. What are the key HR considerations for operating in such an industry?
4. Make a judgement about how attractive an industry like this would be to invest $5 million.

Defining what an industry is vital for your analysis. As such, it is wise to look at an industry from a *demand-based* perspective than a *supply-based* perspective. You may like to start by analysing each of the key forces and its sub-considerations in the provided space below for answering the allocated questions.

Porter's five Forces Model

1. Barriers to entry	2. Bargaining power of suppliers
3. Intensity of rivalry	4. Bargaining power of customers/buyers
5. Threat of substitutes	

Bibliography

Barney, J. B. (1991). Firm resources and sustained competitive advantage. *Journal of Management, 17* (1), 99–120.
Boxall, P., & Purcell, J. (2011). *Strategy and human resource management.* Basingstoke: Palgrave Macmillan.
Boxall, P., Purcell, J., & Wright, P. (2007). *The Oxford handbook of human resource management.* Oxford: Oxford University Press.
Cascio, W. F., & Boudreau, J. W. (2012). *Short introduction to strategic human resource management.* Cambridge: Cambridge University Press.
Child, J. (1972). Organizational structure, environment and performance: The role of strategic choice. *Sociology, 6*(1), 1–22.
Child, J. (1997). Strategic choice in the analysis of action, structure, organizations and environment: Retrospect and prospect. *Organization Studies, 18*(1), 43–76.
De Wit, B., & Meyer, R. (1998). *Strategy: Process, content, context–An international perspective.* London: Thomson.
Grant, R. (2010). Chapter 1: The concept of strategy. In *Contemporary strategy analysis* (7th ed., pp. 3–30). London: Wiley.
Legge, K. (1995). *HRM: rhetoric, reality and hidden agendas. Human resource management: A critical text,* p. 33.
Leopold, J., & Harris, L. (Eds.). (2009). *The strategic managing of human resources.* Pearson Education.
Malik, A., & Rowley, C. (Eds.). (2015). *Business models and people management in the Indian IT industry: From people to profits.* Oxon: Routledge.
Mintzberg, H., & Lampel, J. (2001). Chapter 2: Reflections on the strategy process. In M. Cusamano & C. Markides (Eds.), *Strategic thinking for the next economy* (pp. 33–54). San Francisco: Jossey-Bass.
Porter, M. (1985). *Creating and sustaining superior performance.* New York: Free Pess.
Porter, M. (1996). What is strategy? *Harvard Business Review, 74,* 61–78.
Porter, M. (2008, January). The five competitive forces that shape strategy. *Harvard Business Review, 86,* 78–93.
Prahalad, C. K., & Hamel, G. (1990). The core competence of the corporation. *Harvard Business Review, 68,* 79–91.
Whittington, R. (1993). *What is strategy—And does it matter?* London: Routledge.

Strategic HRM & ER: Best-Practice Versus Best Fit

Ashish Malik

Key Learning Outcomes
At the end of this chapter, you should be able to:

- *Differentiate between the best-practice and best-fit school of SHRM*
- *Identify the key types of fit in strategic HRM*
- *Evaluate the key tenets of best-fit and best-practice schools*
- *Apply the concepts of integration and fit to SHRM practices*

Introduction

Building on our the understanding of key terms in chapter "HRM and ER: A Strategic Perspective", this chapter dwells upon two of the most popular schools of thought in the study and practice of SHRM: the best-practice and best-fit schools. While the analysis of a firm's business and industry environment allows the dominant coalition to make strategic choices about its business and competitive positioning, this choice also has direct implications on how people are managed and work is organised in a business. Even though this has intuitive appeal and reinforces the importance of externalities, there are some schools of thought, such as the best-practice school, which adopts a *universalistic* approach, or, in other words, assumes a more prescriptive character in the design and implementation of SHRM and ER practices. The best-fit school, on the other hand, as the name suggests, adopts an 'it depends' on the context approach. Best-fit approach considers numerous contingency factors that affect and shaping of the final set of HRM practices. A related

A. Malik (✉)
Faculty of Business and Law, Central Coast Business School, The University of Newcastle, Ourimbah, Central Coast, NSW, Australia
e-mail: ashish.malik@newcastle.edu.au

topic evident in both these approaches is the concept of *integration* and *fit*. Integration between strategy and HRM practices is critical and a key skill that business leaders will be expecting from HR leaders. Millmore (2007) noted several levels of integration and fit that operate in an organisational context. These include: downstream strategic integration (also referred to as top-down integration), upstream strategic integration (also referred to as bottom-up integration), intra-functional integration (also referred to as horizontal integration or integration between various activities in a functional area) and inter-functional integration (which focuses on integration between various business functions e.g. HR, marketing, legal and so on).

Best-Practice School of HRM

The universality of HR practices in all contexts is emphasised in the best-practice view of SHRM theories. The rationale followed by proponents of this approach is that there is *one best way* of achieving a highly effective and high performing organisation. Boxall and Purcell (2003: 61) suggested that the universalists highlight the need to "have top management support and commitment for certain key HR practices; undertake research on the cutting edge and successful HR practices; create awareness and commitment towards these successful HR practices; measure and monitor progress of these practices; put in place mechanisms to reward managers for implementing the selected practices." Other theorists have suggested that "All else being equal, the use of High Performance Work Practices [HPWPs] and good internal fit should lead to positive outcomes for all types of firms" (Huselid 1995: 644). The work of Kaufman (2010: p. 289) provides a good critique of both the approaches-best-practice (BP) and best-fit (BF) and notes where some of its variants such as HPWPs fit: "The key hypothesis of the BP model is that a set of HRM practices exist that universally lead to superior organizational performance. Thus, the BP and Universalistic perspectives are largely equivalent; this implies, in turn, that HPWPs are largely synonymous with "advanced" or "transformed" practices of the Universalistic model, such as employee involvement, extensive training, and self-managed teams…. In a BP world, the use of HPWPs dominates in all firms." In a similar vein, Comb et al.'s (2006: 502) meta-analytic review of the field summarised: "Human resource practices that SHRM theorists consider performance enhancing are known as high-performance work practices (HPWPs). HPWPs include, for example, incentive compensation, training, employee participation, selectivity, and flexible work arrangements. SHRM theory asserts that these practices increase employees' knowledge, skills, and abilities (KSAs), empower employees to leverage their KSAs for organizational benefit, and increase their motivation to do so. The result is greater job satisfaction, lower employee turnover, higher productivity, and better decision-making, all of which help improve organizational performance."

What follows from the above is that BP theorists identify a set of HRM practices and mount a case for its universal use, irrespective of the context in which these HRM practices are to be implemented. This approach can be linked it back to earlier scientific management approaches of Fredrick Taylor, however, for sake of brevity, here the discussion is confined to the most popular conceptualisations such as that of Pfeffer's model (1998) of seven key successful HR practices and Walton's (1985) control versus commitment model. Readers are advised to review some of the other variants of the approach under the umbrella of high commitment management (HCM) (e.g. Arthur 1992), high involvement work systems(HIWS) (Lawler et al. 1998), high performance work practices (HPWPs), or high performance work systems (HPWSs) (e.g. Huselid 1995) for a systems level understanding of managerial control, commitment. Another popular conceptualisation is that of the AMO (ability, motivation and opportunity) framework (Applebaum et al. 2000; Bailey 1993). Pfeffer (1998, 96), in his model of key HRM practices stated, "Effective management of people can produce substantially enhanced economic performance" and that high performance or successful organisations are characterised by the following set of seven HR practices: (1) employment security; (2) selective hiring of new personnel; (3) self-managed teams and decentralisation's of decision making; (4) comparatively high compensation contingent on organisational performance; (5) extensive training; (6) reduced status distinctions and barriers, including wage differences across levels; and (7) extensive sharing of financial and performance information throughout the organization, as the key drivers of high performance.

Walton's (1985) work is premised on the tenets of managerial control theory wherein he argues that in the strategic management of a firm's resources, its leaders have two strategic choices: follow a low-commitment or high-commitment HR policy choices. Depending on the choice implemented, the HR system will differ significantly in the set of values and management philosophy that is consistent with the approach. These choices will shape not only the firm's culture (e.g. follow either a rule-based or an empowerment-based culture), but it will also affect wider strategic choices in terms of the organisation structure, technology use in work design, and the final choice of a range of HR practices.

As observed by Combs et al. (2006), the major emphases is on bringing to action the HRM-Performance link by implementing a "bundle" of universally applicable practices. The proponents of this school further argue that HPWS or HPWPs not only lead to higher business performance, but they also result in better HR outcomes such as low employee turnover, high satisfaction by users of HR practices, better knowledge and skills, alignment and fit with goals and improved employee attitudes and behaviours. In line with this, many subsequent studies have come up with their own bundle of 'magic lists' or 'silver bullets'. For example, Purcell et al. (2003), employed the classic performance eq. (P = fAMO) and suggested a set of 11 inter-related HRM practices. They further highlight the critical role of line managers in ensuring these practices are implemented successfully. Implied in the above is that managers have a choice in implementing and indeed interpreting some of these practices, which may or may not conform to what the HR leaders conceived of in their design.

Best-Fit School of HRM

Best-fit (BF) models of HRM rely on the logic of contingency theory. Such a conceptualization stems from the premise that high performance in organisations varies with context as each firm operates in a slightly different environment. Differences in context is argued to have a direct bearing on the way firms organize their production function. The basic assumption of the BF approach is that high performance and HR practices relationship is not linear; it is mediated and/or moderated by a set of contingency variables such as strategy, size, technology, regulation, market segment and so on. The focus should be on achieving the most desired fit between these factors. BF theorists emphasize the importance of strategic alignment and fit between HR practices and the contextual factors, such that, the better the integration and fit, the more likely a firm is to deliver high performance. The notion of integration and fit was introduced earlier in the chapter. Thus, it is important to achieve *integration* and *fit* at various levels. Boxall and Purcell (2011) highlight the importance of fit at the following three levels: societal or institutional fit (this will be explored in greater detail in chapter "SHRM&ER: Institutional Theory"), industry fit and organisational fit. The latter two types of fit put constraints on managerial thinking as evidenced through Porter's industry analysis. Boxall and Purcell (2011) refer to certain table stakes that are necessary for a given industry if a firm has to survive. Similarly, studies of commitment and control highlight the impact certain types of culture and managerial ideologies have on people and the types of people that need to be hired and integrated to support the desired cultures. This line of thinking is important in implementing the HR practices of recruitment and selection as well as induction and socialization for the desired person-organisation fit.

As with the BP tradition, research in the BF stream is also voluminous and finds support for their thesis, though, the problem is more theoretical–one of parsimony– as the number of contextual variables to account for can be huge and a challenging enterprise. As noted earlier, fit manifests itself at numerous levels: strategic or vertical, internal or horizontal and external or institutional/contextual. Integration of the above different fits is considered important in the effective design and implementation of HR practices. Ichniowski et al. (1996), for example, argued for three levels of fit: *fit between innovative practices* so that the whole is greater than sum of parts; fit within a bundle of management practices; and achieving fit with the *external environment*. Employing a differentiated workforce model approach (Becker et al. 2009), the authors argue that for different employee groups different set of HRM practices may be a desirable way forward for achieving what has been described as a configurational approach. Fombrun et al. (1984) noted the need for *internal strategic fit* and delineated a set of strategic HR choices in recruitment, selection, training and development, and rewards and remuneration, depending on the firm's strategic configurations. For example, training activities should be closely aligned and support an organisation's strategic needs. Within the BF school, additional set of contingency influences include the *business life cycle model* (Baird and Meshoulam 1988), wherein firms HR practices must evolve in line with a firm's growth, maturity, stability and decline stages in a way that the emphasis of certain

HRM practices will be high or low at each phase of an organisation's growth. For instance, recruitment and selection will assume strategic importance during times of high growth and managing change and headcount during times of recession, even more so, at times when the industry is experiencing a shakeout. Best-fit models draw upon extensively on Porter's (1985) classification of three generic *competitive strategies*: differentiation, cost-reduction, and focus. The seminal BF work in this area has been by Schuler and Jackson (1987), who argued that firms can pursue any of the three generic strategies as long as they concurrently also develop certain values and behaviours among employees to support each of the three generic competitive strategies of cost leadership (efficiency), differentiation (innovation) or focus. The chosen competitive strategy would have varying levels of demands on the nature and extent of HRM practices and value systems implemented. For instance, when cost-leadership strategy is adopted, training and skills development would not be very high on an organisation's agenda, rather, a control-oriented workflow design would be a key focus. Employing the classic "make" or "buy" decision as applied to study of HRM, and using Porter's set of generic strategies, Stewart and Brown (2009) advanced a model based on an organisation's orientation towards its investment in labour – a make decision (or having an internal orientation) versus buy decision (or having an external orientation)) on one axis and a firm's competitive strategy on the other. Such an approach yields different configurations of strategic HR choice menus for each of the two commonly used generic competitive strategies of cost leadership and differentiation.

Application Examples

While the above application of generic competitive strategy is widely employed in the literature, some researchers (DeSabro et al. 2005: 49), in a similar vein, have employed Miles and Snow's (1978) classic framework of four groups of firms (prospectors, defenders, analyzers and reactors) based on their strategic orientation. In analyzing firms in an industry and how they might employ different SHRM and management practices, Miles and Snow (1978) noted that *prospectors* are leaders in their industry and are known to shape the direction of the product market and the speed at which the market changes. They do so by continuously launching new products and/or identifying new marketplace opportunities. Apple and Intel are prime examples of prospectors. In essence, these firms follow differentiation and innovation strategies. The nature of strategic alignment HR practices have to achieve for this group of firms is one that encourages innovation and risk-taking behaviours. *Defenders,* on the other hand, try to prevent competitors from shaving away their gains by delivering on a secure and niche market area. An example of this type would be SAP from Germany who offer a specialized enterprise resource planning application. They offer a single software product that is a highly stable and specialized product. SAP focuses more on exploiting its competencies and strengths to the core thereby achieving resource efficiency and reducing its service/product production costs. The opportunities for HR design here will be very different to the prospectors. HR would want to drive standardization and control over its established and proven best practices for most of the work groups. The *Analyzers,* similar to the prospectors and defenders, cautiously and selectively enter only those markets that may offer potential. They may initiate product or market development, but are "more likely to follow a second-but-better strategy". Companies like Advanced Micronics Devices (AMD) and IBM would fall into this category. The first three categories would have a distinct advantage over the *Reactor* firms, which, as the name suggests, are firms that will be slower than second movers and their responses to changes in environmental conditions are unsynchronized and to say the least, appear, disjointed.

While there is a pattern of stability in HRM practices in most manufacturing firms, service industries are much more dynamic and change frequently. As such the nature and extent of change of HR responses in services is varied and highly differentiated. It depends on the nature of markets served. Boxall (2003), developed a typology of HR strategic responses based on the competitive dynamics and market characteristics of service sector firms. Boxall developed a framework for identifying whether there are opportunities for implementing HPWPs in some segments of the industry more than others. Using Herzenberg et al.'s (1998) classification of types of work systems in services industries—starting from highly control-oriented, Taylorist forms of service work organisation through semi-controlled to high-skills and highly autonomous structures—and overlaying such forms of work with Porter's generic competitive strategies, three types of markets are: the mass-service markets, a mix of mass markets and higher value-added segments or *slightly differentiated markets*, and very significantly, if not totally *differentiated markets*. The first type of service markets is often typical of what is seen in the fast food and petrol stations segment of the services market. The second type of markets requires slightly higher and complex level of skills such as that evident in nursing and age care staff. Finally, in the highly differentiated markets, complex and higher-order learning and skills are required such as that found in legal practices and software development firms. Boxall argues that the opportunity for implementing HPWPs in these latter two market segments is greater than in the first. Boxall (2003) suggests that there are opportunities to implement HPWPs (including quality management approaches).

From the above analysis and discussion, the primacy of context is highlighted and that there exists no single or universal solution that is applicable to all industries. Such is the nature of complexity of HR decision-making that managers have to deal with. Not having a model approach to combat the dynamic environment may be unsettling for the novice or less prepared HR practitioner. Boxall and Purcell (2011) summarise that relative to BP (the universalistic school), BF (contingency school) is a clear winner. They argue that this does not mean one should discount BP approaches totally, rather, HR managers should use BP modules as guiding principles for developing HR solutions to suit their specific contexts.

Critical Reflections of the Best-Practice and Best-Fit Schools

Critique of Best-Practice Models

Critics of best-practice models (Marchington and Grugulis 2000; Kaufman 2010) challenge the universal application of these prescriptive lists of HR practices on the basis that, organisational and business complexity must pay attention to contextual and environmental factors before we can expect a generic set of prescriptions. Further, it has been argued that the sophistication and sometimes the prohibitive costs of the excessively long list of these practices makes their application possible only in large and diversified businesses. Finally, others too, have highlighted the need for investing in complementary capabilities, a view that is widely dealt within the resource-based view of the firm (Barney 1991) and will be covered in the next Chapter.

Further, in the absence of any agreed definition or list of HRM best-practices, there is little understanding of the 'best' HRM practices and for whom do these universalist prescriptions apply? Some have argued that the best-practice school is grounded in a unitarist approach. It is also not very clear which practice is most important creating the problem of strategic ambiguity (Purcell 1999). On a rational and logical front, this prescriptive approach does not take into account influences of national cultures and the dynamic business environment. This school of thought also ignores the differences in HRM practices due to a firm's life cycle of development and evolution. Equally problematic is the notion of high-performance work practices or high-performance work systems and its impact on individual outcomes, as there have been studies that report adverse impacts on employee well-being and health from some of these bundles of practices. A common critique is that performance comes at a human cost. Lepak and Snell (1999) argue that it is not clear which HR practices are interdependent and which ones are independent of management practices. It may be possible that some management practices indirectly influence HR practices in achieving high performance. Boxall and Purcell (2003) conclude there is some merit in regarding these practices as generic guidelines or general principles for labour management rather than as a prescriptive list of universally accepted practices for achieving high performance. There is also some disagreement on what might be the agreed and enforceable standards, if one were to implement these sets of HR best practices. While the HR professional bodies promote ethical code of conduct as a guide for shaping HRM best practices, the membership of HR professionals into this community is voluntary and as such may not always result in any enforceable HRM standards. Furthermore, there are differences between HR professional bodies and the emphases varies from one country to another.

Critique of Best-Fit Models

Researchers focusing on contingency perspective or best-fit school, according to critics have a disproportionate focus on a top-down approach. For effective HRM, HR practices must align with the chosen competitive strategy. As covered in the earlier chapters, the notion of achieving a strong strategic, institutional societal and horizontal fit requires organisations to follow a pluralistic approach to strategy. Achieving fit is particularly relevant in the case of multidivisional firms who are operating in more than one market and offering differentiated and segmented products and services. As Boxall and Purcell (2011) noted, organisations cannot be viewed as isolated entities–they are deeply entrenched in a society and its norms. The pressures imposed by institutions and other macro influences such as religion, culture, language and customer's expressed and latent need cannot be underestimated. Boxall's (2003) classification of the three service markets, is too simplistic. Take the case of, for example, an organisation's learning and development function: will an organisation invest negligible amounts in training if it belongs to Type 1 (mass services market segment) and more if it belongs to Type 3 (highly differentiated services), and if it does, what is the nature of knowledge and skills that will be developed in each? Will firms in a Type 1 market employ on hiring more from the external labour markets low-skilled employees? Will they focus on developing people in-house for a Type 3 market? Would a high skills road be required for high-end products that are typical of a Type 3 market? Evidence of this is equivocal. Studies in the UK suggest the need for a high skills road for a differentiated product market is not always the case (Mason 2005). Similarly, differentiated product markets are not always associated with the use of highly skilled workforce (Sung and Ashton 2005).

Illustrations and Skills Sandpit

Integration and fit between HRM practices and strategy is easily observable in a number of service sector firms. For example, in call centre firms, those focusing on simple and high volume transaction processing work, for example, selling internet connections or fundraising and competing on the basis of price of the service. These providers often tend to rely on hiring youth and recent college graduates, paying a bit over the minimum clearing wage. Compare this to call centres that are offering complex services and solutions, for example, legal, medical and counselling services, who tend to employ medium to highly skilled and experienced resources, paying significantly above the minimum clearing wage and offering extensive training and benefits for dealing with the complex nature of service. Often the size of the enterprise may necessitate making significant investments in training and development infrastructure by call centre operators. This is evident in the case of large call centres and consulting firms such as IBM services, Accenture and Genpact where these firms invest significant extensive volumes of training for providing client-, domain- and industry-specific training to their employees. They also offer training modules in the areas of cultural integration for a better person-organization fit. Other forms of training include, for example, Six Sigma training and certification at Genpact, which is a widely acknowledged strength of this offshore outsourcing major for bringing about process improvements and service excellence.

Concept Integration with Cases and Learning Activities

Aspects of the application of SHRM & ER best-practice and best-fit approaches is evident in the Dorian LPG's rapid fleet growth case study and to some extent in the Crisis and IHRM case study of a Greek MNC that decided to grow by expanding overseas. These cases highlight the need for maintaining integration and fit between the parent firm's values and culture and their HRM practices.

Conclusion

Overall, this chapter highlighted the two most common approaches to strategic HRM. Even though there is extensive support from meta-analytic studies exploring the HRM-Performance link, Combs et al. (2006), in line with Boxall (2003), suggested differences between manufacturing and services sectors, in that, the nature of HPWPs in each would be different due to the distinctiveness of various service work market segments. The challenge therefore for future inquiries is to uncover additional contextual variables that can be systematically analysed as part of the HPWP systems that consider both an organisation's business environment and strategy.

Glossary

Best-practice HRM school advocates the adoption of a universally applicable set of HRM practices, which, if implemented collectively, can be a source of sustained performance for organisations.

Best-fit HRM school advocates that it is unwise to assume that a given set of HRM practices are universally applicable. Rather, this school highlights the importance of achieving alignment and fit between an organisation's strategic choices and its wider internal and external contextual factors.

Context refers to an organisation's internal and external environment.

Organisational fit in relation to SHRM &ER refers to achieving integration and fit between an organisation's SHRM & ER practices with its culture and values.

Strategic or vertical fit refers to achieving integration and fit between an organisation's SHRM & ER practices with its competitive strategy.

Horizontal or internal fit refers to achieving integration and fit by developing and implementing SHRM & ER practices that are internally consistent and mutually reinforcing.

Key Questions and Learning Activities

Question. 1 As an HR practitioner, how would you carry out a strategic analysis from an HR perspective?

Question. 2 Analyse three influences on a firm's contextual environment. How are such influences likely to impact the strategic HR choices it may want to exercise?

Question. 3 Identify three examples of poor horizontal fit in HRM. What might be the common reasons for it?

Learning Activity: Analysing the Integration and Fit in the Call Centre Industry

With the increasing use of communication technologies, a number of call centres have sprung up in different parts of the world. A leading multinational company (MNC) has opened up subsidiaries and entered into a third party contracts with service providers in India and the Philippines for a range of call centre operations due to costs and skills arbitrage opportunities. Despite the economic rationale, this poses an interesting challenge for the MNC in managing its strategic fit and integration. This relates to differences between the subsidiary operation and/or in dealing with the third party providers. Your task is to:

- Identify the key issues of integration and fit in each scenario;
- Analyse the contextual conditions; and
- How might these issues be dealt with?

Bibliography

Applebaum, E., Bailey, T., Berg, P., & Kalleberg, A. (2000). *Manufacturing advantage: Why high-performance work systems pay off*. Ithaca: Cornell University Press.

Arthur, J. (1992). The link between business strategy and industrial relations systems in American steel minimills. *Industrial and Labor Relations Review, 45*, 488–506.

Bailey, T. (1993). Organizational innovation in the apparel industry. *Industrial Relations, 32*, 30–48.

Bailey, T., Berg, P., & Sandy, C. (2001). The effect of high-performance work practices on employee earnings in the steel, apparel, and medical electronics and imaging industries. *Industrial and Labor Relations Review, 54*, 525–543.

Baird, L., & Meshoulam, I. (1988). Managing two fits of strategic human resource management. *Academy of Management Review, 13*(1), 116–128.

Barney, J. (1991). Firm resources and sustained competitive advantage. *Journal of Management, 17*(1), 99–120.

Becker, B. E., Huselid, M. A., & Beatty, R. W. (2009). *The differentiated workforce: Transforming talent into strategic impact*. Boston: Harvard Business Press.

Boselie, P. (2010). Chapter 2: Strategic human resource management and context. In *Strategic human resource management: A balanced approach* (pp. 17–45). Berkshire: McGraw Hill Higher Education.

Boxall, P. (2003). HR strategy and competitive advantage in the service sector. *Human Resource Management Journal, 13*(3), 5–20.

Boxall, P., & Purcell, J. (2003). *Strategy and human resource management*. UK: Palgrave Macmillan.

Boxall, P., & Purcell, J. (2011). *Strategy and human resource management* (3rd ed.). London: Palgrave Macmillan.

Child, J. (1972). Organizational structure, environment and performance: The role of strategic choice. *Sociology, 6*(1), 1–22.

Child, J. (1997). Strategic choice in the analysis of action, structure, organizations and environment: Retrospect and prospect. *Organization Studies, 18*(1), 43–76.

Combs, J., Liu, Y., Hall, A., & Ketchen, D. (2006). How much do high-performance work practices matter? A meta-analysis of their effects on organizational performance. *Personnel Psychology, 59*(3), 501–528.

Fombrun, C., Tichy, N. M., & Devanna, M. A. (1984). *Strategic human resource management*. New York: Wiley.

Huselid, M. A. (1995). The impact of human resource management practices on turnover, productivity, and corporate financial performance. *Academy of Management Journal, 38*(3), 635–672.

Kaufman, B. E. (2010). SHRM theory in the Post-Huselid Era: Why it is fundamentally misspecified. *Industrial Relations: A Journal of Economy and Society, 49*(2), 286–313.

Lawler, E. E., Mohrman, S. A., & Ledford, D. E. (1998). *Strategies for high performance organisations: Employee involvement, TQM and reengineering programs in fortune 1000 corporations*. San Francisco: Jossey-Bass.

Lepak, D. P., & Snell, S. A. (1999). The human resource architecture: Toward a theory of human capital allocation and development. *Academy of management review, 24*(1), 31–48.

Marchington, M., & Grugulis, I. (2000). Best practice' human resource management: Perfect opportunity or dangerous illusion? *International Journal of Human Resource Management, 11*, 1104–1124.

Mason, G. (2005). *In search of high value added production: how important are skills?* London: Department for Education and Skills.

Millmore, M. (2007). *Strategic human resource management: Contemporary issues*. UK: Pearson Education.

Pfeffer, J. (1998). Seven practices of successful organizations. *California Management Review, 40*, 96–124.

Porter, M. (1985). *Creating and sustaining superior performance*. New York: Free Pess.

Purcell, J. (1999). Best practice and best fit: Chimera or cul-de-sac? *Human Resource Management Journal, 9*(3), 26–41.

Purcell, J., Kinnie, N., Hutchinson, S., Rayton, B., & Swart, J. (2003). *Understanding the people and performance link: Unlocking the black box*. London: CIPD.

Schuler, R. S., & Jackson, S. (1987). Linking competitive strategies with human resource management practices. *Academy of Management Executive, 1*, 207–219.

Stewart, G., & Brown, K. (2009). *Human resource management: Linking strategy to practice*. Hoboken: Wiley.

Walton, R. (1985). From control to commitment in the workplace. *Harvard Business Review, 52*, 77–84.

Further Study Resources

Baron, J., & Kreps, D. (1999). Consistent human resource practices. *California Management Review, 41*, 29–53.

Bamber, G., Gittell, J. H., Kochan, T., & von Nordenflycht, A. (2009). *Up in the air: How airlines can improve performance by engaging their employees*. Cornell: ILR Press.

Brown, C., Reich, M., & Stern, D. (1993). Becoming a high-performance work organization: The role of security, employee involvement and training. *The International Journal of Human Resource Management, 4*, 247–275.

Cappelli, P. (1985). Competitive pressures and labor relations in the airline industry. *Industrial Relations, 24*(3), 316–338.

Gittell, J. H., & Bamber, G. (2010). High- and low-road strategies for competing on costs and their implications for employment relations: International studies in the airline industry. *The International Journal of Human Resource Management, 21*(2), 165–179.

Harvey, G., & Turnbull, P. (2010). On the go: Walking the high road at a low cost airline. *The International Journal of Human Resource Management, 21*(2), 230–241.

Hoque, K. (1999). Human resource management and performance in the UK hotel industry. *British Journal of Industrial Relations, 37*, 419–443.

Ichniowski, C., Kochan, T., Levine, D., Olson, C., & Strauss, G. (1996). What works at work: Overview and assessment. *Industrial Relations, 35*, 299–333.

MacDuffie, J. P. (1995). Human resource bundles and manufacturing performance: Organisational logic and flexible production systems in the world auto industry. *Industrial and Labor Relations Review, 48*, 197–221.

Miles, R. E., & Snow, C. C. (1978). *Organizational strategy, structure and process*. New York: McGraw-Hill.

Pfeffer, J. (1994). *Competitive advantage through people: Unleashing the power of the workforce*. Boston: Harvard Business School Press.

Pfeffer, J. (1998). *The human equation*. Boston: Harvard Business School Press.

Stavroua, E., Brewster, C., & Charalambous, C. (2010). Human resource management and firm performance in Europe through the lens of business systems: Best fit, best practice or both? *International Journal of Human Resource Management, 21*(7), 933–962.

Whitfield, K., & Poole, M. (1997). Organizing employment for high performance: Theories, evidence and policy. *Organization Studies, 18*, 745–764.

SHRM & ER: The Resource-Based View

Ashish Malik

Key Learning Outcomes
At the end of this chapter, you should be able to:

- *Define the terms competencies, capabilities and sustained competitive advantage*
- *Define the key elements of the VRIO framework*
- *Analyse how resources can be the basis for sustained competitive advantage*
- *Evaluate the role of SHRM practices in applying VRIO*

Introduction

The earlier chapters focused on an 'outside-in' view of strategy as applied to SHRM & ER. In some ways this approach brings balance to the literature on strategic management, which in the early stages of its development had an extensive reliance on rational, outside-in views of strategy. Therefore by including an inside-out approach to strategic analysis, an alternate and exciting avenue of investigation and analysis allows us to understand how a firm's internal endowments can be leveraged for sustained competitive advantage. Labelled as the resource-based view (RBV) of a firm, this approach to managing people has its foundations in Penrose's (1959) work. Penrose described a firm as an administrative structure and collection resources that are put to productive use for achieving an organisation's production goals. Through their subjective interpretation of the firm's strategic mileu, senior management team decides the nature of (heterogeneous) resources they need to

A. Malik (✉)
Faculty of Business and Law, Central Coast Business School, The University of Newcastle, Ourimbah, Central Coast, NSW, Australia
e-mail: ashish.malik@newcastle.edu.au

develop for achieving sustained competitive advantage. Penrose further argued that it is *how* a firm implements and organizes these bundles of resources and capabilities that forms the basis of an organisation's competitive advantage, rather than relying on possessing value creating resources and capabilities. The focus on resources and capabilities has also been popularised by the work of Prahalad and Hamel (1990). This chapter examines the resources and organisational capabilities that matter and how firms ought to organize resources for achieving sustained competitive advantage.

Managers are affected by the limits of their rationality and the challenges posed by asymmetrical market information about the nature and extent of competition. It is through their subjective and partial interpretations that managers make choices and take decisions about how they may be able to remain competitive in a market. Firms that are successful achieve competitive parity or have a clear competitive advantage over their competitors. When they are able to do so over sustained periods of time, they are said to have achieved sustained competitive advantage (SCA). The key focus of the RBV is to create SCA through investing in and organising their resources and capabilities. These resources can be tangible (e.g. physical and financial) or intangible (organisational, patents and skilled human resources). In the context of managing people, we are most interested in how human resources management policy choices and organisational strategies help in achieving SCA.

Resource-Based View of the Firm

The RBV, following Penrose's seminal work in late 1950s regained momentum in 1980s when Wernerfelt (1984), Barney (1991) and Barney, Ketchen and Wright (2011) developed the idea further and applied it to the field of strategy. The RBV's current conceptualisation proposes a framework for analysing how firms may achieve sustained competitive advantage. Using the VRIO (value, rarity, inimitability, and organisation) framework proposed by Barney and Hesterly (2010), managers and researchers must answer following four questions about a resource or capability before they can determine the competitive benefits such resources or capabilities may offer: the question of value, rarity, inimitability and organisation of resources to an organisation's productive use (Barney 1991; Barney and Hesterly 2010).

Illustrations and Skills Sandpit

Applying the VRIO Framework in Practice

Analysing each element of framework, examples from practice are presented here for some clarity of its application. With regards to the first question on focusing on *value* (**V**) adding resources, Barney and Hesterly (2010) suggest managers need to ask whether resources in question help overcome threats or exploit an opportunity?; does it enhance a firms competitive position in the market? By answering questions whether a resource is valuable one can proceed to examine the subsequent questions of rarity and inimitability. Are the resources controlled by a small group of competing firms. Consider a range of resources that are rare. For example, owning **real estate near Sydney Opera House** is an example of how a physical resource will continue to be valuable and deliver rents on a sustained basis. Such a resource is also rare and cannot be substituted in full. Similarly, take the example of an intangible resource, ESPN's "**X-games**" sport channel, is rare, at least temporally till other channels develop alternate media to compete in its position (Barney and Hesterly 2010). Even if other channels want to imitate (I) this channel, they might find it extremely hard to do so in a way that ESPN does. Barney and Hesterly (2010) cite the unsuccessful example of NBC with Gravity games, which wasn't as successful as ESPN. From my research of firms operating in the Indian IT industry, there are several examples of product development firms and how their resources have created barriers that are difficult to imitate. For example, at a large US MNC specialising in embedded chips and microprocessor design firm, this MNC requested several customisation requests for its People Management ERP (enterprise resource planning) software module to the software company, such that any competitor wishing to copy it would render it an extremely expensive exercise. Further, the software may still not be fully transferable to the firm wishing to copy and adopt that software application.

Even though these seminal works have had a significant impact in shaping the inside-out view of strategy, they are not free from its detractors. For example, Kor and Mahoney (2004) offer a rejoinder to Rugman and Verbeke (2002) who underestimated the contributions made by Penrose's original work from the late 1950s. They argue that Penrose offered enough clarity of how this approach can be a source of competitive advantage to firms. Penrose, for example, noted the following in relation to creating value: "There is a close relation between the various kinds of resources with which a firm works and the development of the ideas, experience, and knowledge of its managers and entrepreneurs, and we have seen how changing experience and knowledge affect not only the productive services available from resources, but also 'demand' as seen by the firm. Unused productive services are, for the enterprising firm, at the same time a challenge to innovate, an incentive to expand, and a source of competitive advantage. They facilitate the introduction of new combinations of resources – innovation – within the firm (Penrose 1959, p. 85; emphasis added)."

Additional considerations of whether a resource hard to imitate or copy by competitors is also a critical consideration? Penrose argued that not only it is important for firms to acquire resources that are valuable but also invest in maintaining them so they remain relevant over a period of time. Penrose stated in this regard (1959: 136–7) "In entering any new field, a firm must consider not only the rate of return it might expect on its new investment but also whether or not its resources are likely to be sufficient for the maintenance of the rate of investment that will be required to keep up with competitors' innovations and expansion in its existing fields as well as in the new one. Even when a firm enters a new field armed with a revolutionary innovation and is able to ward off competition with patent protection or other restrictive devices, it must expect that in time it will be overtaken if it fails to continue to develop its advantage." In this regard, imperfect inimitability can be achieved if the firms without such resource face considerable disadvantage in acquiring or developing it. This can be achieved by developing barriers to imitation through aspects such as path dependence or unique historical conditions, causal ambiguity, social complexity and protection via patents (Barney 1991; Barney and Hesterly 2010). In relation to the above, Penrose argued that 'the services that resources will yield depend on the capacities of the men using them, but the development of the capacities of men is partly shaped by the resources men deal with. The two together create the special productive opportunity of a particular firm' (pp. 78–9).

Finally, the resource in question should be organised in such a way that it cannot be easily copied or transferred to other organisations. Does the resource have context 'stickiness'? It depends on how a firm's organisation structure and design prevents imitation or creates barriers for it. Additionally, the intangible managerial and HR practices, management values and philosophy is considered important in the organisation of such resources. Finally, the extent to which a firm invests in the development of higher order capabilities (Barney 1991; Barney and Hesterly 2010) also ensures the resource to remain a source of SCA. Penrose maintained the importance of tacit and firm-specific knowledge that managers in an organisation would possess. Such knowledge along with collective shared experiences of other managers is extremely valuable. As highlighted by Penrose (1959: 46), "Existing managerial personnel provide services that cannot be provided by personnel newly hired from outside the firm, not only because they make up the administrative organization which cannot be expanded except by their own actions, but also because the experience they gain from working within the firm and with each other enables them to provide services that are uniquely valuable for the operations of the particular group with which they are associated."

Critical Reflections

Even though the RBV has remained a popular approach within SHRM and strategic management literature, Priem and Butler (2001) identify several difficulties in the RBV, most of which share common concerns about the weak operationalisation of its somewhat abstract constructs. The authors even challenge whether RBV is a theory? This is especially the case as the empirical evidence is often hard to collate on the VRIO elements of the framework. Second, the independent (Value and Rarity) and dependent (SCA) variables are defined in terms of value, which creates problems in assessing the logic of this approach empirically. As with any approach on assessing the *performance* of a system, one has to always deal with the performance black box, as there often are a number of internal and external factors affecting it. There is also some critique levelled at this approach

Table 1 The VRIO framework and competitive advantage

Valuable?	Rare?	Costly to imitate?	Exploited by the organisation?	Competitive implications	Strengths or weaknesses
No	–	–	No	Competitive disadvantage	Weakness
Yes	No	–		Competitive parity	Strength
Yes	Yes	No		Temporary competitive Advantage	Strength and distinctive competence
Yes	Yes	Yes	Yes	Sustained competitive advantage	Strength and sustainable distinctive competence

Source: Adapted from Barney and Hesterly (2010): 84, Tables 3 and 4

regarding the excessive dependence on *internal* resources and a firm's ability to deploy and use it. Limited attempts have been integrate the 'inside-out' with 'outside-in' approaches, as one can logically argue that firms also need to be cognisant of the external markets in relations to the goods and services they plan to offer. The literature on RBV suggests that this approach may be more applicable to older and established firms as they would have had certain path dependencies and organised their resources in a manner that offers rarity and uniqueness. Because of the social complexity, unique and historical path dependence, and stickiness of the context, it is very difficult for others to understand through the RBV, how rare, unique and non-substitutable resources are developed in the first place or how and which HR practices need to be aligned for the development of certain capabilities in different contexts. As some have argued that excessive focus on core capabilities and competencies may potentially result in a firm developing core rigidities, which in times of a dynamic and volatile environment may make these firms more vulnerable (Leonard-Barton 1992). Finally, Priem and Butler (2001) argue that the RBV is tautological and needs more clarity and rework before it can be empirically tested.

The extent to which a resource or capability is valuable, rare, inimitable will determine the extent of its competitive advantage as shown in Table 1 above.

Applying RBV to SHRM

However, as focus is on applying RBV to HRM, Prahalad and Hamel's (1990) idea of a 'core competence', is relevant here. The authors note this as a set of skills and technologies that represents a firm's ability to use them productively for current and future business needs. Firms always have choices where to invest and which resources they need to invest in.

Wright et al. (1994) differentiated between human capital (key quality of resources) from the approaches (specific HR practices) that are used in managing human capital to create value, rarity, inimitability and non-substitutability. They argued that while human capital is critical, getting the right behaviours is vital. Lado and Wilson (1994), on the contrary argue and highlight the need for a collective system of HR practices to be a source of uniqueness and inimitability. Building on these discourses, Boxall (1996) introduced the idea of human capital advantage (HCA), wherein firms, through effective approaches of human capital management (i.e. by recruiting and retaining people with high-value, tacit knowledge and skills) and human process advantage (HPA) or superior social capital (i.e. by managing people in unique ways to secure their trust, cooperation and commitment) achieve SCA. Notationally, they expressed human resource advantage (HRA) as a function of HCA and HPA or HRA = f (HCA, HPA). Wright, Dunford and Snell (2001), building on Penrose, Wernerfelt (1984) and Rumlet's (1984) work, provide an excellent account of how the RBV can be applied to the study of SHRM. In their conceptualization, they argue for the role of HR practices in building both the human capital and critical behaviours and relationships between the employees. Related to the above, Boxall and Purcell (2011) caution the problem of appropriation of the value thus generated through deployment of resources within the organisation. The underlying argument is that value and benefits accruing from the above may not always translate into higher profits due to the political processes of appropriation of value and profits by the dominant coalition of stakeholders, who created and captured value in the first place. This dominant coalition can also destroy the value created through misappropriation of profits and value.

Conclusion

To conclude, while individual HR policies alone are less likely to generate SCA or superior value, a collective set of *HR systems* can along with the right pool of human capital and organisational capabilities. In the RBV of a firm, HCA and HPA collectively, can be a source of SCA. To capture value, firms need to think of developing resource heterogeneity and barriers to imitation by focusing on aspects such timing, nature of learning, social complexity and causal ambiguity. Finally, not all resources are equal in enabling a firm to build similar capabilities in its industry; some have the potential to generate distinctive value, while some resources can have a negative impact on value creation and indeed some managerial actions of misappropriation of profits can indeed lead to destruction of value.

Glossary

Capabilities of an organisation can be viewed as the organisation's ability to utilize its resource base in a way that it effectively and efficiently delivers on its business objectives. In short, it is those set of activities that a firm does very well. For such capabilities to be a source of competitive advantage, a firm must utilise these better than other firms.

Competencies can be defined as a set of knowledge, skills and abilities that are needed to successfully perform a set of tasks.

Sustained Competitive advantage is a firm's ability to remain successful over a long period of time in relation to its competitive peer group through its resource and capability endowments

Key Questions and Learning Activities

Question. 1 Competing at a professional level requires you to offer something that is distinctive, inimitable and rare. Can you identify any aspects of your personal HR competency(ies) and capability(ies) that provide you with an advantage? If so, how might you try and apply these to a business setting?

Question. 2 Thinking about your organisation's resources and capabilities, analyse and identify the resources that are rare, valuable, inimitable and organised in a way that allows your firm a source of competitive advantage. What barriers do you think might preserve such an advantage?

Question. 3 Thinking about your organisation's resources and capabilities, analyse and identify the resources that is neither rare, nor valuable and are organised in a way that allows imitation and is a cause of competitive parity or disadvantage. What investments or acquisition of new resources might offer your firm some competitive advantage?

Learning Activity: Applying the RBV to Disneyland

Using the VRIO framework, analyse the key resources that allows Disneyland Resorts a source of competitive advantage. Ensure you discuss each of the four elements of the **VRIO** framework.

Bibliography

Barney, J. B. (1991). Firm resources and sustained competitive advantage. *Journal of Management, 17*(1), 99–120.

Barney, J. B., & Hesterly, W. S. (2010). *Strategic management and competitive advantage: Concepts.* New York: Prentice hall.

Barney, J., Ketchen, D., & Wright, M. (2011). The future of resource-based theory: Revitalization or decline? *Journal of Management, 37*(5), 1–18.

Boxall, P., & Purcell, J. (2011). *Strategy and human resource management.* London: Palgrave Macmillan.

Boxall, P. (1996). The strategic HRM debate and the resource-based view of the firm. *Human Resource Management Journal, 6*(3), 59–75.

Kor, Y. Y., & Mahoney, J. T. (2004). Edith Penrose's (1959) contributions to the resource-based view of strategic management. *Journal of Management Studies, 41*(1), 183–191.

Lado, A. A., & Wilson, M. C. (1994). Human resource systems and sustained competitive advantage: A competency-based perspective. *Academy of Management Review, 19*(4), 699–727.

Leonard-Barton, D. (1992). Core capabilities and core rigidities: A paradox in managing new product development. *Strategic Management Journal, 13*(S1), 111–125.

Penrose, E. G. (1959). *The theory of the growth of the firm.* New York: Wiley.

Prahalad, C. K., & Hamel, G. (1990). The core competence of the corporation. *Harvard Business Review, 68*, 79–91.

Priem, R. L., & Butler, J. E. (2001). Tautology in the resource-based view and the implications of externally determined resource value: Further comments. *Academy of Management review, 26*(1), 57–66.

Rugman, A. M., & Verbeke, A. (2002). Edith Penrose's contribution to the resource-based view of strategic management. *Strategic Management Journal, 23*(8), 769–780.

Rumelt, R. P. (1984). Toward a strategic theory of the firm. In R. Lamb (Ed.), *Competitive strategic management* (pp. 556–570). Englewood Cliffs: Prentice-Hall.

Rumelt, R. P. (1991). How much does industry matter? *Strategic Management Journal, 12*, 167–185.

Wernerfelt, B. (1984). A resource-based view of the firm. *Strategic Management Journal, 5*(2), 171–180.

Wright, P., McMahan, G., & McWilliams, A. (1994). Human resources and sustained competitive advantage: A resource-based perspective. *International Journal of Human Resource Management, 5*, 301–326.

Wright, P., Dunford, B., & Snell, S. (2001). Human resources and the resource-based view of the firm. *Journal of Management, 27*(6), 701–721.

Institutional Theory and SHRM

Ashish Malik

Key Learning Outcomes
At the end of this chapter, you should be able to:

- *Analyse the impact of institutional mechanisms in shaping SHRM & ER practices*
- *Analyse the limits of institutional theory in developing differentiation*
- *Examine and analyse the relationship between institutional fit and SHRM & ER*

Introduction

In addition to the major schools of thought impacting the study of SHRM and ER, this chapter highlights the importance of institutions from a people management perspective. The impact of contextual environment, especially the influence of institutional mechanisms in shaping the nature and extent of SHRM practices is quite pervasive. This chapter begins by revisiting the importance of the wider external context and how various types of institutional mechanisms at work shape HRM practices. This requires a brief understanding of the core assumptions of institutional theory. Building on the author's recent research on India's information technology (IT) industry, a brief account is offered of how various institutional forces (Malik and Blumenfeld 2010; Malik 2013, 2015, 2017) and actors in a system (Malik and Nilakant 2015) shaped the nature and extent of HRM practices and the IT industry's growth (Nilakant 2005).

A. Malik (✉)
Faculty of Business and Law, Central Coast Business School, The University of Newcastle, Ourimbah, Central Coast, NSW, Australia
e-mail: ashish.malik@newcastle.edu.au

© Springer Nature Singapore Pte Ltd. 2018
A. Malik (ed.), *Strategic Human Resource Management and Employment Relations*, Springer Texts in Business and Economics,
https://doi.org/10.1007/978-981-13-0399-9_5

Within the domain of SHRM, some argue that work design and management of people in workplaces is governed by strategic choices exercised by the dominant coalition of stakeholders (Gooderham et al. 1999). For example, the authors argue that institutional norms, rules and structures can shape the final work and workplace practices. Still others who have attempted to adopt an inclusive approach by integrating the two theoretical approaches of institutional theory and strategic choice theory, argue for analysing their combined impact (Child 1972, 1997) in shaping work and workplace practices (Arthur 1992; Holman et al. 2009; Hunter 2000). Noting the debates on best-practice and best-fit theories in the SHRM literature, Paauwe and Boselie (2003) propose that the field is ready for an alternate explanation, as HRM practices, in much as they are shaped by internal strategic choices and context, they are also influenced by, and embedded in, a country's national institutional environment. Thus, many learnings from the tenets of institutional theory can be employed in furthering our understanding of SHRM & ER. Making a case for differences in institutional environments, say between the Anglo-Saxon nations such as the UK and US and Rhinish countries such as Germany, France and the Netherlands, Paauwe and Boselie (2003) proposed the concept of new institutionalism and highlight how the institutional context shapes the nature and extent of practices between regions.

Importance of Context

Boselie (2010, p. 42) notes that "Context represents the set of facts or circumstances that surround the organisation". He offers a further differentiation between internal and external contextual environment. In the main, Boselie argued that internal context includes an organisation's unique historcal paths, heritage and covers aspects such as the founder of the firm, the number of years since its establishment and the nature of its work organisation. As part of the work environment, the internal context focuses on the structure, how the production function is organised, its systems and procedures for managing workflow and the prevailing culture among the workers. In relation to the external environmental context, DiMaggio and Powell (1983), Pauwee (2004) and Boselie (2010: 23), noted two mechanisms: *market* and *institutional mechanisms*. While the former focuses on developing an understanding of the nature and extent of competition in a given firm's product and /or service markets, the latter focuses on the nature of regulatory pressures, controls and restrictions that are imposed by the environment. Such pressures also form the basis, albeit partially, on an organisation's procedures, formal and informal norms, routines, and choices of expressed and unstated value systems. Building on the above external environment classification, Deephouse (1999) suggests firms need to differentiate between its *general* and *population* environments. While the former environment is akin to DiMaggio and Powell's (1983) market and institutional environment, the latter (*population environment*), focuses on the meso-level differences at an industry level, similar to Porter's model of a firm's key competitors, suppliers and other organisations that contribute directly or indirectly to its value-chain. By explicating the contextual factors as per above, the following section focuses on key terms relevant in developing our understanding of institutional theory and how it might impact a firm's HRM practices.

Types of Institutional Mechanisms

Buidling on the seminal work of Scott (1995), institutions are defined as (p. 33): "cognitive, normative, and regulative structures that provide stability and meaning to social behaviour. Institutions are transported by various carriers- cultures, structures, and routines- and they operate at multiple levels of jurisdiction". Based on the above definition, the literature on institutional theory has three pillars: regulative, normative and cognitive pillars that variously impact people and organisations in a society (See Table 1 for details).

DiMaggio and Powell (1983) argue that both the market and institutional mechanisms have a homogenising impact on a firm, as a result, its business and HR practices tend to assume isomorphic forms or a state that is close to an equilibrium state. The authors further argue that socio-economic institutional mechanisms shape 'sameness' due to coercive, normative and mimetic pressures the above institutional mechanisms have on firms (see Table 1) (DiMaggio and Powell 1983, 1991; Scott 1995). The nature of pressure imposed by these three mechanisms is briefly discussed. For example, *coercive mechanisms* come into force through the political responses and for dealing with the issues of organisational legitimacy.

Applying Institutional Mechanisms

The key institutions herein that have an impact include: the trade unions, government legislation, work councils and so on. A number of legislative and compliance approaches require businesses to behave and comply in a certain way or else experience sanctions. For example, Workplace Health and Safety legislation, HIPPA and Sarbanes Oxley Act compliance requirements are good examples of how the industry has adopted their business and HR practices to deal with *Coercive mechanisms*. *Mimetic mechanisms* focus on firms to adopt standardised HRM practices in times of business uncertainty. In such cases, typically, firms copy HR and other business practices of highly successful or leading firms in a market. As in the past, people in

Table 1 Institutional theory- key approaches

	Regulative	Normative	Cognitive
Mechanism	Coercive	Normative	Mimetic
Logic	Instrumentality	Appropriateness	Orthodoxy
Indicators	Rules, laws, sanctions	Certification	Prevalence
Basis of legitimacy	Legally sanctioned	Morally governed	Culturally supported
Nature of knowledge	Social realist		Social constructionist

Adapted from Scott (1995)

IT procurement world would have said, 'nobody got fired for buying an IBM computer system'. There are many such examples that are considered as the gold standard in making certain decisions or indeed following development protocols for certain products and services that becomes the industry's norm e.g. The Toyota Production System or GE's application of Six Sigma and subsequently Lean Six Sigma for operational and process excellence. *Normative mechanisms* focus on what 'we ought to do' and emanates from organisations such as professional and educational bodies. In line with the above, Pauwee and Boselie (2003) applied the above mechanisms to the study and practice of HRM and noted that the above influences of coercive mechanisms leads to establishing the rules of the land and compliance as a result of regulation, mimetic mechanisms lead to adopting HRM 'blueprints' of best practices. Normative mechanisms will lead to 'formalised professional education' and 'homogeneity' of the HRM profession (Paauwe and Boselie 2003). It is not surprising to see similarity in the core modules typical in an undergraduate or a postgraduate HRM degree. Recently, the Australian Human Resource Institute, Australia's professional HR organisation, launched its certification and articulation pathways for recognising the competencies of HR practitioners by mapping these against their HR competency framework. The content similarity points to the isomorphic pressures, even though there may be some differences evident in the form of how the delivery of such content occurs. But in the main, the core curriculum studied and the competencies expected of HR practitioners remain more or less the same. The above points to an increased level of homogenisation of HRM practices and conduct by HR practitioners. Increasingly most HRM professional bodies, who have developed a code of conduct or a competency-framework for assessment and credentialing paints a similar picture.

Thus, while the issue of institutional isomorphism is very real in business environment, it does not help us understand how *institutional isomorphism* or sameness can be a source of sustained competitive advantage. This is an important point as firms typically need a 'space' for differentiation to be able to offer value that can command rent on a sustained basis. Building on the idea of reducing the degree of sameness in an organisation's internal and external contextual environment, Boon et al. (2009) argue that the extent to which firms can manoeuvre and exercise strategic choice is first of all is dependent on the nature of the wider institutional environment.

Overcoming Institutional Isomorphism: The Case of the Indian IT Industry

The institutional environment can sometimes be too restrictive or for some industries, as noted in the case of the Indian IT industry (Malik and Nilakant 2015), it can be expansive or less restrictive. Malik and Nilakant (2015) and Nilakant (2005) argue that at a time when the Indian IT industry was still finding its feet in the 1980s in establishing its identity, certain players in the Indian IT industry–from both the public and private sector–convinced the Indian government to liberalise the industry and allow several tax-incentives to attract foreign direct investment if the country wanted to boost its foreign exchange reserves, which, in the late 1980s, were at their lowest level in the history of India's economic development following the post-colonial era. Certain individuals succeeded in changing the nation's *dominant logic* of self-reliance and as a result convinced the key players in the government to allow several concessions and setting up of tax-free export processing zones for the Indian IT industry. What this illustration shows is that people, firms and industries always have some degree of *leeway* in exercising strategic choices and the role of *human agency* in the exercise of managerial and leadership *choices* exists, even if there are adverse legislative and institutional conditions. The role of human agency was also noted in a recent study of how firms navigated and in some cases circumvented the adverse impacts of the global financial crisis in the Indian IT industry (Malik 2017). In this context, it can be argued that the degree of leeway to manoeuvre is higher in a growing market. *Institutional pressures,* Boon et al. (2009) argue are often mediated by an organisation's power, politics, culture relationships and forces of change. In any environmental setting then, organisations can and do have the ability to manipulate constraints and therefore expand or constrict the degree of leeway in exercising its strategic choices. In such cases, Boon et al. (2009) note three possible types of institutional fits: first, a *conformist fit,* wherein nothing much changes and firms succumb to institutional pressures and maintain a status quo simply because the human agency is passive or neutral. Second, for an *innovative fit,* however, Boon et al. (2009) argue that by pursuing active developmental agentic choices, firms can expand their degree of leeway and implement innovative solutions even in a constrained institutional environment. This occurs when firms and its human agency actively look for solutions that are outside the box and convince the dominant stakeholders in various institutional bodies to change their dominant logic and allow for the emergence of a new and innovative fit. Such a fit was evident in the firms in the Indian IT industry, who, in a post- global crisis environment went back to their clients and/or their parent firms to allow space and avenues to explore new business and services rather than making several employees redundant during the GFC. Details of such strategic choices are covered in the next chapter where, in a similar vein, strategic choice theory is examined in terms of its influences on HR and management practices. Finally, the third strategic fit, a *deviant fit,* was also proposed by the authors as a mechanism to raise voice against the isomorphic institutional pressures. This is a common occurrence in the direct and indirect forms of employee voice evident in trade union bargaining and individual negotiations with the key stakeholders who may be able to offer greater degree of leeway and choice when active human agency is exercised. Boon et al. (2009) through their research demonstrated how through human agency, the menu of strategic choices can be expanded thus allowing additional leeway to deal with institutionally imposed constraints.

Critical Reflections

While the importance of contextual factors and the need for maintaining an institutional fit has been highlighted by several researchers, Boon et al. (2009) have found that excessive institutional pressure decreases the degree of differentiation a firm can have in its SHRM practices and consequently result in sub-optimal levels of performance. Further, not having a right balance between different institutional mechanisms may also result in competitive disadvantage. Thus, there is a need to maintain an appropriate balance between institutional and competitive pressures and its interactions with human agency to achieve a desired institutional fit.

Illustrations and Skills Sandpit

The role of *human agency* is critical in changing the dominant institutional logic. Strategic choice theory also points to the politically negotiated nature of strategic choices that are evident in business decisions. Thus, it becomes necessary for the HR practitioner for achieving an institutional fit that is creative. Following actions are critical in developing such a fit:

- *Develop political acumen and skills to be able to successfully navigate through the political processes of institutional and resource-based decisions*
- *Develop their leadership skills to challenge the status quo*
- *Engage in lateral thinking for breaking the mould that prevails as a result of institutional isomorphism*

Concept Integration with Cases and Learning Activities

Aspects of the application of institutional theory are highlighted in three cases on *Crisis and IHRM, Recontextualizing diversity: The German Case* and *Patanjali: The Black Swan*. In these case studies, there is ample evidence of various institutional mechanisms at work and how the human agency employed in the case studies creates an opportunity for the business.

Conclusion

While institutional mechanisms have a pervasive impact in shaping the behaviour of people and people in society through normative, cognitive and mimetic mechanisms, from a strategic HRM point of view, the relationship between institutional theory and SHRM dominant schools, on the surface seems to be at odds as firms seek legitimacy of their actions. Through institutional isomorphic pressures, firms often struggle to deliver differentiation, a core theme in strategic HRM literature. The examples used in this chapter highlight the importance of interactions between context, human agency and institutional environment to deliver three types of institutional fits, of which two fits (deviant and innovative fit) can be a source of differentiation and sustained competitive advantage. The extent of this will vary in each context, and depends on, the quality of human agency in each organisation's strategic milieu.

Glossary

Environmental fit refers to that fit when a firm aligns its business objectives to meet some aspects of the wider business and institutional environment.

General environment refers to that part of the business environment which focuses on the macroeconomic business environment affecting a firm's business.

Institutional fit is said to be in operation when a firm chooses to align its business and HR practices to any one or all three of the institutional mechanisms.

Institutional mechanisms are the three commonly understood mechanisms of institutional pressures on businesses that emanate from legislation (coercive), professional or ethical norms (normative) and copying market best-practices (mimetic).

Population environment refers to that external environment of a group of business organisations that belong to a particular population e.g. an industry.

Key Questions and Learning Activities

Question. 1 Explain the concepts of leeway, strategic choice and human agency as applied to the concepts covered in institutional theory.

Question. 2 What are the key influences of various contextual factors in shaping HRM and ER practices in organisations?

Question. 3 What are the different choices of fit typically available to HR practitioners and managers in overcoming institutional isomorphism?

Learning Activity: Applying Institutional Theory

Thinking of your current or past work organisation, identify the three institutional mechanisms from institutional theory and discuss how some or all of these mechanisms might be in operation at these organisations.

Bibliography

Arthur, J. B. (1992). The link between business strategy and industrial relations systems in American steel minimills. *ILR Review, 45*(3), 488–506.

Ashton, D., & Sung, J. (2006). *How competitive strategy matters? Understanding the drivers of training, learning and performance at the firm level* (Research paper no. 66). Oxford: Oxford and Warwick Universities, Centre for Skills, Knowledge and Organisational Performance.

Bélanger, J., Edwards, P., & Wright, M. (1999). Best HR practice and the multinational company. *Human Resource Management Journal, 9*, 53–70.

Boon, C., Paauwee, B., Boslie, P., & Hartog, D. (2009). Institutional pressures and HRM: Developing institutional fit. *Personnel Review, 38*(5), 492–508.

Boselie, P. (2010). *Strategic human resource management: A balanced approach*. Berkshire: McGraw Hill Higher Education.

Boselie, P., Dietz, G., & Boon, C. (2005). Commonalities and contradictions in HRM and performance. *Human Resource Management Journal, 15*(1), 67–94.

Boxall, P. (2003). HR strategy and competitive advantage in the service sector. *Human Resource Management Journal, 13*(3), 5–20.

Child, J. (1972). Organizational structure, environment and performance: The role of strategic choice. *Sociology, 6*(1), 1–22.

Child, J. (1997). Strategic choice in the analysis of action, structure, organizations and environment: Retrospect and prospect. *Organization Studies, 18*(1), 43–76.

Deephouse, D. L. (1999). To be different or to be same? It's a question (and theory) of strategic balance. *Strategic Management Journal, 20*(2), 147–166.

DiMaggio, P. J., & Powell, W. W. (1983). *The new institutionalism in organizational analysis*. Chicago: University of Chicago Press.

DiMaggio, P. J., & Powell, W. W. (Eds.). (1991). The new institutionalism in organizational analysis. Chicago: University of Chicago Press.

Gooderham, P. N., Nordhaug, O., & Ringdal, K. (1999). Institutional and rational determinants of organizational practices: Human resource management in European firms. *Administrative Science Quarterly, 44*(3), 507–531.

Holman, D., Frenkel, S., Sørensen, O., & Wood, S. (2009). Work design variation and outcomes in call centers: Strategic choice and institutional explanations. *ILR Review, 62*(4), 510–532.

Hunter, L. W. (2000). What determines job quality in nursing homes? *ILR Review, 53*(3), 463–481.

Malik, A. (2013). Post-GFC people management challenges: A study of India's information technology sector. *Asia Pacific Business Review, 19*(2), 230–246. https://doi.org/10.1080/13602381.2013.767638.

Malik, A. (2015). The role of HR strategies in change. In A. Goksoy (Ed.), *Organisational change management strategies in modern business* (pp. 192–214). Hershey: IGGI Global Publishers.

Malik, A. (2017). *Human resource management and the global financial crisis: Evidence from India's IT/BPO industry*. London: Routledge.

Malik, A., & Blumenfeld, S. (2010). *Temporal analysis of evolving organisational capabilities in India's information technology (IT) sector*. Paper presented at the 2010 academy of management meeting, Montreal, Canada.

Malik, A., & Nilakant, V. (2015). Context and evolution of the Indian IT industry. In A. Malik & C. Rowley (Eds.), *Business models and people management in the Indian IT industry: From people to profits* (1st ed., pp. 15–34). Abingdon: Routledge.

Mason, G. (2005, May). *In search of high value added production: How important are skills?* (Research report no. 663). Nottingham: Department for Education and Skills.

Nilakant, V. (2005) *Institutional dynamics in the evolution of the Indian software industry*. Paper presented at the academy of management meeting.

Paauwe, J. (2004). *HRM and performance: Achieving long-term viability*. Oxford: Oxford University Press.

Paauwe, B., & Boslie, P. (2003). Challenging 'strategic HRM' and the relevance of institutional setting. *Human Resource Management Journal, 13*(3), 56–70.

Scott, W. R. (1995). *Contemporary institutional theory, chapter 3 in institutions and organizations*. Thousand Oaks: Sage Publications.

Strategic Choice and SHRM & ER

Ashish Malik

Key Learning Outcomes
At the end of this chapter, you should be able to:

- *Apply the concept of strategic choice to the study and practice of SHRM & ER*
- *Identify the common strategic choice options and its impact on SHRM & ER*
- *Analyse the role of HRM and ER in post-merger integration*
- *Critically evaluate the contribution of SHRM in M&A contexts*

Introduction

While there are similarities in the concepts covered in the previous chapter on institutional theory and the role of human agency with the notion of strategic choice, strategic choice receives a much broader treatment in the study of strategic management. Keeping in line with the pluralist approach adopted in this book, this chapter examines the application of concepts from strategic management literature and applies these to SHRM and ER. One mustn't forget that strategy is not just the exclusive domain of management; even unions and other forms of employee associations have strategies, which can have a profound impact in shaping the nature and extent of employment relationships and a range of employment outcomes. Additionally, for firms to grow, not only do they exercise strategic choices in terms of their business, competitive and functional strategies, additional strategic choices are available to firms to operate in new markets and seek growth through different strategic choices in each. While one dominant view in line with planning school of

---

A. Malik (✉)
Faculty of Business and Law, Central Coast Business School, The University of Newcastle, Ourimbah, Central Coast, NSW, Australia
e-mail: ashish.malik@newcastle.edu.au

© Springer Nature Singapore Pte Ltd. 2018
A. Malik (ed.), *Strategic Human Resource Management and Employment Relations*, Springer Texts in Business and Economics,
https://doi.org/10.1007/978-981-13-0399-9_6

strategy is that firms and its leaders exercise strategic choices based on a systematic and rational analysis of their internal and external environments, another view from the organisational theory focuses on the theoretical lenses of sociology and social psychology (Child 1972, 1997). The central idea of this latter view is that managers and leaders in organisations play a critical role in influencing the organisation by making strategic choices. This is essentially a dynamic and political *process*. The role of human agency in navigating through the political processes is a powerful one as rationality sometimes gets challenged and people (leaders engaged in such process) may sometimes exercise choices that serve their vested interests. The study of these processes must be context-specific as each organisation has its unique historical path dependence and organisational learning processes that have been developed in response to its external environment over a period of time. Further, each organisation will have its own intensity of political and power exchanges between the key and diverse set of stakeholders. Hence, by implication, firms offer some differentiation in any institutional environment however, harnessing this in a positive way for sustained competitive advantage is often a political process and in some cases such a process may not yield the most desirable results.

Firm Growth and Strategic Choices: Internationalization and Cross-Border Acquisitions

Strategic choices in the literature on strategic management focuses on a menu of options firms can select from, for pursuing their growth strategies (Child 1972). This assumption stems from a view that firms are operating in a market-based economy and have to pursue a growth strategy in order to survive in the longer term. The literature, from an Anglo-Saxon context, highlights three distinctive forms of organisation for pursuing growth: generic expansion (which may be in home country or across international borders), mergers and acquisitions, or a hybrid/network strategy (Contractor and Lorange 1988; Penrose 1959; Yip 1982 as cited in Peng and Heath 1996). The moment the strategic choice of expanding operations to international context is taken, a firm may have embarked on its path to becoming a multinational corporation (MNC). This decision has huge set of resourcing implications and development of skills and resources that require a higher level of complexity than would have been expected in a domestic context. The core activities of HRM: procure, allocate and utilize will require further considerations such as of managing home, host and other country's cultural and institutional influences and the nature of resources. The nature of resources will also become diverse: in that, the internationalising firm will end up invariably employing some mix of parent country nationals, host country nationals and third country nationals (Dowling 2008). Strategic management of these diverse groups of employees is always challenging (Schuler et al. 1993). The entire HRM function suddenly receives a major revamp in terms of its orientation. For example, for procuring human resources, this will now involve sending organisationally assigned expatriates–the most common form of international assignments, which will require firms to invest in extensive cross-cultural training for sensitizing to the new cultural and national context of the host country. Apart from selecting expatriates, the additional issues of expatriates' familial needs such as accommodation, kids' education and medical needs and ensuring the cultural assimilation and integration processes are smooth, pose additional challenges for the HRM function. The related topic of expatriate compensation requires a very different understanding of local tax laws and ways of maintaining parity with the current levels and ensuring additional compensation is offered in the form of difficulty allowance and cost of living allowance, in the host country. Similarly, the performance management needs to be contextualized in relation to the local norms and should not be judged by the parent firm's current approaches, as some of these might not be culturally relevant and applicable in the host country. A key debate in this decision is whether a firm wants to focus on global integration of its practices or is accepting of locally responsive practices (Prahalad and Doz 1987). Others have looked at these issues as whether a firm wants to press for convergence of its HR and management best-practices or does it want to allow divergence in the form of accepting local host and third country influences or a hybrid approach called crossvergence in HRM practices and values (Ralston 2008).

Boxall and Purcell (2011) noted several differences in a MNC's strategic response from an HRM perspective. In brief, they argue that MNCs have the added task of coordinating the activities of subsidiary operations and other partners across its global value chain of production networks around the world. This is a very demanding enterprise. It is inherent with social, political, cultural and economic complexity and firms are often presented with balancing the dualities of local responsiveness with global integration. A common issue that most large MNCs face today is the issue of social legitimacy of their actions, as there are numerous instances wherein MNCs have been accused of putting profits over people and shying away from their global citizenship responsibilities. These developments have led to the formation of global codes of corporate governance by MNCs in a bid to 'fix' the problem but the ground realities are far from what is being practised. In the main, the short-term profit maximization agendas prevail and MNCs do not shy away from implementing changes to (or more specifically shifting) their production bases to economies where the labour cost and skills arbitrage offered is the highest. Some MNCs have also been accused of siphoning off profits through tax havens and not contributing to taxes in the host countries from where they profit. In view of the above, one can imagine the complexity HRM role can witness through such a strategic choice. Thus, multiple influences are expected through such a decision shaping the nature and extent of strategic HRM and ER practices.

The second approach focuses on growth through a network of inter-organisational collaborative relationships (Contractor and Lorange 1988). Depending on the strategic choice exercised, the nature and extent of a firm's SHRM and ER practices will vary significantly. Again, these networks of inter-organisational collaborative relationships can be in a domestic or an international context. If it is in the latter, the degree of complexity will be much higher as it will involve different sets of relational and hierarchical market contracts to manage the performance of these networks. This will necessarily require a different set of relational skills in ensuring a firm's production chain functions effectively. Finally, among key strategic choices for growth, mergers and acquisitions (M&A) is regarded as a major strategic choice available to grow and expand a firm's portfolio of products and services and/or to enter new markets (Bauer and Matzler 2014). For example, when a firm exercises merger and acquisition as a strategic choice for growth, they need to be cautious of not only the purpose and benefits that such a decision will have on its growth (Haspeslagh and Jemison 1991), but also keep in mind, right from the start, how to manage the post-merger integration processes, especially if, the merger and acquisition is cross-border in nature. Following on from Haspeslagh and Jemison's (1991) influential work on the commonly noted structures that result following an M&A activity, for example, absorption, preservation, symbiotic and a subsidiary of a holding company, the authors suggest that the nature and extent of effort that will be required by bidder and target firms will vary depending on the preferred structure of the post-merger integration. Based on the preferred integration structure, the bidder firm will have to reconfigure and integrate its capabilities and competencies to fully realize the benefits it seeks to achieve from the M&A choice. The decisions are often irreversible and carry major resource allocation implications. Although it is vital for bidder firms to successfully integrate their target firms, there is sufficient indication in the literature that suggests of failures in a post-merger integration stage (Cartwright and Schoenberg 2006; Haleblian and Finkelstein 1999; Tuch and O'Sullivan 2007). Among the commonly noted reasons for M&A failure include: absence of a cultural fit between the acquirer and the acquired (e.g. Graebner et al. 2017), impracticable expectations on part of the buyer firm, overconfidence of the buyer firm in handling the integration (Roll 1986), lack of trust between the bidder and the target, and finally poor post-merger integration capability of the bidder firm. In most M&As, there are significant people management issues at stake, right from the due diligence process, to reducing stress and anxiety levels of employees at the target firm. This is particularly the case in enabling functions where there are high levels of skill and role relatedness. While the above discussion gives an idea of the impact of strategic choices on HRM and ER issues, the following section provides an overview of strategic choices in relation to ER strategies.

Employment Relations Strategies

A strategic approach to employment relations encapsulates a pluralist approach adopted by a firm's managers. Such an approach adopts a longer-term view, and takes into account the expectations of both the workforce and the demands placed by a range of stakeholders. In other words, ER strategy in all businesses, public or private sector is that part of an organisation's strategy, which is related to industrial/ employment/employee relations. Depending on the context, ER strategy of a firm may well be part of an organisation's HR strategy, or is separate to and /or even dominate a firm's HR strategy. Building on Child's (1972) strategic choice theory, Kochan et al. (1984) identified how a key actor in an industrial relation system– the employer–implements strategic choice adopting a pluralist framework that is typically associated with the study of industrial relations. One criticism of such a system is that it stresses on the importance of the interests and roles of unions and governments and focuses, in the main, on the process of strategy formulation rather than it's content and outcomes. The authors further argue that *strategic choice* is bound by two conditions: "Strategic decisions can only occur where the parties have discretion over their decisions; that is, where environmental constraints do not severely curtail the parties' choice of alternatives" (p.21). By discretion Kochan et al. mean the ability to exercise *fully and freely* one's judgement. They provide examples such as how government policy can impose constraints over the extent of unionisation, collective bargaining or other market conditions, which then affects the pricing of product and services a firm can offer or indeed the appropriation of profits by senior management teams and/or its employees' remuneration decisions. The authors argue that the degree of discretion is a function of the nature of the goals pursued. For instance, there is scope for some leeway for parties if they formulate goals in an ambiguous style so that it is exposed to diverse understandings and offers them flexibility. Kochan et al. (1984) further note that "Strategic decisions are those which *alter* the party's role or its relationships with other actors in the industrial relations system". (p.22). Thus, in analysing or developing an ER strategy, some of the critical factors that should be considered include: (a) *Agency factors*: a concept popularised by the influential industrial relations framework developed by Dunlop. Agency (human agency) covers actors under your (or someone else's) control and is also influenced by an organisation's assumptions and managerial values; and (b) *Contextual factors*, which were covered earlier to include internal and external contextual factors, which creates constraints and opportunities for organisations. The influence of the above two factors in shaping ER strategic choices are profound as Kochan et al. highlight in their 'industrial relations decisions matrix'. These decisions occur at various levels and how different actors in the industrial relations system are either affected by or can have an influence on employment practices. As mentioned earlier, ER strategies are not limited to decisions flowing from business level strategies. In a number of industry and even national settings, even unions have strategies. It would be unrealistic to assume that strategy is the exclusive domain of management. Unions and management strategies are generally viewed as competing with each other, though, it can also be argued that the two complement each other and the main issue at hand is of how to balance the two. Based on the nature of agency and contextual pressures in a given environment, the rules of employment relationship and decisions pertaining to employment are finally shaped.

Critical Reflections

In the preceding chapters, an account of different theoretical perspectives and dominant schools of SHRM and ER was presented. The diversity of schools and perspectives requires an evaluation as well as what the empirical evidence suggests in terms of its application to the real world. Numerous scholars have offered a systematic critique of the role and scope of HRM in modern society. Legge (2001) and Keenoy

(1999) are excellent overviews of the dominant themes embedded in the HRM discourse and the authors do an excellent job in delineating the rhetoric from the reality and analyse the underlying assumptions of HRM. Quite apart from the ideological positions, the debate also focuses on definitional issues, goals of HRM and the choice of SHRM models (e.g. Goddard 2001; Guest 2011).

In almost three decades of theorizing and empirical studies, while a large body of literature suggests that HRM has a strong impact on business performance, the evidence is not unequivocal (Boselie et al. 2005; Combs et al. 2006; Guest 2011). Additionally, most research focuses on the *association* between HRM and performance rather than establishing any causation. While intuitively, the best-fit approach seems like a superior approach to theorizing, the evidence nevertheless is much stronger for universalistic prescriptions (Combs et al. 2006). One of the common issues in the critique of HRM revolves around the *ethicality of HRM* and its companion—industrial and employment relations. Scholars have called for progressing the field by employing more qualitative and longitudinal designs, minimizing single response bias in surveys by including a wider range of stakeholders, and undertaking multilevel research designs –namely between managers and employees who are, respectively, the designers and users of HRM practices.

There are several challenges that relate to the application of strategic choice theory in practice. The dynamics of cognition and information asymmetry limits the managers to fully comprehend and implement the nature of strategic choice menus available to them. The menu of influences are broad, affecting therefore, the limits of bounded rationality. Similarly, the intent of choices managers exercise may not be fully appreciated by the wide range of stakeholders, especially if the decision pertains to strategic activities such as mergers and acquisitions. In such situations, attempts to undermine or simply a lack of empathy and interest towards the wider pool of stakeholders may render the acquisition an epic failure. The literature on this topic is peppered with examples of failure of strategic choices.

Illustrations and Skills Sandpit

Strategic choices such as mergers and acquisitions often fail due to inattention to issues such as cultural integration between the bidder and the target firm, due diligence, choice of language strategies employed by the bidder at the target firm, misalignment in the purpose of acquisition and its integration by the bidder. Even the target's expectation of merger with a large bidder may lead to undermining by the target firm employees. Attention must be paid to above aspects, to make the strategic choice a success. Unfortunately, a number of times, firms tend to focus on one major group of stakeholder–the shareholders and emphasize more on profit maximization goal by driving cost efficiencies without realizing the other bases for value creation and realization at target firms. In such events, value creation often results in value destruction. Allowing sufficient time for bidder firm's managers to interact with target firm's key employees and managers before optimization efforts are rolled out might be a better way to realise longer-term and sustained value creation and realisation.

There are several examples of M&A failures due to culture and language issues. Key among these include, for example, the M&A between New York Central Railroad Company and Pennsylvania Railroad (Jacobsen 2014). In the above case, past animosity and lack of cultural integration resulted in both firms filing for bankruptiecs. Daimler (Mercedes Benz) and Chrysler's (US) also encountered major cultural and language problems by US employees in integrating with the German ways of working. The AOL/Time Warner merger also failed due to poor mismatch between culture, leadership and communication styles. Malik and Bebenroth (2017, 2018) note the importance of language strategies in such choices. Employing Haspeslagh and Jemison's (1991) seminal work on four integration structures following an M&A event: absorption, preservation, symbiotic and a subsidiary of a holding company, Malik and Bebenroth (2017, 2018) developed language strategies for a non-English speaking pair of bidder and target firms. The authors highlight different set of language strategies for each structure such as common corporate communications, translation services, and other hybrid approaches.

Concept Integration with Cases and Learning Activities

The case study titled *Japanese cross border M&A and German target employee alienation issues* by Bebenroth and Bartnik is a good illustration of the unexpected outcomes for the bidder and target firms. Sometimes, it becomes an issue of managing expectations of both the parties and communicating clearly the purpose of the acquisition. Managing subsequent issues of employee alienation and stress faced by the target firm employees, the authors ask pertinent questions regarding how autonomous should target firms be left after the M&A deal has gone through. The literature on post-merger integration contrasts the degree of autonomy with the degree of interdependence. The case demonstrates how the German firm target has a high degree of autonomy in its operations in the European market whereas, the Asian market was fully left for the Japanese firm to decide how they want to operate and leverage the acquisition.

Conclusion

This chapter brings to an end of the multiple theoretical foundations that are generally applied to the study and practice of SHRM and ER. One could argue that the one-best way or universalistic approaches are inherently problematic as the role of context, institutions, human agency and other contingency variables play a critical role in shaping the final HRM practices. While best-fit, RBV, institutional and strategic choice approaches offer more hope and flexibility in their logic, we can argue that it is neither possible nor practicable to incorporate in an organisation's cognitive frame all the possible contingent variables, their interrelationships and path dependencies so as to establish a clear path for implementing the most appropriate set of HRM practices to support the HRM-performance link (Purcell 1999). The logic of a theory of practice, unfortunately does not exist. What we do have, however, are a number of alternate approaches and explanations that need to be used in a phronetic manner even though we know that phronesis (or practical wisdom) is often hard to develop and requires the investigator to be also mindful of the vested interests and power and politics at play in any organisational context. The role of human agency in navigating and negotiating through this is a challenging enterprise but something we must endeavor and continue to explore and develop for the wider benefit of the field.

Glossary

Strategic choice is the extent to which a firm has leeway in making decisions from a strategic perspective

Human Agency in an organisational context refers to the key individuals tasked with exercising choices and making key decisions that may have an enduring impact on the scope and sustainability of an enterprise.

Post-merger integration (PMI) refers to the processes through which firms integrate the soft (people, culture, leadership and language) and hard (such as strategy, M&A performance and benefit realization) issues following the merger of a firm.

Language strategies in a cross-border PMI context refers to a range of language choices that firms may employ to make the integration process more successful. Firms may choose from adopting a common corporate language, such as English, where both the target and bidder firms are non-native language speakers, to a combination of home or host country languages. In some cases, translation services might be deployed as a useful and cost effective language strategy.

Key Questions and Learning Activities

Question. 1 Explain how strategic choices impact the nature and extent of HRM practices.

Question. 2 What HRM skills are necessary for realising value while exercising strategic choice in relation to mergers and acquisitions?

Question. 3 In a M&A context, discuss whether the use of a common language at the target firm by the bidder firm is a better strategy for ensuring a successful post-merger integration.

Learning Activity: Analysing Language Issues in Post-merger Integration

Looking at the *Japanese cross border M&A and German target employee alienation issues* case study by Bebenroth and Bartnik, propose a language strategy that might be most relevant. Ensure you provide a reasoned answer for your choice.

Bibliography

Bauer, F., & Matzler, K. (2014). Antecedents of M&A success: The role of strategic complementarity, cultural fit, and degree and speed of integration. *Strategic Management Journal, 35*, 269–291.

Boselie, P., Dietz, G., & Boon, C. (2005). Commonalities and contradictions in HRM and performance research. *Human Resource Management Journal, 15*(3), 67–94.

Boxall, P., & Purcell, J. (2011). *Strategy and human resource management* (3rd ed.). London: Palgrave Macmillan.

Cartwright, S., & Schoenberg, R. (2006). Thirty years of mergers and acquisitions research: Recent advances and future opportunities. *British Journal of Management, 17*(S1), S1–S5.

Child, J. (1972). Organizational structure, environment and performance: The role of strategic choice. *Sociology, 6*(1), 1–22.

Child, J. (1997). Strategic choice in the analysis of action, structure, organizations and environment: Retrospect and prospect. *Organization Studies, 18*(1), 43–76.

Combs, C., Liu, Y., Hall, A., & Ketchen, D. (2006). How much do high-performance work systems matter? A meta-analysis of their effects on organizational performance. *Personnel Psychology, 59*(3), 501–528.

Contractor, F. J., & Lorange, P. (Eds.). (1988). *Cooperative strategies in international business*. Lexington: Lexington Books.

Dowling, P. (2008). *International human resource management: Managing people in a multinational context*. Hampshire: Cengage Learning.

Godard, J. (2001). Beyond the high-performance paradigm? An analysis of variation in Canadian managerial perceptions of reform programme effectiveness. *British Journal of Industrial Relations, 39*, 25–52.

Graebner, M., Heimeriks, K., Huy, Q., & Vaara, E. (2017). The process of post-merger integration: A review and agenda for future research. *Academy of Management Annals, 11*(1), 1–32.

Guest, D. (2011). Human resource management and performance: Still searching for some answers. *Human Resource Management Journal, 21*(1), 3–13.

Guest, D., & King, Z. (2004). Power, innovation and problem-solving: The personnel managers' three steps to heaven? *Journal of Management Studies, 41*(3), 401–423.

Haleblian, J., & Finkelstein, S. (1999). The influence of organizational acquisition experience on acquisition performance: A behavioral learning perspective. Administrative Science Quarterly, 44(1), 29-56.

Haleblian, J., Devers, C. E., McNamara, G., Carpenter, M. A., & Davison, R. B. (2009). Taking stock of what we know about mergers and acquisitions: A review and research agenda. Journal of Management, 35(3), 469-502.

Haspeslagh, P. C., & Jemison, D. B. (1991). *Managing acquisitions: Creating value through corporate renewal*. New York: Free Press.

Jacobsen, D. (2014). *6 Big mergers that were killed by culture (And how to stop it from killing yours)*. Globoforce Blogg. Accessed 1 Aug 2017.

Keenoy, T. (1999). HRM as hologram: A polemic. *Journal of Management Studies, 36*(1), 1–23.

Kochan, T., & Rubinstein, S. (2000). Toward a stakeholder theory of the firm: The saturn partnership. *Organization Science, 11*, 367–386.

Kochan, T., McKersie, R., & Cappelli, P. (1984). Strategic choice and industrial relations theory. *Industrial Relations: A Journal of Economy and Society, 23*, 16–39.

Legge, K. (2001). Silver bullet or spent round? Assessing the meaning of the high commitment management performance relationship. In J. Storey (Ed.), *Human resource management: A critical text* (2nd ed., pp. 21–36). London: Thomson Learning.

Leonard-Barton, D. (1992). Core capabilities and core rigidities: A paradox in managing new product development. *Strategic Management Journal, 13*(S1), 111–125.

Malik, A., & Bebenroth, R. (2017). *Mind your language!: Role of target firm language in post-merger integration* (No. DP2017-15).

Malik, A., & Bebenroth, R. (2018). Mind your language!: Role of language in strategic partnerships and post-merger integration. *Journal of Global Operations and Strategic Outsourcing, 11*(2), 1–31.

Martinez Lucio, M., & Stuart, M. (2004). Swimming against the tide: Social partnership, mutual gains and the revival of 'tired' HRM. *International Journal of Human Resource Management, 15*, 410–424.

Peng, M. W., & Heath, P. S. (1996). The growth of the firm in planned economies in transition: Institutions, organizations, and strategic choice. *Academy of Management Review, 21*(2), 492–528.

Penrose, E. T. (1959). *A theory of the growth of the firm*. New York: Wiley.

Prahalad, C. K., & Doz, Y. L. (1987). *The multinational mission: Balancing global integration with local responsiveness*. New York: The Free Press.

Purcell, J. (1999). The search for "best practice" and "best fit": Chimera or cul-de-sac. *Human Resource Management Journal, 9*(3), 26–41.

Ralston, D. A. (2008). The crossvergence perspective: Reflections and projections. *Journal of International Business Studies, 39*(1), 27–40.

Roche, W., & Geary, J. (2002). Advocates, critics and union involvement in workplace partnership: Irish airports. *British Journal of Industrial Relations, 40*, 659–688.

Roll, R. (1986). The hubris hypothesis. *Journal of Business, 59*(2), 197–216.

Schuler, R. S., Dowling, P. J., & De Cieri, H. (1993). An integrative framework of strategic international human resource management. *Journal of Management, 19*(2), 419–459.

Tuch, C., & O'Sullivan, N. (2007). The impact of acquisitions on firm performance: A review of the evidence. *International Journal of Management Reviews, 9*, 141–170.

Professionalism and Ethics

Ashish Malik

Key Learning Outcomes
At the end of this chapter, you should be able to:

- *Differentiate between commonly used ethical frameworks*
- *Compare and contrast the core competencies required of an HR practitioner in different national contexts*
- *Explain the concept of moral intensity*
- *Analyse the sources of conflict and dilemmas that HR practitioners are confronted with from an ethical viewpoint*

Introduction

Up to this point, the preceding chapters have offered some major theoretical foundations of SHRM and ER. The profession of HR expects its community and practicing members to possess certain core HR competencies. HR managers must learn and follow a code of practice that is acceptable to the profession and society they operate in. Almost each country has its HR professional body though some nations have adopted or simply transferred the US or UK professional body competency models to their contexts in a bid to emulate global best practices. This chapter focuses on the HR practitioner– the competencies they need and the code of professional ethics they must apply in their day-to-day workings. The field of applied ethics such as HRM must be viewed and practiced as one that is built upon ethical foundations.

A. Malik (✉)
Faculty of Business and Law, Central Coast Business School, The University of Newcastle, Ourimbah, Central Coast, NSW, Australia
e-mail: ashish.malik@newcastle.edu.au

The chapter begins with a discussion of the commonly understood HR competencies and its basis and then explores the role of values and ethics in the life of an HR practitioner.

HR Competencies and the HR Professional

One can argue that in order to effectively perform HR activities, HR managers or practitioners must develop the core HR domain knowledge and skills. Such a knowledge base is vital for the design and implementation of a range of HR practices. This specialism also gives, to some degree, legitimacy to the HR function and its practitioners. In light of the complexities of content and related contingency variables that are at play in the management of people in organisations, it would be fair to say that the profession has little room for people who are less prepared, skilled, trained and experienced in handling complex HR and ER issues. A broad knowledge base along with experience from different contexts of HR issues is vital, as is deeper and narrow understanding of the sub-specialisms that exist within the broader domain of the HRM and ER knowledge-base. In practice though, job competencies generally operate in a very narrow space. For a broader conceptualisation of competency, its measurement and management in HR space has been suggested by Losey (1999) who notes competency to be a sum total of an individual's intelligence, specialist education received in a field, relevant work experience in that field, understanding of ethical issues affecting that field and an individual's specific interest(s) in a particular sub-specialisation within a field of practice. This would suggest that there are distinctive sub-specialisations within the field of HRM and ER that HR practitioners choose to specialise in. Notably among these would be: a recruitment and selection specialist (which in the hiring industry is quite different from an in-house recruitment and selection role), training and development specialist, compensation and benefits administration, organisational development and change management, building high performance teams, industrial and employment relations advisor, a mentor and so on. While most of these roles can be broadly grouped into HR specialist roles, there are opportunities also for HR practitioners to perform a generalist role. While larger organisations can afford both specialists and generalists, however, the latter role is generally found in small- to medium-sized organisations. Further, one can expect that parts of the HRM function or in some cases even the full function can now be totally outsourced in organisations and much of the HRM assumes an advisory role or carried out by line managers in addition to their main roles, with some support by HR managers.

HR Roles and Models

In addition to the competencies and roles noted above, researchers have classified HRM function into specific and somewhat broader classification schemas such as from performing an *administrative expert* role to a *strategic* and *change management agent* role (Ulrich 1997). Kramar et al. (2011), noted four key sets of competencies as essential for any HR professional. These are: business competence (knowledge of the business); professional and technical knowledge (HRM and ER domain knowledge); integration competence (ability to integrate business, strategy and people needs); and ability to manage change in organisations. Another widely adopted model of HR roles was developed by David Ulrich (1997). Popularly described as the *HR champions' Model*, Ulrich (1997) proposed four key roles for HR practitioners: HR as an *administrative expert* (carrying out and implementing administrative people management polcies including activities such as compliance and reporting for legislative and administrative purposes); perform the role of an *employee champion* between the employer and employees as someone who can be the linking pin to articulate employee voice and understand their needs; a *change agent* for dealing with routine and non-routine change events; and finally a *strategic business partner*, wherein HR practitioners not only are at the executive table to execute strategic decisions affecting people, but they can also inform and shape the formulation of such decisions. Based on the developments in the field, different professional bodies have developed models of HR practice and conduct in their respective countries.

In Australia, for example, the Australian Human Resource Institute (AHRI), Australia's professional HR body developed four key objectives and six key HR capabilities that HR professionals need for successfully performing in a range of roles. These are captured in AHRI's Model of Excellence- HR objectives and capabilities. The HR objectives of the institute are to: contribute to a profitable and sustainable organisation; increase workforce competency and engagement; develop excellence in people management; and create a dynamic and productive work environment. Similarly, AHRI expects certain behaviors from its professional members as well as a set of HR 'I am' behaviours and following competencies: 'I know' and 'I do' competencies. In the former group, these are being: business driven and strategic architect (similar to Ulrich's strategic business partner role), an expert practitioner (similar to Ulrich's administrative expert); ethical and a credible activist (akin to Ulrich's employee champion), whereas the latter group of competencies include being a: stakeholder mentor and coach (similar to Ulrich's employee champion role), a culture and change agent (similar to Ulrich's change agent), and a workplace and workforce designer (similar to Ulrich's administrative expert). Similar lists and objectives of varying degrees of emphases can also be found in the other professional bodies from the Anglo-Saxon countries e.g. in the US–SHRM, the UK–CIPD and the Human Resource Institute of New Zealand – HRINZ in New Zealand.

We can note similarities in the above models especially in HR roles such as that of being a *change agent* and an *administrative expert* (e.g. payroll, recruitment etc). Despite the ample clarity these professional body institutions offer to HR practitioners, the on ground reality of its implementation is a bit ambiguous. For example, as Legge (1978) noted three common reasons of why such ambiguity exists: limited power to influence HR practices and overlaps between line and HR functions; lack of clarity about who owns the success or failure of HR outcomes; and whose interests are being served–management or employees? The dominant view is that HR serves management more than the employee constituencies. There is a need to restore some balance in terms of power inequalities before we can expect to see any meaningful changes. While there are encouraging signs of a strategic role HR is playing in some organisations, a widespread proliferation of this strategic role is not visible and in the main, HR is often seen as the 'implementer' of strategic decisions.

In a bid to understand the changing landscape in the field of HRM, in 2007, a Human Resource Competency Survey (HRCS) was undertaken covering nearly 10,000 survey respondents from the HR community from different regions around the globe to come up with the key competencies required by HR practitioners (Ulrich et al. 2007). The study found six key clusters of HR competencies that were essential for HR practitioners. The focus for HR practitioners is to become: credible activists; operational executors; business allies; talent managers and organisational designers; culture and change agent stewards; and a strategic architects. In line with previous studies, the survey posted major similarities in the expected thrust areas of HR competencies. However, the researchers noted differences in emphasis in some competency groupings, reflecting the diverse contextual environments surveyed around the world. The above research points largely to a convergence thesis in the competency models of HRM. However, in terms of implementation, again there were ambiguities, dualities, paradoxes and tensions noted due to competing interests of different stakeholders, a view that was highlighted in the previous chapter. Therefore, it appears that the role of an "HR professional", at the coalface, is often peppered with dilemmas and ethical tensions.

Ethics and Professionalism

The focus here is not on reviewing knowledge of various ethical theories (for example, deontological, teleological, stakeholder, and contingency theories) but to reinforce the issue of business ethics in routine and non-routine business decisions, including abiding by the ethical code of conduct instituted by the professional body organisations in an HR practitioner's country as well as the ethical code of conduct of an organisation. Briefly, the key thesis of deontological view is that ethics is all about following rules whereas teleological ethics focuses on the greater good or the impact of the consequences on the affected people (hence is also referred to as consequentialist view). Virtue ethics, by its very meaning focuses on the character and virtues that people possess or need to be educated in, in order to be ethical in their conduct. Stakeholder theory in the applied area of business ethics argues that managers and leaders need to take into consideration the competing demands of different stakeholder groups for resolving societal, business and individual ethical dilemmas. The underpinning logic of this perspective is that firms cannot survive without paying serious attention to the different stakeholder needs. As such businesses should embrace the concept of fairness for all stakeholders rather than one. Often the neglect happens when business supports one group–the shareholders over other stakeholder groups. If the practitioner is a member of the professional body,

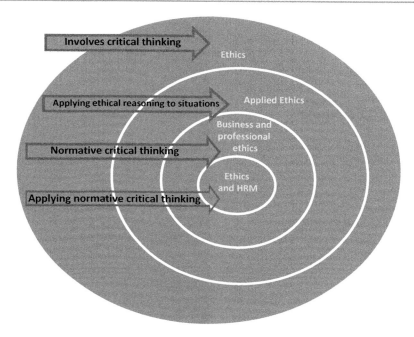

Fig. 1 Ethics and HRM

s/he may also have to consider his/her employing organisation's code of ethics and values. This may or may not be in dissonance with the individual's personal ethical frame and moral intensity. In today's multifaceted, interrelated, interdependent and inter-reliant business setting, managing people is a cerebrally challenging enterprise and often also a politically charged one. Often HR practitioners and managers are faced with ethical quandaries. Despite the presence of their professional skills and codes of conduct, the solutions to some problems are not always easy. Although there is evidence to suggest that being a professional would prevent such issues (Donaldson 2000), however through the complex overlaying of three possible (individual, organisational and professional) value systems, decision-making and ethical actions can at times be challenging. One way to understand the multiple layers of relationship HRM has with ethics is to consider Fig. 1, wherein, at the first level individuals must be able to engage in critical thinking, an important critical attribute for engaging in ethical conduct and decision-making. The focus then shifts to applying ethical reasoning and critical thinking to the domain of business and professional decisions. More narrowly, we have the presence of normative frameworks for engaging in critical thinking in an applied business and professional setting. This may mean applying normative critical thinking to HRM scenarios.

Within this space, practitioners are generally guided by, but are not restricted to, theoretical lenses other than professional codes of ethics. While the study of ethics allows us to recognize our moral values and how we should treat people, the integration of ethics in HRM has witnessed an intense debate within the academic community, wherein several questions were raised: for example, these range from "is HRM ethical?" to "Can HRM be ethical?" Consider the use of terms resource management and use in HRM, as these raise questions of an ethical nature and points to an ethically deficient nature of HRM.

Critical Reflections

One might question, to what extent is contemporary thinking in the area of business ethics influenced by history? The idea that people can learn to behave ethically has its roots in early thinking of Socrates who argued that it is possible to teach people to do the 'right thing'. Socrates further noted that people need to develop them in certain knowledge areas to behave ethically. Building on this idea, Aristotle noted that education regarding how to think critically is a first step in being ethical in one's decisions as it is through critical thinking that one can develop the skills of *phronesis* (prudence or practical wisdom), which is an essential beginning for conducting oneself ethically. Additionally, people need to engage in introspection and reflect on their experiences along with essential knowledge or educational grounding. It is not surprising then to see that a number of business schools are advocating in their educational programs, an element of ethics education. What is current in debate is the extent to which it occurs, whether ethics is taught as part of a program in the form of a standalone course or is an embedded and applied across several units in a program. Additionally, recent research (Erlic 2014) has examined and found support for the idea that a person who has formal training and education in ethics and philosophy is most suited to teach business ethics in business educational programs. It is not surprising then to see a vast majority of business programs not teaching ethics as a standalone course.

Practitioners also need to differentiate between what is *morally* right or wrong from what is *legally* right or wrong. While the latter offers guidelines through legislation and established case law, the former requires engaging deeply in ethical reasoning and by implication critical thinking about what's right and wrong. Some might even argue that people have inert tendencies to behave in an ethical or unethical manner.

Illustrations and Skills Sandpit

There are many examples from practice one can think of that requires moral reasoning in the sphere of HR decisions. For example, you may like to reflect and examine the following question: is the use of drug-testing ethical in selection processes? Another very widely reported unethical issue is that of sexual harassment at the workplace. O'Leary-Kelly and Bowes-Sperry (2001), for example, noted that a number of times people who get embroiled in this situation often do not see this as an act that has a moral issue. Consequently, they do not engage in making moral judgements or establishing their moral intent in resolving the moral issue. As a result, they do not take moral actions. O'Leary-Kelly and Bowes-Sperry (2001) further argue that it is therefore important to build people's moral intensity before they can be expected to engage in moral judgements and decision-making. Moral intensity depends on a number of contextual and contingency factors. These include factors such as in the case of sexual harassment, the authors found it was affected by: the perpetrator's (the person engaging in sexual harassment) understanding of magnitude of consequences; degree of social consensus; probability of the effects; temporal immediacy of actions; similarity of actor and target; and the concentration of responsibility of people in dealing with such events.

Concept Integration with Cases and Learning Activities

The case study *To Cyber-Vet Or Not To Cyber-Vet: An Ethics Question For HRM* by Holland and Jeske investigates an increasingly topical area of Cyber-vetting. What role does an organization's code of conduct and social media policy has on the practice of engaging in social media screening and background checks. The case introduces to the learner the associated complexities in developing an exhaustive policy that covers this issue as well as explores the need to pay attention and thoughtful consideration to who the stakeholders are and the kinds of data and sources to consider? The case study entitled *Patanjali: The Black Swan* by Shukla explores the related themes of context, ethics (albeit briefly) and leadership theory in examining how ethical is it to use symbols by leaders in framing their leadership persona.

Conclusion

The development of competency frameworks and code of conduct although sets in place institutional isomorphism, the question remains how can we ensure all HR practitioners conduct themselves ethically in a manner that satisfies the needs of the professional body and their employing organisation. While it is certainly possible that the two can be achieved in some, if not all situations, a more pressing point is whether practitioners are able to engage in critical thinking in mid-career? Can we teach critical thinking to someone at a later stage in life? Can ethics be taught? These are some of the questions the field has some but not full answers to. A similar question was put forth by Plato to Socrates: "Can you tell me, Socrates, whether arete is something that can be taught? Or is it not taught, but acquired by practice? Or is it neither acquired by practice nor learnt, but does it arise in people by natural aptitude or in some other way?" (Plato and Meno, 70a 1–4). The literature presents competing views whether ethics can be taught (see for instance studies by Boyd 1982 and Martin 1982). A key point to remember is that most HR strategies evolve as a result of ongoing negotiation and political process between various stakeholders and the way managers (including HR managers) interpret the circumstances around them. Ethical considerations must be kept in mind in such processes.

Glossary

Business ethics is an applied branch of ethics that requires the exercise of ethical reasoning and critical thinking skills to a range of business situations, decisions and practices which has an ethical component (the rightness or wrongness).

Stakeholder theory asserts that firms must follow a longer-term strategy which gives thought and consideration to balancing the vested interests of a wider group of stakeholders in a business. Such an approach necessarily has to rely upon ethical reasoning and for managers and leaders to engage in critical thinking in making business decisions.

Shareholder theory asserts that the primary role of managers is to maximise the wealth for its shareholders.

Key Questions and Learning Activities

Question. 1 Explain what is meant by the term business ethics as applied to the study and practice of HRM & ER.

Question. 2 Identify an ethical dilemma for each of the following HRM practices and comment how you would resolve each of the identified ethical dilemmas:
1. *Performance Management*
2. *Training and Development*
3. *Workplace Change*

Question. 3 Comment on the effectiveness of the use of a professional code of conduct by HR professional body organisations. In your view, do members of these institutions see this as a requirement for upholding professional ethics or an unnecessary impost?

Learning Activity: Statistical Discrimination in Hiring

Consider the situation when employers discriminate people in hiring based on the applicants' characteristics such as being a smoker, or belonging to a particular geographical area or other demographic characteristics e.g. height, weight and personal preferences that are not usually covered by human rights legislation. Analyse the above using relevant ethical theories.

Bibliography

Banaji, M., Bazerman, M., & Chugh, D. (2003). How (un)ethical are you? *Harvard Business Review, 81*(12), 56–64.

Boyd, D. P. (1982). Improving ethical awareness through the business and society course. *Business and Society (pre-1986), 20, 21*(2, 1), 27.

Davis, M. (1999). Professional responsibility: Just following the rules? *Business and Professional Ethics Journal, 18*(1), 65–87.

Donaldson, T. (2000). Are business managers 'professionals'? *Business Ethics Quarterly, 10*(1), 83–94.

Erlic, S. (2014). *Business ethics education and faculty teaching expertise: Are business school educators equipped, trained and capable to teach normative ethical theory?* Unpublished doctoral thesis, University of Newcastle, Australia.

Greenwood, M. (2002). Ethics and HRM: A review and conceptual analysis. *Journal of Business Ethics, 36*(3), 261–278.

Human Resource Institute of New Zealand— Competency Framework. http://www.hrinz.org.nz/Site/About/What_is_HRINZ/framework.aspx

Kramer, R., Bartram, T., De Cieri, H., Noe, R. A., Hollenbeck, J. R., Gerhart, B., & Wright, P. M. (2011). *Human resource management in Australia-strategy, people, performance*. North Ryde: McGraw Hill.

Legge, K. (1978). *Power, innovation, and problem-solving in personnel management*. London: MacGraw-Hill.

Losey, M. (1999). Mastering the competencies of HR management. *Human Resource Management, 38*(2), 99–102.

Martin, T. R. (1982). Do courses in ethics improve the ethical judgment of students? *Business and Society (pre-1986), 20, 21*(2, 1), 17.

O'Leary-Kelly, A. M., & Bowes-Sperry, L. (2001). Sexual harassment as unethical behavior: The role of moral intensity. *Human Resource Management Review, 11*(1–2), 73–92.

Rousseau, D., & Barends, E. (2011). Becoming an evidence-based HR practitioner. *Human Resource Management Journal, 21*(3), 221–235.

Ulrich, D. (1997). *Human resource champions: The next agenda for adding value to HR practices*. Boston: Harvard Business School Press.

Ulrich, D., Brockbank, W., Johnson, D., & Younger, J. (2007). Human resource competencies: Responding to increased expectations. *Employment Relations Today, 34*(3), 1–12.

Van Buren, H., III, Greenwood, M., & Sheehan, C. (2011). Strategic human resource management and the decline of employee focus. *Human Resource Management Review, 21*, 209–219.

Wiley, C. (2000). Ethical standards for human resource management professionals: A comparative analysis of five major codes. *Journal of Business Ethics, 25*, 93–114.

Part II

HR Profession and Design and Implementation of Strategic HRM and ER Practices

Work Design and HR Planning: A Strategic Perspective

Ashish Malik

Key Learning Outcomes
At the end of this chapter, you should be able to:

- *Define the terms HR planning and work design from a strategic perspective*
- *Describe the dominant approaches to HR planning*
- *Evaluate the effectiveness of commonly used analytical HR planning techniques*

Introduction

The second part of the book focuses on the strategic application of functional HRM and ER practices. This chapter focuses on two key preliminary HRM practices: work design and human resource planning, which are core elements of an individual's employment lifecycle and trigger recruitment and selection. Appropriate work design choices must suit the business needs so one can decide how to plan the resourcing of people needed for the jobs they have to perform. The nature of work design ranges from a "control-oriented" to a "commitment-oriented" continuum, wherein firms can decide and plan for how they can balance the goal of organisational flexibility and autonomy with control, a key consideration for HR managers. Following a discussion on strategic HR planning and work design, this chapter briefly considers the strategic approaches to recruitment and selection.

A. Malik (✉)
Faculty of Business and Law, Central Coast Business School, The University of Newcastle, Ourimbah, Central Coast, NSW, Australia
e-mail: ashish.malik@newcastle.edu.au

Strategic Human Resource Planning

To begin with, HR planning has been defined as having the right number of people, at the right place, right time, with the right set of knowledge, skills and abilities. From a strategic HR planning perspective, one must focus also on the wider environmental and strategic context in which strategic HR planning exercise occurs. The HR practitioner, at a macro level, should be sensitised to the prevailing labour market conditions, especially in high growth and volatile industries such as mining, software development and health services as there is a constant competition for attracting and retaining talent in all aspects of the employment lifecycle (e.g. HR planning, attracting, selecting, training, rewarding and managing the performance). Strack et al. (2008) noted the following the top five challenges for Australian HRM practitioners such as: managing talent, demographics, change and cultural transformation, leadership development, and transforming HR into a strategic business partner. While these challenges have also prevailed in previous and subsequent studies, this study provides a macro-level background and understanding of the challenges and sets the tone for HR planning and work design. HR managers need to take into account other trends in their planning for human resourcing: industry characteristics and trends; nature of internal and external labour markets; nature of job content and its scope; sorts of skills and employee aspirations; and determine the 'gap' from both an employee and organisational perspective. HR planning also requires attention to legislation, industry and professional requirements (for example, some jobs require continued professional development and training).

At a meso (organisational) level, HR practitioners need to consider organisational influences such as, labour costs as a percentage of the overall production cost, firm's competitive strategy (for example, whether it is following a cost leadership or differentiation or some other combination), its organisation's life cycle stage, management culture, values and orientation towards the people it employs. Orientation towards labour is an important consideration as it informs the classic "make versus buy" decision. Additionally, with the changing workforce demographics, wherein an increasing number of employees are Generation Y workers and will continue to be so for a while, developing an appreciation of their motivations, values and beliefs may result in their successful attraction and retention. This was borne out in a recent study on Generation Y expatriates –or what the authors terms as *Yopatriates* (Pereira et al. 2017). Demographic differences are vital and HR should take into account aspects such as employee's career aspirations, retention and engagement tools, which may be a bit different from managing baby boomers and Generation X employees.

Millmore et al. (2007) argue that for a better understanding of the strategic, operational and process level issues, strategic HR forecasting and planning must employ a reliable and holistic database. From a strategic perspective, HR planners should be able to analyse and forecast a detailed plan regarding the profile of the current workforce and match it with future requirements based on strategic plans, and projected flows of employees in terms of increases or decreases in numbers, at various levels and roles. HR forecasting can lead to one of the three outcomes: reductions in a given area(s), expansion of workforce in existing or new roles, or maintain a status quo. Such forecasting often relies on a combination of quantitative and/or qualitative techniques. From an operational perspective, HR planners consider a number of useful data points: determine past, current and future trends in workforce movements in an organisation. HR planners must also engage and consult with senior leaders, line managers and business development leads for getting a sense of where the organisation might be heading in the short- to medium-term. Once such an understanding is gained, they can look at process level issues of how to plan for the subsequent attraction, retention and/or talent management campaigns. Larger and multidivisional firms have elaborate computerised HR information systems (CHRIS) that can churn out a number of analytical reports on various aspects of the quality and other profiles of its workforce. HR analytics now is much advanced than what it used to be and HR and line managers can 'slice and dice' different analytical reports from their CHRIS. An overview of the sorts of analysis that can be undertaken is discussed next.

HR Analytics for Planning

Illustrations and Skills Sandpit from the Mobile Telephony Industry

From a strategic HR perspective, HR planners should know the nature and extent of key competencies and capabilities an organisation has where the major competency and skill gaps lie. This can and should inform talent management strategies. For example, in a mature mobile telephony industry, the technology infrastructure is generic, the point of differentiation lies in the competencies possessed by sales and service as well as advertising teams for enhancing the overall customer experience. Additionally, the skills of pricing the phone plans can be a key skill for the industry. Thus, customer-centricity may become a key competency for all job roles that involves direct or indirect interaction with the customer. HR planners would need to forge partnerships with line managers in these functional areas to identify the key pain points at every point of customer interaction which may adversely impact quality of customer service experience. However, if the industry is undergoing a shift in the technology platforms and moving to the next curve, this may reflect a surge in either upskilling existing technical talent or develop an aggressive talent hunt program. For keeping up with the 'pulse' of the employee composition, its supply and potential demand, HR planners need to engage in dynamic modelling of current skills with the 'actual number of people' using data points such as past trends of employee turnover rates. For example, this can be calculated for each year using the following or a similar formula:

Annual employee turnover rate = Total number of people leaving in a year/The total number of people in an organisation *100.

Additionally, data points on expansion or contraction/retrenchment plans, age-grade, grade/skills and age-skills matrices can be used for developing a granulated understanding of the required skill composition in different roles. Other metrics that are useful in HR planning include focusing on the average revenue contributions per employee, average cost per full-time staff equivalent (direct and indirect costs), and projected (anticipated) retirement numbers, mix of standard (e.g. permanent) and non-standard (e.g. fixed-term and casual) employment. Ratios such as the proportion of core (revenue earning) and non-core (support and enabling functions) and employee utilisation rates are additional metrics that can inform decisions related to resourcing of people. For managing the flows within an organisation, HR planners can focus on metrics such as the completed length of service profiles in different occupational categories for undertaking a career progression analysis at different levels for informing their compensation and retention plans. Clearly, HR planning is a much more integrated HRM practice and informs almost all practices of the HR employment life cycle.

Workforce Flexibility
While the above set of HR metrics and analysis yields useful and rich insights to aid HR decision-making, there is an increasing focus on maintaining workforce flexibility (Atkinson 1984). Firms respond to changes in macro-economic environments (e.g. social, political, technological and labour market) by implementing different forms of workforce flexibility. These include adopting numerical, functional, financial and temporal flexibility. While there is intuitive appeal of the idea of workforce flexibility a number of researchers have criticised the approach and noted it as a form of neoliberal market managerialism. Although these contracts constitute a small percentage of the total workforce in an economy, the worrying trend is that it is gradually increasing and its incidence is spreading across all levels of employment. There is an increasing trend in zero hour contracts and its proliferation now extends to all levels of the workforce (managerial, professional, technical and manual). There has almost been a doubling, in percentage terms, of zero hour contracts between 2004 and 2011 (Wanrooy et al. 2013). Unfortunately, much of the focus has been on 'organisational' flexibility and somewhat limited focus exists on 'employee' flexibility (Bal and Jensen 2016; Bauman 2000). The latter focus will bring in a balance to a strategic and managerialist approach to achieving flexibility. While there have been several approaches implemented to accommodate employee flexibility in the form of work-life balance programs (Fleetwood 2007; Tomlinson 2007) as well as smart working options (Malik et al. 2016), the issue at hand is the uniform access of flexible working options by employees. Indeed, this is especially an issue for minority groups of employees such as access to work-life balance benefits by Muslim migrant women (Ali et al. 2017).

Work Design
Typically, employers can adopt an internal (make/invest in) or an external (buy/outsource) orientation in meeting their workforce resourcing needs. The need for achieving a strategic and horizontal fit to align their HR planning and work design approaches with their chosen competitive strategy is critical (Stewart and Brown 2009). In designing work, HR practitioners must not forget the AMO rubric

introduced earlier in chapters "Introduction" and "HRM and ER: A Strategic Perspective" of the book. To this end, work design principles should *motivate* (M) employees as well as meet the organisational goals. Such designs are often associated with balancing the tensions between employee commitment with the managerial prerogative of control of workflow and maintaining an efficient structure. From its deep underpinnings in the scientific school of management, most work designs in manufacturing sector today still reflect scientific management principles. It would not be incorrect to say that a number of low-end and less complex service work such as that evident in call centre and transaction processing work also adopts a modified Taylorist approach. One word that summarises this school of work design is control.

Illustrations and Skills Sandpit from the IT & Business Process Outsourcing (BPO) Industry

Call Centre Industry

A number of call centres have been classified as work design centres of excessive control. Phrases like 'an assembly line in the head'(Taylor and Bain 1999) and 'entrapped by the electronic Panopticon' (Bain and Taylor 2000) typify the nature of excessive control evident in work design in call centres. Part of the problem lies in the lack of trust by clients in the service providers that they set up contracts with across borders. As a result, the client dictates the nature and extent of the scripted message, the number of calls an agent has to typically do, the precision and time in which these have to be delivered, all this exemplifies the nature of excessive control in what is essentially a twenty-first century service job. The HR developer has to hire people who can perform in this environment; design their training to support such precise and predictable levels of performance and above all, develop systems for capturing performance tracking for meeting the clients' expectations in line with the contract's service level agreements.

The next major school, although it offered respite for workers in the form of a human relations movement propagating the idea of flexible, team- and empowerment-based design for gaining employee commitment, it wasn't as widespread as Taylor's scientific management. There is ample evidence in the literature, which suggests that by designing work that is motivating (intrinsically and extrinsically) and providing employees with the freedom and opportunity to exercise leeway and choice in structuring their work, will most likely lead to greater satisfaction, retention and longer term commitment. Typically firms design their work somewhere on a continuum of control and commitment, wherein the commitment end typically results in greater job satisfaction. If a firm is following a cost-leadership strategy, it is likely to focus on a control-oriented design, especially if it also has an external orientation towards its employees. There are numerous adverse impacts noted of control oriented designs. These include stress, anxiety and an overall decline in employee well-being.

High-End Software Development and Design Industry

Attracting highly skilled and specialist talent for the high-end software product development and design firms requires a different work design for retaining and motivating knowledge workers who are likely deliver their discretionary and best performance. Work designs for the software development industry require empowerment-based designs to allow employees the freedom and autonomy they need to take calculated risks for proposing new and better solutions to their existing products. Managers will need to allow flexibility and trust their employees to complete their work tasks in an environment that makes them most productive. Some IT firms such as Google, allow up to one full day for employees to engage in creative and new product development projects. The work design for this group of workers will necessarily require a mix of intrinsic and extrinsic rewards. A number of product development firms reward people monetarily for lodging patent applications and celebrate their success with peers through recognition certification programs, and by even allowing employees to lodge patent applications in their name.

Strategic Recruitment and Selection

Recruitment has a positive valence as it involves attracting and adding potential candidates to a pool of talent. Selection, on the other hand has a negative valence as it acts as a sieve for sifting through the talent pool thus created. These two process are triggered once the organisation has an idea of the nature and extent of its resourcing requirements from its HR planning exercise. Organisations need to adopt a systematic and strategic approach to ensure each resourcing decision adds value to the strategic needs of the business. They must tap into the right types of labour markets for their needs.

When it comes to selection, the focus, from a strategic point of view shifts to person-organisation, person-context and person-job fit. The applicant's personality and skills attributes are key areas to assess. Organisations can employ a number of 'sifting' and 'sieving' approaches to choose from a pool of applicants. Depending on the nature of role, these include: assessment centres employing a range of psychometric tests, realistic job previews, referrals, work portfolios, job knowledge tests, integrity tests, situational interviews and so on. Some firms employ values-based testing to assess person-organisation and person-context fit. Although the most popular, the least effective predictor of person-job fit is the job interview. A controversial area that has come into recent discourse is drug-testing and extensive set of medical tests before hiring. The issue of ethicality of these approaches is causing a lot of debate. Maintaining a strategic focus is therefore critical in ensuring the use of a combination of 'good' selection practices to minimize the likelihood of a poor decision. Poor decisions are often costly and hiring the wrong person may have major impacts on work disruptions, demotivation of other employees and negatively affecting organisational citizenship of others. In a highly regulated society that we live in, there are high costs of separation that an organisation may have to bear to get rid of an employee and then start the process again.

Further Illustrations and Skills Sandpit from IT and Software Services Industry

Firms may develop their own campaigns or outsource the entire process to large recruitment firms such as Addeco, Right Talent and so on. A number of firms follow differentiated campaigns for recruiting different categories of employees. These are often implemented in the form of 'Employer of Choice' branding campaigns or expressions of interest through their online jobs portal to generate a right pool of applicants for future client opportunities. Infosys Technologies, a large global IT major, for example receives more than a million applications for its annual hiring of between 10,000 and 15,000 engineers. So, for applicants, messaging matters a lot, as does the orientation–internal versus external–that an organization has. Stewart and Brown (2009) argue that HR practitioners should design advertising communications that meets an organisation's strategic needs. For example, hiring for long-term and with an internal orientation would require a more realistic messaging than for short-term hiring with an external orientation and focused hiring, which would require employing idealistic messaging.

Critical Reflections

One of the major critiques of HR planning is the durability of HR plans. By the time one completes the analytical process and modelling for future needs, the market or the environment changes and most plans require subsequent revisions. Sometimes, changes to the key stakeholders and leadership might also bring in new perspectives on the resourcing models. These may be radical; departing from an internal to an external orientation in a firm's resourcing approach. A related challenge in HR planning, and other sub-functions is that of achieving integration and fit. While this may seem logical and highly desirable, even the best laid out plans are open to interpretation and power dynamics between HR and line managers. It is much easy to observe the performance impact of poor HR plans in service sector firms, as often service sector firms, have a greater adverse impact on business due to delayed resourcing.

Concept Integration with Cases and Learning Activities

The case study *DORIAN LPG's rapid fleet growth: A story of Maritime HR Planning and People Management* by Progoulaki and Tasoulis highlights the critical role of HR planning in times of a major expansion phase in a firm's life cycle. This contingency or best-fit approach to HR practices was also covered earlier in chapter "Strategic HRM & ER: Best-Practice Versus Best Fit" of the book. The case provides a useful account of how business strategy informs people management practices in a large firm experiencing rapid growth related to fleet expansion. The case also provides an opportunity to analyse aspects of internal fit in managing a culturally and professionally diverse employee base. Other strategic HRM practices and their interrelationships with HR planning is also covered in this case study.

Conclusion

The importance of getting the right people, with right skills in a timely manner is vital for uninterrupted performance of a firm's production function. In some industries that are more people intensive, such as in the services industry, performance of HR planning, impacts of recruitment and selection practices, have a profound impact on a firm's bottom-line. In the longer-term, for gaining sustained levels of commitment from its employees, firms need to ensure they offer a job-value proposition that is appealing to not just the new entrants but also to their existing employees. Strong employer branding exercises and developing a parallel set of talent pool will ensure a steady supply of talent. However, to achieve job-, organisation-, culture and people-fit, the HR practitioner will need to employ a combination of hard and soft approaches for optimal results.

Glossary

Employer of choice branding is a set of activities that are targeted to attract a group of applicants and retain existing employees to an organisation by offering a set of employer job value propositions.
Person-environment fit refers to the degree of alignment of a person's attitude and personal attributes to the wider work environment and their job
Person-job-fit refers respectively, to the extent to which the preferred candidate's profile aligns with the requirements of the offered job
Selection is the process of shortlisting from a pool of suitable applicants, the most appropriate candidate for a given job

Key Questions and Learning Activities

Question. 1 What are the main options available to line and HR managers when they discover a mismatch between the job/organisation fit with the person they have hired?
Question. 2 Outline three advantages of person-job fit and person-organisation fit.
Question. 3 Outline three disadvantages of person-job fit and person-organisation fit.

Learning Activity: Analysing Job Design at Neutral Spaces

Recent interest in working at places other than your home or usual place of work i.e. your office, has led to new workspaces such as co-working spaces and Smart Work Hubs (see for example, Malik et al. 2016). Would there be differences in productivity, employee's experience and satisfaction for people who are allowed the opportunity to work at these alternate work spaces as compared to those who work at their usual place of work and home offices? What are the implications of such a design in employer of choice campaigns and balancing work and life?

Bibliography

Ali, F., Malik, A., Pereira, V., & Al Ariss, A. (2017). A relational understanding of work-life balance of Muslim migrant women in the west: Future research agenda. *The International Journal of Human Resource Management, 28*(8), 1163–1181.

Atkinson, J. (1984). Manpower strategies for flexible organisations. *Personnel Management, 16,* 28–31.

Bain, P., & Taylor, P. (2000). Entrapped by the 'electronic panopticon'? Worker resistance in the call centre. *New Technology, Work and Employment, 15*(1), 2–18.

Bal, P. M., & Jansen, P. G. W. (2016). Workplace flexibility across the lifespan. *Research in Personnel and Human Resources Management., 34,* 43–99.

Bauman, Z. (2000). *Liquid modernity.* Cambridge: Polity Press.

Cascio, W. (1998). Analyzing work and planning for people. In Chapter 4, *Managing human resources: Productivity, quality of work life, profits.* Toronto: 5/e McGraw Hill Education.

Cordery, J., & Parker, S. (2007). Work organization. Chapter 10. In P. Boxall, J. Purcell, & P. Wright (Eds.), *The Oxford handbook of human resource management* (pp. 187–209). Oxford: Oxford University Press.

Fleetwood, S. (2007). Why work–life balance now? *The International Journal of Human Resource Management, 18,* 387–400.

Greenlagh,L. (1991). Organisational coping strategies. In J. Hartley, D. Jacobsen, B. Klandermans, & T. van Vuuren (Eds.), *Job insecurity: Coping with jobs at risk.* London: Sage.

Malik, A., Rosenberger, P. J., III, Fitzgerald, M., & Houlcroft, L. (2016). Factors affecting smart working: Evidence from Australia. *International Journal of Manpower, 37*(6), 1042–1066.

Millmore, M., Lewis, P., Saunders, M., Thornhill, A., & Morrow, T. (2007). Strategic human resource planning: The weakest link? In *Strategic human resource management: Contemporary issues* (pp. 236–275). Pearson Education Limited: Essex.

Pereira, V., Malik, A., Howe-Walsh, L., Munjal, S., & Hirekhan, M. (2017). Managing Yopatriates: A longitudinal study of generation Y expatriates in an Indian multi-national corporation. *Journal of International Management, 23*(2), 151–165.

Singh, P. (2008). Job analysis for a changing workplace. *Human Resource Management Review, 18,* 87–99.

Stewart, G., & Brown, K. (2009). *Human resource management: Linking strategy to practice.* Hoboken: Wiley.

Strack, R. et al. (2008). *Creating people advantage: How to address HR challenges worldwide through 2015.* USA: The Boston Consulting Group and World Federation of Personnel Management Association.

Taylor, P., & Bain, P. (1999). 'An assembly line in the head': Work and employee relations in the call Centre. *Industrial Relations Journal, 30*(2), 101–117.

Tomlinson, J. (2007). Employment regulation, welfare and gender regimes: A comparative analysis of women's working-time patterns and work–life balance in the UK and the US. *The International Journal of Human Resource Management, 18*, 401–415.

Van Wanrooy, B., Bewley, H., Bryson, A., Forth, J., Freeth, S., Stokes, L., & Wood, S. (2013). *Employment relations in the shadow of recession: Findings from the 2011 workplace employment relations study*. Basingstoke: Palgrave Macmillan.

Strategic Performance and Commitment Management

Ashish Malik

Key Learning Outcomes
At the end of this chapter, you should be able to:

- *Analyse the key elements impacting individual level performance*
- *Analyse the key elements impacting systems level performance*
- *Evaluate the effectiveness of performance management systems*
- *Explain the causes of poor performance at individual and systems level*

Introduction

A quick way to ascertain how well the performance management system of an organisation is working from a strategic perspective, is to ask multiple employees their understanding of the organisation's strategy, its goals, key performance indicators and how employees think they are contributing to the same (Boselie 2010). Next, verify this understanding with the senior management team. One would most likely find gaps in understanding of expected and actual performance. There are many reasons for this. Performance is a multifaceted and multi-level concept and thus needs attention, at least, at two very distinct levels: a micro (individual level) and a meso-level (organisational systems level) and how high performance is achieved at each level. Of course, many have attempted to unlock the performance 'black box' from multiple disciplinary perspectives including from HR perspective. With an increasing interest and sophistication in research designs, which focus on multi-level and multi-respondent explanations of performance, there is some

A. Malik (✉)
Faculty of Business and Law, Central Coast Business School, The University of Newcastle, Ourimbah, Central Coast, NSW, Australia
e-mail: ashish.malik@newcastle.edu.au

comfort in agreeing that a combination of certain HR and management practices can contribute to sustained levels of organizational level performance.

Individual Level Performance Management

Typically, performance management is a cyclical process, which involves determining first of all, the performance expectations of a role. This is followed by setting and planning an individual's goals, providing the individual with learning and development support where necessary, monitoring their progress and providing ongoing feedback through formal and informal means regarding their actual performance against the expected performance. Performance management in 'HR speak' comprises of numerous factors that can contribute to improving the performance of a system. In the preceding chapters, the performance rubric, $P = f(AMO)$ was introduced, wherein 'A' stands for ability, 'M' for motivation and 'O' for opportunity. It is worth remembering that individual level performance requires the presence of all three factors for achieving high performance. Hiring people who have the relevant knowledge, skills and ability is a key foundation for expecting people to perform well in a given role. HR managers should also focus on a combination of intrinsic and extrinsic motivational approaches to offer satisfying and motivating jobs for employees and hope to improve their performance. Line managers and supervisors play an important part in providing the environment or 'opportunity' for their staff to remain motivated and to apply their abilities to the fullest. From a strategic perspective, the basic tenets of the goal-setting theory are highly relevant here (Locke and Latham 1990). This theory suggests directing employee's attention to goals, regulating the effort, increasing their persistence and encouraging the development of plans to achieve the goals. The goals should be set at the right (stretch) level to motivate employees to aspire to achieve higher and that such goals should be quantifiable and clear. HR practitioners and line managers have a responsibility to deliver on these counts if they are expecting the best out of their employees. The focus here is not to get into different performance management systems such as the MBO, rating scales, Six Sigma, or 360-degree multi-rater feedback, it is more around understanding guiding principles that have worked well in managing performance. An equally relevant consideration here is of *distributive justice*. Managers and HR leaders must ensure that employee perceptions about rewards and its appropriation are fair. The role of line managers and supervisors is extremely critical in clearly communicating the expectations. Where necessary, this has to be supplemented with support by way of training and development and/or a nurturing environment to improve the performance of individual contributors. Equally important is adopting an integrated approach to HRM practices and ensure there is a horizontal fit between HRM practices. For example, recruitment and selection practices should be supported by employee development and motivational support from managers.

The notion of internal fit was also covered in chapter "Strategic HRM & ER: Best-Practice Versus Best Fit" of the book.

Illustrations and Skills Sandpit

Some large and successful firms have put in place forced distribution systems and Six Sigma or even Lean Six Sigma as a means to precisely measure and ensure high levels of performance. This is achieved by removing the root cause of variation in a performance system. Such approaches often rely on giving very clear, prompt and transparent feedback to performers and non-performers. General Electric (GE), Motorola and a number other US firms and more recently offshore contact centres and business process outsourcing firms of large multinationals in India are using these approaches. Aspects of performance metrics and problem-solving approach to managing individual performance is in line with the basic tenets of goal setting theory and does seems to deliver sustained levels of high performance. GE, for example, follows a forced distribution system wherein it distributes scores in a 10% (below average), 70% (Potentials), 20% (high perfomers) distribution. Looking after the 20% and pushing as many people in towards the upper end of the 70% range is a key focus. The remaining 10% are asked to either buckle up or look elsewhere. As with any HR performance management system, the challenge lies in its implementation. But sometimes, even the design of a performance management system is not free from flaws. For example, not having clear performance measures for goals and expectations and inadequate communication and training on what the various range of scores mean are often cases of core flaws in design. Shields (2007) notes that there are some key considerations in designing an effective performance management system. These include, for example, the following: ensuring that the system is valid, reliable, cost-effective and has perceived fairness by its users. Managers and leaders must therefore address each of the above elements for an effective performance management system. They need to know what it takes to apply the design consistently to avoid problems of perceived inequity and poor implementation. Excessive focus on unrealistic 'stretch' goals may lead to unintended consequences such as poor performance and adverse outcomes such as dysfunctional employee turnover, poor employee well-being, stress and fatigue. Most good performance management systems aim to increase their employees' job satisfaction and organisational commitment. As such, efforts must be made to offer a combination of intrinsic and extrinsic rewards to achieve job satisfaction and maintain affiliation with an organisation (Shields 2007). Additionally, employers must also avoid any breaches in psychological contract of their employees through issues of poor design and implementation. Shields (2007) further notes that the most common culprits here are: lack of consistency, perceived or felt unfairness of the system and poor distributive and procedural justice. All of these factors affect an employee's motivation, attitudes towards the job and the firm, which subsequently has an affect on behaviour of employees and their discretionary performance.

Organisational Level Performance–HRM Systems

For achieving high levels of organisational and systems performance through HRM practices, a number of interrelated factors must be considered. For example, these include: creating and managing a desired culture to support the performance expectations; providing the relevant structural elements such as a sound performance management design and other mutually reinforcing HR practices; and finally ensuring 'integration and fit' with the firm's competitive strategy. Key questions for the HR managers to think are: to what extent are there complementarities between HR and other management functions? Are HRM practices mutually fitting and reinforcing–in other words, achieving an internal or horizontal fit? Are they applied consistently across the organisation? Attending to these questions may result in a better fit as per the best-fit school, covered earlier in chapter "Strategic HRM & ER: Best-Practice Versus Best Fit".

While adopting a best-fit thinking yields better alignment, we nevertheless see a number of studies of high performance work practices or systems tend to adopt a universalist approach. Typically, studies in this group are akin to studies of best-practice models wherein a certain bundle of HRM and perhaps management practices, if implemented collectively are likely to have positive impacts on the performance of a system. Careful selection of a 'set' of HRM practices must be implemented collectively and if issues of fit and integration are also attended to then such an approach is most likely to lead to sustained levels of performance. Firms must identify a set of complementary capabilities that help create mutually reinforcing systems for achieving high levels of systems level performance. Therefore, the focus is on identifying the 'right' sets of mutually reinforcing practices to support coherence and fit at a system, practice and competency level. The difficulty, however, in such an approach is that there are several contingencies that need to be considered for each organisation in selecting the right bundle. Some studies highlight the degree of change in performance when firms use high performance work practices. For example, Huselid (1995: 667) noted that "a 1% standard deviation increase in such practices is associated with a 7.05% decrease in labour turnover and, on a per employee basis 27,044 US$ more in sales and 18, 641 US$ and 3,814 US$ more in market value and profits respectively." West et al.'s (2002) study of hospitals in the UK found a strong correlation between teamwork, learning and development and performance appraisals on patient mortality. While the literature is voluminous on the choices in relation to the bundles of HRM practices that are available, these choices depend on the purpose of each organization and its approach to achieve its goals.

More importantly, these choices depend on line manager's discretion and employees' attitudes and behaviour in the chain of links between management's espoused goals and high organisational performance. This argument is well-articulated in Wright and Nishii's model (2004, as cited in Boxall and Purcell 2011), wherein intended HR practices (from senior management) lead to actual HR practices (i.e. as enacted by managers), which then leads to perception of HR practices by the employees and invokes employee responses (attitudes and behaviour), which may/may not then lead to organisational performance. There are opportunities for leakages in the above causal chain at one or more points and therefore, implementation of HPWS may not always result in optimal performance. This line of thinking highlights the gaps between the espoused intentions and actual actions, and performance outcomes will vary, often due to lack of real buy-in by employees due to their perception of managers' intent in implementing these practices.

Critical Reflections

While there are several individual and systems level approaches to choose from, there are problems in achieving transparency, consistency, validity and reliability in the measures employed for both of the above levels. Additionally, the multidisciplinary orientation of different approaches and contextual conditions in which such studies were designed provides little basis for uniform comparison and its application to other contexts. The field of managing performance also suffers from the performance black box problem. What this implies is that there are a number of other factors that may explain the anticipated and unanticipated drivers of performance at an individual, organizational and system levels.

Part of the problem also occurs because of the interpretation and enactment of espoused meanings by managers and employees. There appears to be an increasing consensus that performance can be affected by how employees perceive the way their managers implement these HPWS, which then has an impact on the effectiveness of these practices on business performance.

Concept Integration with Cases and Learning Activities

The case study entitled *Appraisal at Systel Technologies* by Manimala, Desai and Agarwal highlights several problems associated in the design and implementation of performance appraisal systems in a large IT multinational undergoing change. The case study highlights various issues involved in design and implementation of performance management system.

The case also provides a detailed description of the rationale and process of designing and implementing a key performance area (KPA)-based rating system of performance appraisal and offers an opportunity to appreciate its merits and demerits in comparison with those of other systems. It is also evident from the case that employees expect some tangible outcomes from the appraisal in the form of increments, promotions, etc. When such links are established, the issues of objectivity and fairness are likely to re-emerge as major concerns.

Conclusion

Overall the performance–HRM link, though on a strong footing, with a plethora of studies pointing to its positive association with performance, requires further research from under researched geographical contexts, especially from emerging markets, which can further test the evidence base. Also, scholars are beginning to challenge whether it is possible to sustain the tested frameworks in today's neoliberal and managerial approaches. This burning question is logical as there are signs of weakness in the dominant capitalist logic with declining levels of employee well-being and health outcomes, especially when firms continue to implement high-performance work designs and do not effectively balance the demands such practices place on its human resources.

Glossary

High performance work practices is a 'set' or a 'bundle' of HRM practices, which, if implemented collectively can be the source of sustained competitive advantage to firms. Even though there is extensive research on this topic, consensus is far from being reached in terms of the 'set' or 'bundle' of HRM practices that are central to high performance.

Performance Appraisal is a process that involves planning, observing, measuring and evaluating an individual's performance against a set of performance expectations using a set criteria.

Performance Management is a holistic process that focuses on linking an individual's goals to an organisation's overall strategic direction and scope. The process involves goal-setting, development, reward, appraisal and ongoing mentoring and coaching using formal and informal mechanisms including the use of single and multiple feedback systems such as 360-degree feedback systems.

Key Questions and Learning Activities

Question. 1 From your study of organisational behaviour, critically evaluate the contribution of any two theories that are relevant to the study and practice of performance management.

Question. 2 Critically evaluate the contribution of HRM-performance link in the wider literature on SHRM & ER.

Question. 3 Compare performance appraisal system from multisource performance feedback approaches.

Learning Activity: Daily Performance Monitoring at XYZ Call Centre

At XYZ Call Centre in Somewhereland country, a number of call centre agents are considering quitting en-masse due to the incessant pressure that call barging and micro-managing brings for them on a daily basis. For example, call centre agents' length of the call, tone of the call and the quality of the product information disseminated forms part of such daily monitoring. The performance of the process is evaluated on a number of rating scale parameters. Managers at XYZ highlight that the requirement of daily and excessive monitoring is part of the clients' contractual requirements. They have to identify errors and provide a Six Sigma process report on weekly basis to the clients with details of corrective action taken. The organisation currently has an annual employee turnover of 80% and its hiring managers are always fulfilling new hire demands. If you were the HR manager at XYZ Call Centre, what solution(s) would like to propose to rectify this situation?

Bibliography

Boselie, P. (2010). *Strategic human resource management: A balanced approach*. London: Tata McGraw-Hill Education.
Boxall, P., & Purcell, J. (2011). *Strategy and human resource management*. Basingstoke: Palgrave Macmillan.
Huselid, M. A. (1995). The impact of human resource management practices on turnover, productivity, and corporate financial performance. *Academy of Management Journal, 38*(3), 635–672.
Locke, E. A., & Latham, G. P. (1990). *A theory of goal setting and task performance*. Englewood Cliffs: Prentice Hall.
Shields, J. (2007). *Managing employee performance and reward: Concepts, practices, strategies*. Melbourne: Cambridge University Press.
West, M. A., Borrill, C., Dawson, J., Scully, J., Carter, M., Anelay, S., Patterson, M., & Waring, J. (2002). The link between the management of employees and patient mortality in acute hospitals. *International Journal of Human Resource Management, 13*(8), 1299–1310.

Strategic Learning and Development

Ashish Malik

Key Learning Outcomes
At the end of this chapter, you should be able to:

- *Review of key theoretical bases of learning and development*
- *Analyse the dominant drivers of internal career orientations of individuals*
- *Examine and analyse the relationship between strategy and learning and development*
- *Analyse the key drivers of training*

Introduction

Exploring the AMO model, this chapter focuses on building 'A'–or the ability of employees. From a strategic HRM perspective, this chapter examines the role that training, learning, and skill development can play in the development of individual and organisational capabilities necessary for achieving sustained competitive advantage. The extant literature on skills development is extensively well-developed at a macro-, meso- and micro-level. The theoretical underpinnings of this important activity spans across the fields of economics, strategy, public policy and other disciplinary domains. The focus in this chapter will be on skills development in an organisational context, encompassing three distinctive levels: individual, group/team and organisational development. The chapter begins by analyzing the theoretical foundations that explains why firms invest in training and offers an overview of the factors that shape an organisation's decision to invest in training. Dealing with

A. Malik (✉)
Faculty of Business and Law, Central Coast Business School, The University of Newcastle, Ourimbah, Central Coast, NSW, Australia
e-mail: ashish.malik@newcastle.edu.au

© Springer Nature Singapore Pte Ltd. 2018
A. Malik (ed.), *Strategic Human Resource Management and Employment Relations*, Springer Texts in Business and Economics,
https://doi.org/10.1007/978-981-13-0399-9_10

the strategic question of differentiation between firms, this chapter explores why some firms invest more in training than others even if they are competing in the same product markets. In addressing human capability and development issues in an organisation, the HR developers must also consider employees' personal development and career needs. This is especially true for key roles given that talent is scarce. In managing talent there are invariably some tensions between an individual's internal career orientations (or career anchors, see Schien 1996, 2006, for example) and the external career path that an organisation offers.

Managing Employee Learning and Development: Theoretical Foundations

In the wider education and training institutional infrastructure, there are tensions about who is responsible for creating 'industry ready' workers? Is it the individual, organisation or state? While game theorists (Finegold 1992) have modelled these scenarios and argue that the weakest stakeholder group loses. Another theory that traverses all three levels is the human capital theory (Becker 1964), which suggests that for improved wages and increased productivity, investment in human capital is vital. The underlying logic of this theory is that high levels of skills and knowledge enables people to perform better in their jobs, which ultimately raise their productivity. Increases in productivity and presence of higher order skills is rewarded in the form of higher wages. Another hypothesis this theory examines is whether firms should invest in generic and transferable skills or only firm specific and by implementing non-transferable skills (Becker 1964). The theory argues that firms will not invest in generic and transferable skills as these are also of equal value to other employers. Whereas, investment in technical and non-transferable (or firm-specific) skills training is logical as the investing firm can recover the costs of such training during the tenure of an employee and such skills will make the employee more productive in their current job. A variant of this theory, the Neo-Human Capital theory, focuses on investment in training to overcome changes in technology (Acemoglu and Pischke 1998; Bartel and Litechenberg 1987). The neo-human capital theorists argue that firms will invest in generic and transferable skills because of the *information asymmetry* that exists at the time of hiring new employees. Further, the theory postulates that the demand for highly skilled employees will decline with a firm's experience on the use of a given technology, hence with each event of new production, managerial or process technologies, firms can expect a spike in investment in learning. It is interesting to note that most studies of high performance work systems (HPWS) invariably features training and development as a key element in the bundle (Ashton and Sung 2002). Similarly, even the RBV models highlight the importance of investing in firm-specific skills, resources and capabilities to make the resources valuable, rare, and inimitable by the firm's immediate competitors because of the way they are organised in the production function (Barney 1991; Wright et al. 1994).

Given the numerous theoretical explanations of why firms invest in training, one theme that emanates very clearly in the above theories is to improve the performance or productivity of a system. This bears resemblance with Swanson's (2001) conceptualisation of human resource development (HRD) and the role it plays in an organisational context. Swanson (2001) argued that for HRD to survive, the *performance paradigm* should prevail over *learning paradigm*. Building on research undertaken in the UK, Smith and Hayton (1999) analysed the factors affecting the provision of enterprise training in Australia. While a number of other theorisations have since been undertaken in the context of a number of countries and industries, in the main, the key factors affecting a firm's decision to invest in training can be summarised into two groups: *Internal organisational influences* and *external contextual influences*. While the former includes factors such as workplace change, product or process change, enterprise size, industry type, introduction of quality management systems and new technology, the latter group includes factors such as client specifications, government regulation and inadequacies of the educational systems (Malik 2009; Malik and Nilakant 2011; Smith et al. 2004; Ashton and Sung 2002, 2006). From a strategic HRD perspective, Malik (2009) and Pereira and Malik (2015) found that firms that invested greater amounts in training and development were also firms that were operating in a medium- to higher-level product market segment of the IT industry. While this would suggest that high-end product markets demand greater inputs of training investment, this is not always true as even relatively less complex or low-end product and service markets have known to allocate greater investments in training, especially if the industry is growing fast and is witnessing high levels of employee turnover. This may also be the case because of contextual factors such as inadequacies in the educational infrastructure to produce market ready workforce, high growth rates witnessed by the industry and dynamism in a firm's products and service offerings. This trend has been borne out in the study of large IT firms delivering in both simple and complex levels of service delivery. Training in these organisations has played a strategic role in not only keeping the overall workflow steady, but also in the longer term, through sustained investments in learning and development infrastructure, these firms were able to offer a lower unitised cost of training and hence contribute to a firm's bottom line (Malik 2017).

Career Development

As HR developers, apart from focusing on skills development for core roles in an organisation, they are also tasked with retention of key talent in an organisation. This brings to our attention to the topic of managing individual's career aspirations. From a strategic perspective, HR developers must consider the business and competitive strategy before making extensive investments in learning and development and indeed offering employees career paths (Lloyd 2005; Stewart and Brown 2009). There is an ongoing debate regarding whose responsibility is it to invest in an individual's personal learning and career development needs. Schien's (1996) work on career anchor theory, is relevant here as he focuses on first understanding the individual's internal career anchors before offering them with a career path in an organisation. According to Schien, career anchors are a configuration of aptitudes, intentions, and beliefs that help in directing, limiting, stabilizing and assimilating an employee's careers goals. The theory argues that people's career anchors (internal career orientations) take time to get stabilised (up to first 5 years of their working lives) and following this these anchors stabilise and generally do not change over time. According to the theory, people have up to two dominant career anchors from the following list of anchors: *managerial competence, technical and functional competence, pure challenge, creativity, service/dedication, security, autonomy* and *lifestyle*. There is some further research which suggests that career anchors may change over an individual's working life due to major shocks or contextual changes. From a strategic HR perspective, organisations are better placed to identify and place individuals in career paths that match with their dominant career anchors rather than placing people in careers that they are not anchored in. Classic examples of mismatch include people want to pursue *technical* excellence in their respective disciplines are offered to take on a specialist management roles. This creates an internal cognitive dissonance in the minds of such individuals who are more anchored in technical excellence as they do not have excellent people management skills nor are they interested in it. Eventually, this will lead to dissatisfaction at work and may result in voluntary turnover. Read the following case study of managing careers in a multinational firm operating in the UK.

Careers Case Study

Dr Ronan Carbery,
University College Cork, Ireland

A European subsidiary of a US multi-national company operating in the UK has historically endeavored to attract, retain and develop employees identified as critical to the success of the local operation. The organization operates in the ICT sector, offering cloud-computing technologies, and employs over 1500 staff. However, there are a number of issues currently impacting on careers in the organization. This case study presents responses from the organizations' annual employee climate survey. Such responses articulate a sense of belonging and alignment in what employees perceived and identified as being 'their' organization. Social Identity Theory (SIT) developed by Tajfel and Turner (1986) is a useful framework to understand this context. SIT underpins much of the literature surrounding the concept of identity. This involves the self-categorisation of individuals into various social categories. An individual's profession has more relevance to careers than their organizations, as mobility across organizations is more likely than mobility across professions. Hence, professional identification fosters a belief that an individual's career will be rewarded by the profession, which in turn leads to a higher level of career satisfaction.

(continued)

Employees highlight the organization as being an open and culturally welcoming environment and it is apparent that employees feel a strong sense of 'pride' working for such a company. As John, a line-level employee, articulated:

> There's a great work ethic here and a desire to advance and to take on more people and ensure our careers are growing here.

There are obvious feelings of community consistent with a well-developed organizational culture. Whilst it is important for employees to identify with their organization, there is the potential for negative effects on careers, which the HRD function need to be conscious of. Overall however, there is a general positive orientation towards the organization with many employees indicating that working for the organization enhance their career prospects and made them very attractive propositions to other organizations, thus increasing the pride they feel when discussing working for the organization. Indeed one operator, Anne, says that the only way they would leave is if the organization let them go:

> I have no intention of leaving. I'd only leave if they made me go. I like it here. I wouldn't work in a 24/7 culture if I didn't like my job.

The dominant culture in the organization is similar to that of the host US multi-national where a high performance work culture prevails. The performance culture has played a role in influencing how employees view their careers with employees accepting that while career success in the organization is determined by both ability and passion, there is a certain amount of box ticking. As David, a supervisor, noted:

> I think ability and [being] passionate are the two words. You need to have a passion for the organisation to succeed, for the business, for the products. And there is a certain amount of box ticking that goes on definitely but I do think that they are looking for somebody who goes that extra bit, that has that passion, drive, ambition and ability as well.

The emphasis on reaching goals and targets is viewed as critically important towards career success. Reaching targets and branding yourself to the right people is deemed necessary to get promoted. There exists a degree of cynicism around how employees should raise their profile in order to be perceived as talented, indicating that playing the game was more important to be seen as talented rather than actually being talented. According to Sara:

> It's more about branding yourself with you manager and then eventually...if you want to go to another department maybe your manager can say a good word for you but its really branding yourself to senior management.

(continued)

The organization is somewhat of an anomaly in that its attrition rates are considerably higher that its competitors despite it being seen as an attractive employer from a career development point of view. There is a perception that the organizations' historical core products are bankrolling the development of newer products and this might lead to capability issues in the future if new employees join and leave within 2–3 years, thereby taking their knowledge and innovative ways of exploring problems elsewhere. Attracting new staff in in certain organizational functions is challenging so the focus is upskilling existing employees.

In order to improve the high rate of employee attrition, the organization is looking at formalizing an organization career system. Organisational career systems are collections of policies, priorities, and actions that organisations use to manage the flow of their members into, through and out of the organisations over time. Essentially they relate to the set of HR policies and practices, and management actions that are used to direct employees during their employment. One thing to note is that changes in the external environment and an organisations strategy often cause employers to change the supposedly objective nature of the employment relationship and the subsequent composition of career systems.

A key issue for individual careers in the organisation is the nature of the performance management process. The organization use individualized development plans that are co-created by a manager and the employee to assign specific roles and responsibilities to employees who are perceived to be talented or have potential. The role of the manager is vital here – they are expected to set clear guidelines, a specific timeframe and provide coaching to the employee to help them fulfil their developmental objectives. Whilst it is the individual employees responsibility to manage their career, a manager who requests such a plan without authentic coaching renders it an administrative exercise rather than a developmental process. With some employees reporting being on individualized development plans for up to 5 years, it has become apparent that not all managers are willing or able to engage in coaching as Silvio articulates:

> *The company gives you lots of tools and opportunities to develop such as training, etc., but maybe what you need is a consultant, maybe HR to tell you, what is useful for you, what you need to follow a real career path.*

Without such supports the risk is that employees will prioritise managing their own brand without necessarily engaging in strategic thinking and decision-making, which is best enabled by mentoring and coaching. Referring to the need to engage in self-directed learning and development activities, Luis, a supervisor mentioned:

(continued)

> One of the not so good things that I didn't get a chance to mention is high turnover, I've had 7–10 managers over the last 10 years and that inhibits my ability to progress. You're constantly trying to impress, should I put some time and effort into impressing this person? How long will they last? So it's a case of anything I've done development wise I've done myself.

It is clear that there are employee undertaking value shifts, in particular with regard to the need to think differently about learning and development. In a such a rapidly changing environment, employees tended to believe that they needed to evaluate current job and career options and take a more proactive approach to their career development and employability. The need for employees to take responsibility for their own development and initiate learning and development needs is paramount. The perception amongst employees is that, increasingly, only firm-specific skills are provided to facilitate development within the organization and advanced generic transferable skills had to be sourced by themselves. Many employees report taking self-financed external training and development opportunities including night courses and part-time college courses.

Interviews with individual employees suggests that those who pursued these external training and development opportunities have recognised their skills gaps, accepted that change is future oriented and also want to ensure that they broaden their knowledge so that they will be employable elsewhere if needs be. As evidenced above, the organisation cannot be relied upon to provide opportunities for self-development unless actively pursued by the individual.

This presents the organization with a potential dilemma. Employees are likely to view organisation provided learning and development programmes as significantly less marketable than those provided in other ways. This raises the question of whether the organization should provide formal learning and development activities that contribute to the development of generic competencies. The organization needs to recognise the value of learning experiences to the individual and construct conditions that enable and encourage self-direction.

Inidivdual employees also have to consider the extent to which they practice agency to improve their careers. The traditional hierarchical career management framework, within which long-term career planning was possible, is gradually being abandoned by both organisations and individuals. This case emphasizes the role of the individual in career management, and the need for organizations to adjust their career system to new patterns of employment. The engagement of employees is important in this respect. Employees who report being engaged at work demonstrate greater workplace performance and engaged workers possess personal resources, including optimism, self-efficacy, self-esteem, resilience, and an active coping style, that help them to

(continued)

control and impact upon their work environment successfully, and to achieve career success. Both managers and the HRD function are in a critical position to increase or decrease engagement because they deal issues with such as accountability, work processes, compensation, recognition and career opportunities. From a career development perspective, there is often a mismatch between the expectations of employees and the roles offered by the organisation. Therefore, processes should be put in place to check that the career goals of employees are clearly understood and job roles are defined with as close an alignment to career aspirations as possible.

Possible Questions
1. How can organizations balance the provision of learning and development activities with individual career development needs?
2. What can be done to encourage individuals to take more responsibility for their career development?
3. Is SHRD compatible with individual career aspirations?

Critical Reflections

Although there is an increasing body of literature that supports the linkages between competitive strategy and a firm's orientation towards training, even firms operating in the low-to medium-end of the complexity of services continuum report equivocal results in terms of the volume and diversity of training. The policy debate on the political economy of skills literature argues that by adopting a high-skills route, we can aim for a high-wage economy. However, this argument has yielded mixed results. Much of the debate here only focuses on the supply side economics rather than the demand side. The focus should be on creating jobs so investment in high-skills can find its application in relevant jobs. Although scholars have touted the adoption of high performance work organisation designs as a way to deal with this, Lloyd and Payne (2006) argue that the underlying assumptions of this approach or its variants hasn't been given the necessary scrutiny. For example, even in workplaces where such designs are implemented the nature of capitalism hasn't changed. The dominant focus is still on adopting a post-Fordist approach where standardizing of jobs and de-skilling of roles is widespread. How then would one expect the change in demand for higher end skills and consequently high wages? Can the government interfere? Do institutions play a role in regulating employment in high and low skill jobs. This question was examined in the Vocational Education and Training sector in European and UK firms. While regulation can help in the form of 'license to skill' and practice, the results in the European fitness industry were varied and it highlights the strength of institutions and the extent to which they collaborated with the industry matters most in achieving high wages through the high skills logic (Lloyd and Payne 2017).

Illustrations and Skills Sandpit

The provision of skills, training and development based on the competitive strategy has been widely noted in a number of industry sectors. For example, in retail, the quality of skills at a discount store versus premium solutions store varies such that employees in the latter setting would require a range of interpersonal, solutions development and project management skills. Similarly, skills needed in mass service environments such as low-end high volume outbound sales transaction service call centres, compared to complex solutions-based call centres such as those offering legal or medical process outsourcing services, requires employees in the latter group to have high end skills and the need for specialist training.

Concept Integration with Cases and Learning Activities

The book has two cases studies that cover aspects of individual development from a career perspective as well as from a change management perspective. The previous case study by Carbery explored the issue of compatibility of careers within the wider umbrella of strategic approaches to learning and development. It also gives the learners an opportunity to discuss and explore an ongoing debate–whose responsibility is it to develop employees' careers? The case study by De Simone et al entitled *Managing Change and Employee Wellbeing in an Italian School* explores how employee wellbeing outcomes are affected in times of change and how training becomes a critical factor in overcoming anxieties in a change management process. Related to study of change, there is always an element of learning that is involved in a change process. The two are inextricably linked and interdependent. The above would suggest that managing change has implications for learning and development practitioners.

Conclusion

Overall, learning and development is a vital function in the armoury of HRM and has been noted to have direct and indirect impact on business and individual levels of performance. This practice has the capacity to impact and in some ways even shape an organisation's strategic choices for operating in certain markets. There is ample evidence of its strategic approach in the high technology services industry. Increasingly with the emphasis shifting towards innovation, changes in a firm's portfolio of products and services requires new skills and newer ways of working, all of which have implications for the HRD department of a firm.

Glossary

Career Development is a planned and systematic approach to identifying, assessing and formulating a suitable career path for an employee based on their aspirations and goals while keeping in mind the needs and contextual conditions of the wider organisation.

Development has a longer-term time orientation than training and focuses on realising an individual's potential for future roles

Human capital refers to those individual skills, competencies, knowledge and human endowments that firms use productively for deriving economic value from individuals. Human capital stock in a society or an organisation can be developed through the provision of education, training and development.

Learning is a relatively permanent change in one's behaviour has been an all-time classic definition. What follows from the above definition is that behaviour change should be supported by learning and development inputs.

Training refers to the development of skills and knowledge that are germane to an individual's immediate job requirements. Training typically has a short-term time orientation and can foccus on either firm-specific or generic skills training.

Key Questions and Learning Activities

Question. 1 In times of uncertainty whose responsibility is it for developing an individual employee's career? What approach and skills would be most beneficial for individuals to have in such times?

Question. 2 What are the key external factors that may impact the skills formation process in an organisation?

Question. 3 Are institutions and government interventions of increasing the quality and quantity of human capital stock an answer to better wages? Why, why not?

Learning Activity

As much as learning is an individual process, it is also influenced by other team members' willingness to share their knowledge and skills. This is especially true in team-based work environments. Applying your knowledge of HRM practices and other work experience, how can one effectively manage the nature and extent of knowledge sharing especially where members have deep levels of technical and behavioural skills and expertise that others can benefit from?

Bibliography

Acemoglu, D., & Pischke, J. (1998). Why do firms train? Theory and evidence. *Quarterly Journal of Economics, 113*, 79–119.

Ashton, D., & Sung, J. (2002). *Supporting workplace learning for high performance working*. Geneva: ILO.

Ashton, D., & Sung, J. (2006). *How competitive strategy matters? Understanding the drivers of training, learning and performance at the firm level* (Research paper no. 66). Oxford: Oxford and Warwick Universities Centre for Skills, Knowledge and Organisational Performance.

Barney, J. (1991). Firm resources and sustained competitive advantage. *Journal of Management, 17*(1), 99–120.

Bartel, A. P., & Lichtenberg, F. R. (1987). The comparative advantage of educated workers in implementing new technology. *The Review of Economics and Statistics, 69*(1), 1–11.

Becker, G. (1964). *Human capital: A theoretical and empirical analysis*. Princeton: Princeton University Press.

Boxall, P. (2003). HR strategy and competitive advantage in the service sector. *Human Resource Management Journal, 13*(3), 5–20.

Finegold, D. (1992). The changing international economy and its impact on education and training. *Oxford Studies in Comparative Education, 2*(2), 57–82.

Hall, R., Bretherton, T., & Buchanan, J. (2000). *It's not my problem: The growth of non-standard work and its impact on vocational education and training in Australia*. Adelaide: NCVER.

Lloyd, C. (2005). Competitive strategy and skills: Working out the fit in the fitness industry. *Human Resource Management Journal, 15*(2), 15–34.

Lloyd, C., & Payne, J. (2006). Goodbye to all that? A critical re-evaluation of the role of the high performance work organization within the UK skills debate. *Work, Employment and Society, 20*(1), 151–165.

Lloyd, C., & Payne, J. (2017). Licensed to skill? The impact of occupational regulation on fitness instructors. *European Journal of Industrial Relations*. https://doi.org/10.1177/0959680117701016.

Malik, A. (2009). *Factors influencing provision of enterprise training: A study of India's information technology (IT) sector*. Unpublished doctoral dissertation.

Malik, A. (2017). *Human resource management and the global financial crisis: Evidence from India's IT/BPO industry*. London: Taylor & Francis.

Malik, A., & Nilakant, V. (2011). Extending the "size matters" debate: Drivers of training in three business process outsourcing SMEs in India. *Management Research Review, 34*(1), 111–132.

Pereira, V., & Malik, A. (2015). *Human capital in the Indian IT/BPO industry*. Basingstoke: Palgrave Macmillan.

Schein, E. (1996). Career anchors revisited: Implications for career development in the 21st century. *Academy of Management Executive, 19*(4), 80–88.

Schein, E. (2006). *Career anchors: Self assessment* (3rd ed.). Hoboken: Wiley.

Smith, A., & Hayton, G. (1999). What drives enterprise training? Evidence from Australia. *The International Journal of Human Resource Management, 10*(2), 251–272.

Smith, A., Oczkowksi, E., Noble, C., & Macklin, R. (2003). Orgaisational change and management of training in Australian enterprises. *International Journal of Training and Development, 7*(1), 94–110.

Smith, A., Oczkowksi, E., Macklin, R., & Noble, C. (2004). The impact of organisational change on the nature and extent of training in Australian enterprises.International. *Journal of Training and Development, 8*(2), 2–15.

Stewart, G., & Brown, K. (2009). Training for improved performance. In *Human resource management: Linking strategy to practice* (pp. 320–328). Hoboken: Wiley.

Swanson, R. A. (2001). Human resource development and its underlying theory. *Human Resource Development International, 4*(3), 299–312.

Tajfel, H., & Turner, J. C. (1986). The social identity theory of intergroup behavior. In S. Worchel & W. G. Austin (Eds.), *Psychology of intergroup relations* (pp. 7–24). Chicago: Nelson-Hall.

VandenHeuvel, A., & Wooden, M. (1999). *Casualisation and outsourcing: Trends and implications for work-related training*. Adelaide: NCVER.

Wright, P. M., McMahan, G. C., & McWilliams, A. (1994). Human resources and sustained competitive advantage: A resource-based perspective. *The International Journal of Human Resource Management, 5*(2), 301–326.

Managing Employee Voice

Ashish Malik

Key Learning Outcomes
At the end of this chapter, you should be able to:

- *Define the terms employee voice, direct and indirect employee voice*
- *Identify the reasons for differences in employee voice across geographical boundaries*
- *Understand the theoretical basis for employee voice and employee participation*
- *Evaluate the contribution of employee voice*

Introduction

This chapter deals with the 'O' in the AMO framework covered in chapters "HRM and ER: A Strategic Perspective" and "Strategic HRM & ER: Best-Practice Versus Best Fit". While employees may have the necessary skills and motivation to apply those skills to productive tasks, sometimes, the workplace environment poses conditions where employees are unable to have a meaningful say in the key aspects and conditions affecting their employment. This chapter explores the idea of providing employees a voice for creating a healthy workplace environment. The presence of a pluralist approach to managing employment relations is not only necessary for the healthy working of an enterprise, it is increasingly becoming much more widespread. Little conflict is always desirable as it allows discourse and dialogue on issues that are competing in nature and affect wide range of stakeholders. Allowing

---

A. Malik (✉)
Faculty of Business and Law, Central Coast Business School, The University of Newcastle, Ourimbah, Central Coast, NSW, Australia
e-mail: ashish.malik@newcastle.edu.au

employees voice in matters that affects their employment conditions and quality of work life is increasingly becoming a key consideration for employees in their intention to join an organisation. In other words, it is a key element of job value proposition in a number of employer of choice campaigns. Potential applicants develop insights into the real workings of their organisation through messaging–idealistic or realistic so that they will have a say in conditions of their work. In some well-known campaigns, messages can be direct or implied. For example, what is the nature of work climate and culture that one can expect to find at the tech giant Google. What would you expect a Googler to do in their typical day? How much freedom and autonomy would they expect to have in carrying out their routine and non-routine work tasks? How much fun do they have in day? In answering these questions, the messaging approach would provide insights for potential applicants in their decision-making. In most cases, the messages are somewhere on a continuum from idealistic to realistic. Nevertheless, these subtle forms of messaging that employers provide through their recruitment campaigns, gives potential applicants an inkling into the kind of work-life an employee can expect. Information and messaging about the extent of employee voice is a key aspect from an employer's recruitment perspective, but there are other aspects to explore once an applicant decides to commence employment at a workplace.

The industrial revolution had strengthened the role of trade unions in providing employees with indirect, and sometimes the only, voice platform for settling the terms and conditions of their employment. Employees can exercise voice at an individual level or through a collective. There are forms of voice that are direct, for example, forms of voice that individuals exercise through a range of workplace participation mechanisms. It is very likely that individual voice will require some form of support through a senior person or an individual who may have strong bargaining powers. Indirect and collective forms voice often takes the form of trade unions or other formal and informal employee representative groups. Managing employee voice, therefore, is a vital aspect of work life today, as it was earlier and it provides employees with all possible opportunities to have *their say* in matters affecting their employment (Boxall and Purcell 2011). This chapter outlines the nature and extent of employee voice mechanisms that are prevalent in workplaces today and evaluates the main forms and its significance in HRM. From a strategic perspective, regardless of the nature of employee voice mechanisms—direct or indirect voice—the central matter is the degree to which employees should have a say over the decisions that affect their employment.

Terrain of Employee Voice

Employee voice has been in existence for more than a century though its nature and extent has changed tremendously. Almost 60 years ago, the premier journal in our field, *Human Resource Management,* in its second issue published in 1962, had an article highlighting that 'listening is good business' for managing people. Marking the 50th anniversary of this premier journal in 2011, a special issue was dedicated to the topic of *Employee Voice*. This issue captures the variety and the changing contours of employee voice in the last half century or so. Among other influences, the issue covered the impact of technology, attitudes of society and industrial democracy on the nature and extent of employee voice. Earlier work on individual level employee voice has been influenced by the work of Hirschman (1970), who developed the exit-voice-loyalty (EVL) framework in which dissatisfied employees express their *voice* in the form of *exiting* (leaving/quitting) or by complaining. While framework was extremely popular during the peak of the trade unions movement, alternate forms of employee voice, especially more direct forms of employee voice have increased in recent times. By building *loyalty* among employees, this framework argues that employers can reduce the incidence of voice. Loyalty has been described in the framework as a reason for not voicing one's concerns. Following this work, Gehlbach (2006) attempted to extend this framework by including the notion of *employee silence*. Gehlbach (2006) viewed employee silence as a dynamic that is contingent upon the degree of bargaining power between the employee and the employer. *Silence* typically manifests as *apathy* (wherein an employee accepts status quo and accepts the work conditions due to the power imbalance) and *enforced silence* (typically occurs when there is no real opportunity for employees to express their voice–directly or indirectly or when management elects to supress employee voice).

While apathetic employees demonstrate loyalty essentially by remaining silent, however, in the latter case of enforced silence, employees have no constructive mechanisms for raising voice. This situation has the potential to cause *harm* through *neglect* of employees. Such occurrences are increasingly seen in a neoliberal approach to management in today's times. Sustained levels of *silence* can lead to serious psychological harm and lead to adverse well-being outcomes such as stress, anxiety, depression and poor resilience. Benson (2000: 453) argues that, 'for some commentators independent unions are the only source of genuine voice', others Millward et al. (2000) note that employee voice has several channels. For example, indirect voice (through trade unions) other indirect forms of voice (such as through participation mechanisms such as joint consultative committees and work councils); and direct voice mechanisms such as by raising task-related voices directly with one's manager, upward problem solving and by making complaints. For example, direct voice can be exercised in the case of unfair and inequitable treatment of employees using employee involvement and participation programs. The roots of these latter direct voice mechanisms can be traced back to the human relations movement, the Japanese total quality management approaches of employee involvement and other employee participation programs. The extent of participation depends on what the contextual conditions offer and is also a function of the extent to which the institutional environment and labour management relations are at a workplace. The higher the degree of mutual trust the more likely one is expected to witness well-developed employee voice mechanisms. Marchington and Wilkinson (2005, p. 401) advanced the idea of an 'escalator of participation' of individual employees direct participation, wherein at the lowest level of the escalator, people freely share information (typically top-down) to briefings and communications about matters that affect work issues. At the next level, consultation focuses on interacting between managers and employees wherein inputs are sought from both parties. The higher levels of the escalator of participation relates to codetermination where both parties collectively make decisions. Finally, the last stage focuses on control or self-control, wherein individuals and teams are in control of their decision-making.

Impact of Employee Voice

The literature on the impacts of direct and indirect voice mechanisms is voluminous and highlights a range of employee and employer outcomes. For example, organisations that have well developed mechanisms for employee voice have noted a reduction in employee turnover rates, increased levels of employee involvement and commitment, enhanced employee well-being, developing a sense of belonging, greater levels of engagement and improved productivity (Batt et al. 2002; Hirschman 1970; Freeman and Medoff 1984; Marchington and Grugulis 2000). Both employees and employers have a role to play in making a genuine contribution through employee voice mechanisms.

Another popular framework for understanding employee voice and managing employment relations using a pluralist frame is the one proposed by John Budd (2004). Budd argues for a need to have industrial democracy at the workplace. In an democratic industrial society, firms seek industrial democracy by balancing *equity-voice-efficiency*. By fair treatment of employees, we can achieve *equity* in, for example, the distribution of rewards and administration of HR/ER practices. This debate is rooted in the political economy literature. Second, the opportunity to provide your say into decisions that affect your employment i.e. through *voice* or having freedom of speech, and indirect worker participation through unions is vital in an industrial democracy. Finally, to attain economic gains or *efficiency* by producing goods and services in a competitive environment and servicing the needs of all stakeholders (including shareholders), employers can ensure there is a right balance between *equity-voice-efficiency*. Budd argues that unlike equity and efficiency, *voice* cannot be achieved unilaterally.

Critical Reflections

In what is essentially a liberal market environment, where policy makers and employers promote the idea of free trade, having strong *equity and voice* is unlikely as the focus is largely going to be on increasing efficiency. It is not surprising to note then that the International Labour Organisation's idea of allowing decent work for all (Budd 2004) is unlikely as the unions are getting weaker with lower density of membership. Furthermore, the nature of equity allowed by free markets is only restricted to minimum enforced standards of a small safety net for employees. The pro-market sentiment offers limited protections such as job security to employees as employers seek greater flexibility for their workforce mix and the conditions that govern the same. In a bid to address the situation, Budd has argued for an increased role of introducing ethics into the discussion and whether consequentialist approaches to understanding ethics is enough or should one embrace more the ideas of virtue ethics as a means of restoring some balance? The sharpest conflicts are between efficiency on one hand and voice and equity at the other in the current system.

Illustrations and Skills Sandpit

What is also apparent is that a number of managers have started to adopt a hybrid approach wherein aspects of both direct and indirect voice mechanisms implemented collectively seem to deliver better outcomes for both the employer and employees. While there are no magic formulas for an ideal combination, a lot depends on the work culture, degree of trust and willingness between the parties for a genuine employee voice to employees. A stepped approach, similar to the escalator of participation can be gradually introduced, to build, over time, trust and hybrid forms of employee voice that are most effective for a given context.

Concept Integration with Cases and Learning Activities

The following case study provides a short scenario of conflict at workplace. The case explores how conflictual situations have an adverse impact on the wellbeing of employees. This is a much too common a situation in a number of high pressure roles typically found in the financial services industry.

Conflict in the Workplace and Need for Wellbeing (A)

Dr. Vidya S. Athota and Dr. Stephen Treloar, University of Notre Dame, Australia.
Work design at a Sydney Office
The workers at head office traditionally get along quite well but in recent times tempers have become a little frayed and outbursts of anger have emerged. On the fourth-floor, there is a team of around 80 people, comprising journalists, sub-editors, office support personnel and clerical support people. It is an open plan style of office layout with extensive use made of approximately two-metre high partitions with various nests of work stations in combinations of four to six workstations per unit.

It is an old building in Sydney's CBD and the windows face west. Senior executive staff are on the sixth-floor and have more modern office facilities, including air conditioners with individual and separate control settings for each office. While the entire fourth floor has so called climate control ducted air conditioning system, it is over 20 years old and probably in need of

(continued)

updating. Due to limited budget, preference was not given for updating air conditioners. The environment at workplace was not up to the standard.

Conflict has escalated between small groups of staff members on this floor whom claim, "the air conditioning is too cold", or conversely, others are complaining "the air conditioning is too hot". Outbursts have included "I can't work in this bloody heat any longer", and "people keep changing the temperature setting on the control and should leave it alone!". Furthermore, some of the staff members come from different parts of the world including the United States, UK, China, India and Japan. Some of the staff members wanted warm and some other preferred cold air conditioning. One of the staff member suggested that weather at his home country was warm and so he likes to have warm air condition while working. Another staff member mentioned that he was from Edinburgh and prefer cold air conditioning. These conflict preferences caused uneasiness and promoted some kind of uncomfortableness among some staff members.

An otherwise harmonious workplace on the fourth-floor is being eroded by this long standing and ongoing problem although complaints seem to have intensified since there were rumours emerging about possible redundancies at head office, due to the growth of digital media and its threat over traditional print media. Office kitchen became central place for discussing these rumours. Some staff members using their lunch time discussing about possible redundancies. Some senior members of the company are open for redundancies. The senior members thought that it would be easy for them get job in other palaces based on their seniority and redundancy was actually win-win deal for them. Some non-senior staff members were started to look for jobs in other companies and unable to give complete attention to the workplace activities. The negative attitude of these staff members was quite noticeable. Moreover, union representations have been made claiming the business is operating outside the legislation relating to workplace health and safety. There have even been 'talk of a work stoppages" (strikes)" to be called at "no to little notice." The frustration of the staff members was reaching to its peak. Negative emotions of the staff members produced negative attitudes towards work commitment. Union representatives called for an emergency meeting to discuss the situation. Request for the Union membership was dramatically increased. Majority of the staff joined in Union in order to protect their jobs and any other consequences of redundancy. Meanwhile, overall productivity was dramatically decreased in the company. The staff members were visibly not unhappy and showed no commitment to work related activities.

On the fifth floor of the same business, another workplace issue has arisen. The 50 workers who work on this floor are involved in pre-press layout, artwork and photography of the same newspaper group that covers all regional newspapers in the group. The Manager for the department has a reputation of being "old school" and routinely yells and raises his voice in angst against

(continued)

workers. He has also been known to use colourful language at times in making a point. He meets the criteria for bullying at workplace. He goes on heavy on the staff who come from Asian countries. It appears to be the manager assumes that immigrant staff members do not speak against their authorities. It seems like the manager taking advantage of this opportunity. He also meets the criteria for racial discrimination. The morale was low among majority of the staff members. Some of the staff members openly talking about leaving the company. Absenteeism has noticeably increased and there are reports that a claim for bullying and harassment will shortly be lodged with the Fair Work Commission (the legislative arm of the Australian industrial relations authority). There has also been an increasing number of staff either arriving late for work, or taking breaks longer than their allocated time. The department manager prides himself on his "third-generation Australian heritage" and at times expressed views that might be considered racist, especially against those from certain Asian countries. Some observers note that there seems to be "one rule for Aussies, and another rule for Asians". The department manager has banned the cooking (heating) of brought-from-home Asian dishes in the adjoining lunch room, due to the "pungent smell they emit". Furthermore, Asian staff members felt that they were disadvantaged in promotion opportunities. One of the staff member was working for 10 years in same company without a promotion despite many Aussie staff members were promoted to senior levels. Staff members from Asian background were exhibited withdrawn behaviours on several workplace situations. They have come to terms with that their career will be negatively impacted. Aussie staff members were able to see discrimination was taking place in the company. It was clear overall productivity was effected due to lack active role all the staff members at the company. Overall, majority of the staff members emotional wellbeing was at its peak and far from happiness at work.

Finally, on the executive sixth-floor. The offices are lavishly furnished, with quality carpet, artwork, indoor plants and above all, superior air-conditioning that has separate control panels for the ten different offices, and reception area. Three years earlier there were 18 senior executives working in the business, located on this floor. With the downturn in business across print media business, the executive staff has been reduced down to just 10 executive people. While all remaining executive are relatively well paid, there is now an unwritten "rule" that executives are virtually on call, 24 h a day in the event of an emergency, or 'breaking news story". Executives are now working an average of 60 h per week and as they are equipped with laptops and mobile phones, they are expected to be "contactable" as required. The boundaries of work-life balance dramatically decreased. Some executive were working hard during the weekends. This has put tremendous pressure on their families. A small number of executive feel anxious and continue to think about work related things during weekends. The average age of executives is 55 and there

(continued)

are signs of burn-out beginning to appear with some of the more senior executives. The wellbeing and happiness of the executives was not in its best. The owner of the business is an Australian living in London and this newspaper group is one of many for which he owns. It is now only marginally profitable. Despite all the existing problems there were no specific policies to promote organisational health and safety, and wellbeing.

Questions of the Case Study
1. What is occurring in this case and identify the parties affected by events reported in the case.
2. What are the general responsibilities of parties for workplace health, wellbeing, and safety in the workplace? How might these be addressed in the case?
3. What steps should be taken to address any undesirable phenomena?
4. What steps should be taken in promoting fairness in promotion opportunities?
5. What are the risk management exposures revealed in the case? And, how might these be addressed?

Conclusion

The three competing concepts of *equity, efficiency* and *voice* need to be managed and balanced in an employment relationship. The effectiveness of implementing employee voice depends on whether there is true intent or voice is simply deployed as a managerial add-on. If it is the latter, then it has the potential to become a fad and a means of gaining control over employees. The organisation will, in such instances, find it hard to win over the trust and buy-in of its employees–both of which are critical in gaining employee commitment and managing organisational change. Some might even argue that achieving balance in these competing goals is simply not possible in a laisse-faire market environment and a relatively weak institutional set of labour protection standards. Free markets demand efficiency and weak labour standards reduce equity, both of which will have an adverse impact on employee voice.

Glossary

Employee voice refers to the conditions where employees are allowed to have a meaningful say in matters affecting their terms and conditions of employment. This may be through individual or collective mechanisms and can also be direct or indirect.

Industrial democracy is an idea that is rooted in the political economy literature and argues that workers should further their emancipation and involvement in workplace decisions that have an impact on their conditions of employment.

Trade unions represent a lawful and an institutionalised form of employee representation for the purposes of bargaining the rights and responsibilities of employees towards their organisation. They can operate at a worksite level through an industry to a national level and sometimes may have a wider role than setting the terms and conditions of employment. For example, a number of trade unions in the services industry also provide a platform for skills and professional development and other benefits to their members.

Work councils is another form of institutionalised employee representative council that seeks to protect the conditions of employment of workers in an organisational setting.

Key Questions and Learning Activities

Question. 1 Discuss to what extent is employee voice an important consideration in your decision to work at an organisation?

Question. 2 If given a chance, would you undertake a role of employee participation representative and engage in collaborative decision-making? Provide a brief rationale for your choice.

Question. 3 Trade unions are losing their might and more hybrid forms of employee voice will be needed in future to provide sustainable conditions of employment that offer decent work. Discuss the above statement.

Learning Activity: Conflict in the Workplace and Need for Wellbeing (B)

Dr Stephen Treloar and Dr Vidya S. Athota, University of Notre Dame
The Insurance Arm of a Leading Australian Bank
My name is Stephen Treloar, sometimes I get approached to provide executive coaching direct to employees of companies and organisations, whom make contact with me (rather than being contracted by an employer) – this was the case with Jennifer. Jennifer was personally financing her own executive coaching, unlike the norm where executive coaching is financed by the employer. The Bank owned and operated its own insurance company as part of its widening of services to its customers, whilst the insurance company operated under its own insurance name brand, it was staffed by employees of the bank who were 'seconded' to work exclusively for the insurance company

(continued)

but under separate employment arrangements. The aim of the bank was to promote high performance work practices. But in reality not enough resources were provided to the staff members.

Jennifer was the newly appointed Claim Manager and was second in command in the business unit, she reported to the General Manager (of the insurance company), and had six direct reports. Jennifer was personally responsible for considering and approving all claims, with claims over 1 million dollars beings referred to the General Manager for sign-off approval. The insurance company was a relatively new arm of The Bank in having traded for less than 5 years. The company management did not conduct personality assessment if Jennifer was suited for the job. They assumed that Jennifer would be able to perform the high demand job.

Jennifer needed assistance in how to handle a situation which was having dire consequences on her health, well-being, and happiness in the job. During a particularly heavy period for insurance claims (there had been widespread damage caused by an abnormal number of bushfires) Jennifer reported she had been working 7-days per week for the past four consecutive months and was tired and weary! Based on the nature of the job, Jennifer needed pay attention to all details in the application. This required all her personal and family time to spend on reading the applications and assessing them. The boundaries between work-life balance were significantly decreased. She has been preoccupied her weekends and majority of evenings about work related issues. During these stressful times, she did not realise the severity of emotional wellbeing. Furthermore, Jennifer brings her stress and anxiety related issues to the work place. Fellow staff members started to observe this in Jennifer. It was clear that Jennifer health was going to be effected.

She was the delegated officer to assess and approve (or disapprove) claims, and was overwhelmed with both the workload and expectation from her employer. Jennifer clearly understood the consequences of disapproving (or reducing the value of claims) on claimants, for whatever reason but was also been driven to ensure the insurance business remained profitable with claims only approved in accordance to strict conditions of the insurance company's own underwriter pursuant to its agreement.[1]

Jennifer was on an annual salary of $80,000 (plus super) and had been promoted from within the insurance company, taking over from her predecessor who had suddenly left the company due to ill-health. This was a significant promotion for Jennifer and she wanted to do a great job and be recognised for

(continued)

---

[1] It is normal practice for insurance companies to cover their own insurance exposure by having an Insurance Underwriter "underwrite" claims against it to spread the risk of exposure across a much wider base of insurance providers. However, claims must be considered considering the terms and conditions of the underwriting, as well as complying to statute law, including consumer legislation.

her efforts and didn't mind doing "whatever it takes". It was her first appointment into a management role and was formerly a Claims Officer for the same company, on an annual salary of $55,000 (plus super). There was no provision for overtime, nor was there any "time off in lieu" provided for in her new role. In her former role, she was employed under an Enterprise Agreement, whilst in her management role was employed under a Contract of Employment. There were certain promises made about the possibility of performance bonuses in her new role but these were not specifically included in her Contract of Employment. She was hopeful this might be amended once she had "proven herself". No bonuses had been offered to her or had been paid, nor had she been offered any time-off in lieu or other inducement or recognition for her service.

Jennifer was almost 12-months into her new role and was happy with being promoted to the job, however, when the bushfire season hit, she was deluged with work and, as earlier reported, was working 7 days per week for the past four consecutive months. She was exhausted, physically, mentally, and emotionally. Moreover, the pressure from work somewhat confused her thinking and had completely forgotten an important family reunion celebrating her parents 40th wedding anniversary. Jennifer was planning to arrive late in the afternoon on a Sunday after attending work that day but had "some-how" completely overlooked the occasion, despite having an entry in her diary. This caused a great deal consternation with her immediate family whom (wrongly assumed) she failed to recognize the importance of the occasion. Given the nature of her provider, Jennifer was able to access a housing loan of just 1.5% PA enabling her and partner to purchase a unit in the burgeoning Sydney market. She was also able to exceed the normal borrowing ratio of loan given in recognition of the nature of her employment.[2] The downside was she felt "trapped" insomuch as committed to a mortgage through her employer knowing that if she left her current employment she would struggle financially to either replace the loan with another loan provider, or at the very least pay a much higher interest rate if she continued the loan through her current employer.

When asked "had she spoken to her Supervisor about her dilemma?" Jennifer responded, "she had" but "...the General Manager was not very responsive to her concerns or need". The General Manager was described, by her as "old school" quoting that "...young people moving into management, had to earn their stripes". She felt 'trapped' and was also concerned about the effect long hours was having in the personal relationship with her partner.

(continued)

---

[2] Lending providers generally loan within limited levels of LVR (loan valuation ratio) meaning the amount of money that will be provided as a loan based on a multiple of factors, including equity of the loan, and earnings which determine a borrower's capacity to repay loan repayments, as well as other considerations.

Jennifer's partner was demonstrating annoyance and frustration with her high work levels and time away from home; he was becoming increasingly "snappy and short" – beginning to show signs which resent the situation of long absences away at work. Jennifer felt uncomfortable and frightened that her relationship might entering "rocky-ground". At home, Jennifer was preoccupied these unpleasant thought and experiences. The Bank, and its independently operated insurance arm adopted a culture of 'high performance work practices' with promotion and the payment of bonuses heavily weighted to performance. The insurance company arm had met or exceeded all its growth KPIs for new customers and premiums since Jennifer took up the role, for which the General Manager seemed to have taken took most of the credit for. Whilst there was a 'blow-out' in expected claims due to the unprecedented number of recent widespread bushfires, these were mostly covered under its own underwriter risk management protection policy. In short the insurance company appeared to be going very well although the General Manager didn't provide any positive feedback of accomplishments. This also led to unhappiness to Jennifer and her team which was beginning to affect their motivation, enthusiasm and even physical/medical wellbeing. Jennifer was becoming very unpopular with her direct reports as she allocated increased workloads to each staff member. The absentee rates from her direct reports were running at over 15% and she had "heard by the grapevine" that one of the employees (although unsure which one) was planning to report oppressive work conditions to Work Cover.[3] Jennifer's wellbeing started to negatively impacted by workplace challenges.

Questions of the Case Study
1. Identify each of the parties affected by events reported in the case.
2. What are the issues of concern for each of the affected parties?
3. What are the general responsibilities of parties for workplace health, wellbeing, and safety in the workplace? How might these be addressed in the case?
4. What are the risk management exposures revealed in the case? And, how might these be addressed?
5. What advice would you provide to Jennifer?

---

[3] WorkCover is a government agency operating in the NSW jurisdiction, responsible for investigating industrial employment issues related to workplace, health, and safety. It has a policy of investigating all complaints made against employers, including complaints made anonymously.

Bibliography

Batt, R., Colvin, A. J. S., & Keefe, J. (2002). Employee voice, human resource practices, and quit rates: Evidence from the telecommunications industry. *Industrial and Labor Relations Review, 55*(4), 573–594.
Benson, J. (2000). Employee voice in union and non-union Australian workplaces. *British Journal of Industrial Relations, 38*(3), 453–459.
Boxall, P., & Purcell, J. (2011). *Strategy and human resource management* (3rd ed.). London: Palgrave Macmillan.
Budd, J. W. (2004). *Employment with a human face: Balancing efficiency, equity, and voice.* Itacha/New York: Cornell University Press.
Budd, J., Gollan, P., & Wilkinson, A. (2010). New approaches to employee voice and participation in organizations. *Human Relations, 63*(3), 303–310.
Dundon, T., & Gollan, P. J. (2007). Re-conceptualizing voice in the non-union workplace. *International Journal of Human Resource Management, 18*(7), 1182–1198.
Freeman, R., & Medoff, J. (1984). *What do unions do?* New York: Basic Books.
Gehlbach, S. (2006). A formal model of exit and voice. *Rationality and Society, 18*(4), 395–418.
Hirschman, A. O. (1970). *Exit, voice, and loyalty: Responses to decline in firms, organizations, and states.* Cambridge, MA: Harvard University Press.
Kaufman, B. (2004). *Theoretical perspectives on work employment and the relationship.* Champaign: Industrial Relations Association.
Marchington, M. (2007). Chapter 12: Employee voice systems. In P. Boxall, J. Purcell, & P. Wright (Eds.), *The Oxford handbook of human resource management* (pp. 231–250).
Marchington, M., & Grugulis, I. (2000). 'Best practice' human resource management: Perfect opportunity or dangerous illusion? *International Journal of Human Resource Management, 11*(6), 1104–1124.
Marchington, M., & Wilkinson, A. (2005). Direct participation and involvement. In S. Bach (Ed.) *Managing human resources: Personnel management in transition* (Chapter 15, pp. 398–423). Oxford: Blackwell Publishing Ltd.
Millward, N., Bryson, A., & Forth, J. (2000). *All change at work?: British employment relations 1980-98, portrayed by the workplace industrial relations survey series.* London: Routledge.
Pfeffer, J. (1992). Understanding power in organizations. *California Management Review, 34*(2), 29–50.
Sako, M. (1998). The nature and meaning of "voice" in the European car components industry. *Human Resource Management, 8*(2), 5–18.
Storey, J. (1992). *Developments in the management of human resources.* Oxford: Blackwell Publishing.

Managing Change and HRM

Ashish Malik

Key Learning Outcomes
At the end of this chapter, you should be able to:

- *Analyse the key barriers to change*
- *Describe the four tasks of managing change*
- *Examine and analyse the relationship between managing change and HRM practices*
- *Identify the key competencies needed by an HR practitioner in managing change*

Introduction

Managing Organisational Change

Managing change has aspects of the AMO framework covered in the previous chapters. The literature on managing change highlights that most change management initiatives fail. Nearly one in three fail. This would suggest that the designers and implementers of change must be doing something wrong that would lead to such a poor performance track record of change management initiatives. It is not surprising then that a number of HR professional body organisations around the world have recognized change management as one of the most important tasks and a key competency for HR practitioners to master. There is an acknowledgement also in the literature that managing change requires higher order skills and that it is a strategic activity, often involving senior leadership's commitment. Change is not like taking a cookbook approach, wherein, by

---

A. Malik (✉)
Faculty of Business and Law, Central Coast Business School, The University of Newcastle, Ourimbah, Central Coast, NSW, Australia
e-mail: ashish.malik@newcastle.edu.au

simply implementing a prescriptive 'list of things to use' one can deliver a successful dish. The importance of managing change cannot be emphasized enough in a post global financial crisis era when most organisations were reeling under severe financial and people management pressures (Malik 2013, 2017).

In today's dynamic environment, strategic HRM practices under the best-practice approach are unlikely to deliver the solutions for dealing with the dynamic challenges businesses face. The importance of context is emphasized here again, and value can be realised through adopting a best-fit and an institutionally grounded approach, wherein, the importance of strategic choices exercised by the human agency are vital in delivering on the most realistic changes in a dynamic environment (Malik 2017). HR practitioners need to get an appreciation of what's required before delivering on the change agenda and must manage the transition and transformation processes carefully. Given the high rates of failure and costs associated with change management programmes, it is important that HR practitioners develop change management capability. Although there are numerous prescriptions of managing change, Nilakant and Ramnarayan offer a tested framework for developing an understanding of the key tasks of change as well as managing the change process. Employing Nilakant and Ramnarayan's framework (2006), Malik (2016) proposed a set of HR strategies in managing change in the Indian IT industry. The key tasks of managing change were overlayed with the role HRM can play at various stages of the change management process. This is presented in Table 1.

Table 1 Change management and key HR tasks

Change management: four tasks	HRM: key tasks
Appreciating change	Communicating the need;
	information dissemination about markets trends;
	system of knowledge sharing (e.g. Performance metrics) and;
	develop a shared understanding of market needs
Mobilizing support	Identify and develop managers who believe in the change;
	Communicate the change widely and frequently (key behaviours and measures of success);
	Empowerment via job redesign;
	Manage employee voice
	Employee and stakeholder involvement in change initiatives (e.g. redesign rewards and quality management schemes)
Executing change	Transparent implementation of positive reinforcement via rewards and benefits (e.g. gain sharing schemes);
	Capture and communicate benefits realised from changes;
	Transparent performance measurement and management;
	Critical role played by HRD/Learning and development for equipping people with the skills to carry out the change
Building change capability	Institutionalise the changes made
	Reward changed behaviours
	Monitoring through performance management systems
	T&D for ongoing change management capabilities at different levels

Nilakant and Ramnarayan (2006) argue that the key reason for ineffective change management outcomes is due to an organisational and individual property called *'inertia'*. Inertia is present in all human beings and organisations as it is manifest in their customs. The first barrier in overcoming change is to be cognizant that inertia is natural and it subsists. Nilakant and Ramnarayan (2006) outline three steps that are critical managing change. They further state that change is not about restructuring or downsizings, it is about *changing the mindsets of people*. Changing *mindsets* is problematic because people and organisations display inertia. This is one of the reasons why change management is regarded as a higher order cognitive and relational skill. Their framework lists four common tasks of change for leaders and HR champions to successfully design and execute. Broadly, these tasks are: *create an awareness of the need to change*; *create a motivation or willingness to bring about change*; *develop supporting capabilities*; and *build capacity and knowledge to deal with change*.

Changing mindsets are not easy as they are made up of routines that are enmeshed in values, assumptions and beliefs. Schein identified two opposing forces in action in any change situation: learning anxiety (which blocks change) and survival anxiety (which facilitates change). Nilakant and Ramnarayan (2006) argue that for change to occur *survival anxiety* must exceed *learning anxiety*. Reducing the learning anxiety is a better way to change people, a point that was long stated in seminal work of Kurt Lewin's approach to change and organisational development. Lewin emphasized that it is easier to bring about change by weakening the forces of stability than by weakening the forces of change and that both these forces of change exist inside every organisation. HR should take a proactive role in designing and managing the implementation process. HR can perform the key change management roles identified by Nilakant and Ramnarayan (2006) to successfully manage change.

These roles are: **appreciating change**–this involves a deeper understanding of the business environment and how it impacts the business model. Why is there a need to change?; **Mobilising support**–this involves creating a strong working coalition within the organisation to ensure the commitment of employees and senior management in managing change; **Executing change**–improving enabling capabilities and bringing in key resources that will assist in executing the change and demonstrating the benefits accruing from the change initiative. The timeframes for executing change should be realistic and the change management team should celebrate small wins and remove any conflicting messages; and **Building change capability**–involves not only institutionalising the key changes made but also taking steps to ensure that the organisation does not falter to the old ways and routines due to inertia.

HRM tasks needed for the management of four change tasks are stated in Table 1.

Change management initiatives can operate at different levels and involve interventions at each level. An earlier approach that gave birth to the modern day change management approaches is the foundational field of Organisational Development (OD). OD interventions operate, in the main, at three levels: individual, group/team or organisational systems level. An intervention in the OD sense is a series of planned steps that are implemented to improve the effectiveness of a given system. The focus could be on improving individual, group, team or organsiational effectiveness and this could take the form of one or several initiatives. While most change interventions are aimed at improving the performance of a process, teams/groups or organisational systems, we often ignore at our own peril, some of the individual level interventions, which could potentially impact the other two levels noted above.

Critical Reflections

One of the common problems in managing change is the inability to overcome inertia due to lack of understanding of cognitive, volitional and action barriers. In addition to this, managers and leaders want to retain their legitimacy and thus often indulge in political behavior and exercise their dispositional power in ensuring their positions are safeguarded. Much of the critique often focuses on lack of a holistic understanding of the key tasks of change and the interrelationships between each of them. All four tasks or for that matter any set of successful change management bullet lists, should be collectively implemented for an enduring and successful change outcome. Poor and ineffective communication during the change management process can also undermine the entire initiative as people tend to become skeptical about the change project. To this end, celebrating small wins and where necessary, rewarding the right behaviours (or indeed actively discouraging inappropriate behaviours), which is also often ignored, could go a long way in cementing the success of a change management initiative.

Illustrations and Skills Sandpit

The following real-life case study explores an OD consulting assignment at an organsiation in India. A bidder firm (the company acquiring stake) acquired a small target (the acquired firm), serving in a specialist niche technology market. A new CEO was brought in by the group bidder firm's management to manage the post-acquisition phase.

Read this short case on how a CEO can have an adverse impact on effectiveness:

> **A CEO Shoots the System**
>
> *Author: Joseph George, PhD, Workplace Catalysts Inc, Bangalore India*
> **Hiring a new CEO**
> A small-scale Indian engineering unit in a Southern Indian state was acquired by a larger business from Western India. In order to make the acquisition

(continued)

changes successful, a new CEO was hired externally from a large organization. This CEO would potentially assume neutral ground as there are no vested interests of the incoming CEO in either the target or the bidder firm. Upon selection, the CEO was eager to leave a mark and thought of this as his swan song before ending his career. As a first indication this position, the CEO invited an OD consultant for change facilitation assignment, on the recommendation of another CEO from their group company.

About the Organisation

Here are some initial points of attention based on which the consultant suggested the use of OD consulting for the problem at hand. The acquired unit had a patent for a porous membrane technology, with minimal maintenance required for the product. The bidder firm valued the innovation, as the membrane served cooling purposes without the use of compressor gas-based cooling. It appears that the potential of this patent was not effectively understood by the target firm, despite the potential and value it offered to its clients. Its original client base included marquee clients whose brand capital was not effectively marketed and operationalised by the target firm. The business operations of this engineering firm included operations such as fabrication of sheet metal, assembly and erection of pumps, motors and air-duct sections with a supply of steady recyclable water at client utilities such as office buildings and manufacturing shop-floors and warehouses. The value proposition was in replacing stale air-conditioned air with fresh air-cooled supply at ambient temperatures suitable for employees and customers at any work or commercial space. E-commerce warehouses, automotive factories and shop floors found such installations both highly energy efficient and appropriate for people at the workplace. The opportunity to contribute to environment friendly technology was inviting.

The new CEO and his assessment

The new CEO was selected from a publically listed company, whose strength was in large project implementations in the energy and environment industry sectors. In initial contact meetings to scope out the pressing issues and probable paths ahead, the incoming CEO described the workforce as disoriented from the marketplace. He felt they needed handholding in the change, as he would spearhead the marketing of the concept leveraging his own strengths. In the meantime, the original promotor of this target firm was allowed to ease out of the day-to-day operations, although his trusted aide from manufacturing division was given an extension of employment until the acquiring company was able to stabilize their operations in the target (acquired) unit.

(continued)

The salesforce of the target firm was scattered over the country, and positioned somewhat closer to client locations in all major Indian cities. The sales team represented a mix of highly experienced and less experienced employees. During the transition and acquisition phase, the project team however lost their key implementers as they quit for greener pastures overseas. So, a decision was taken by the incoming CEO to replace the projects wing with a person who had experience in the services industry but also had a strong service orientation and posst-sales maintenance and installation care experience.

All said and done, the consultant offered the incoming CEO and his think tank, which comprised of the–R&D partner from the acquirer group and another CEO confidante from another group business unit–a step-through details of the process of his proposed OD consultation approach. All three agreed on the OD consultant's suggested approach.

For organisational development to happen towards effective change, it had to commence and signal clearly that the OD intervention had strong support from the top management. Therefore, it was decided that the CEO would offer himself to feedback from his direct reports from all functional areas such as HR, Finance, Manufacturing, Sales and Projects to provide clues to him on his personal leadership style and make him aware of their concerns about the acquisition context using an anonymized feedback process of using the OD consultant to offer consolidated feedback in a thematic form.

In preparation for this intervention, the OD consultant asked the participants to think of the following pointers from their experiences to provide the consultant with feedback for the CEO. These pointers include:

Handling of common issues of the team
Approachability of the CEO as a team leader
Ability of representing team issues to the top management
Dealing with customers and business partners
Impact of the CEO on business strategy
Impact of the CEO on operations and the execution of business strategy

The CEO was enthused and agreed to a facilitated feedback process. An excerpt from the communication that was sent to the participating employees is stated below.

"What is the Objective of this Leadership Assimilation meeting?

*Any leader needs feedback in order to develop himself. Receptivity to feedback is a strong predictor of one's leadership capability. In the appraisal process, one receives feedback from the top, i.e. from their immediate boss. Through this **Leader Assimilation Process (LAP)** that we will engage in, we will generate feedback for the leader from his direct reports; and where*

(continued)

necessary from his peers too. It is essentially a discussion process of about the Leadership style of the recipient leader. It does not refer to the leader as a technical professional or as an individual citizen of the business group. The point of the process is his effectiveness as a leader in his role. Your CEO has volunteered to be the first feedback recipient. You are invited to this important process to share your frank & objective thoughts for his own development. Mutually, we all benefit from the process, as we learn to organise our thoughts and express them responsibly in an anonymized feedback mode."

The *"OD Process"* to be followed was clarified between consultant and the CEO again, before he communicated the launch of change initiative with his team members. A quarterly review event was chosen to kickstart the process of change, so that leaders from different parts of the country could be face-to-face in the same room. A couple of participants from the field offices dialled into through an audio bridge medium. The participants were brief and they were well prepared by the OD consultant with points of unique disclosure, and the OD facilitators' consulting process enabled clarification of expressions between team members. In the spirit of the intervention process, the leader was subsequently called into the room, after the consensual agreement on feedback content was arrived at in an anonymized form in the room. The facilitator had run the anonymized content through the team for their consent before the leader was called in and given the same feedback. The CEO listened to the feedback, and where necessary, asked clarificatory questions of the facilitator / consultant. The OD consultant helped by offering explanations and clarifications as needed. Following this, the participants thanked the consultant for the clarity and integrity of the OD consulting process. A few weeks later, the R&D head from the acquirer firm called up the consultant to say, that the CEO was not receptive to the feedback that was presented at the meeting, and that the fears of the target firm's team came true. These included an overemphasis on micro-managing each direct report's activities. He said, "We do not know if his style can sustain the growth phase". Other pertinent concerns included remarks about the CEOs background, "Technically he is not strong, so he is dependent on others to estimate the effects on execution. He is overestimating on plans for the business more often".

Despite an anonymized feedback and cordially agreed process, the participants of change did not see the leader translate his commitment to the feedback process in action, as originally indicated in the message. The R&D head felt that the consultant should intervene with the group Chairman, especially in the interest of the acquired unit. The consultant considered this to be beyond his brief of engagement. The CEO finally disengaged the consultant's services, although officials who participated in the feedback session, had a healthy respect for the consultant years after the episode. They keep a silence on the origin of their association however, the new CEO

(continued)

continues to present the team with newer challenges to work on. Surprisingly, the firm has garnered greater market share under the CEO's leadership.

Based on the above short scenario, answer the questions that follow
Q1. At what level(s) was this OD intervention scoped?
Q2. What in the OD process consultation went well? Provide reasons for your answer.
Q3. What in the consulting process became ineffective? What may have been the reasons?
Q4. What lessons in OD contracting does this case represent?
Q5. What lessons in intervention design, does this case represent?

Concept Integration with Cases and Learning Activities

The book has two case studies that deals with the related topic of managing change: the first is by De Simone et al. entitled, *"Managing change and employee wellbeing in an Italian school"* and the second case titled, *"Gender Inclusive Leadership for Innovation and Change – an HR Head's reflections"*, by Jayashree, Sevaldsen and Lindsay. Both case studies deal with change. While the first case study highlights the adverse outcomes of poorly managed change initiative and how it impacts on employee wellbeing, the second case study provides an interesting account, from an HR practitioner perspective, when a large multinational firm introduces gender diversity for inclusive leadership in managing innovation and change. There are aspects of these cases that are useful for other chapters as well (e.g. chapters "Strategic Learning and Development" and "Special Topics in SHRM & ER").

Conclusion

The above discussion highlights the importance of change management capability for HR practitioners and leaders who are tasked managing with the key tasks of change. This chapter provides an established framework for managing change successfully and also links the tasks of change to different HR practices, offering a useful inventory of HRM activities for the busy HR practitioner. As managing change is a higher order skill, there will be a need to remain flexible, and manoeuvre and modify some of the activities to suit the change tasks at hand.

Glossary

Change agent can be an internal (usually the HR or OD practitioner) or an external (typically an OD consultant) role that focuses on the effective design and implementation of change management initiatives in an organsiation. The agent –internal or external–must successfully carry out the four or similar tasks of change for successful change outcomes.

Organisational change refers to changes that an organisation wishes to engage in, in response to pressures from its internal and external strategic environments. The nature of such changes can be technical (product or process-related), managerial (process, structural or values) or behavioural (e.g. cultural) and the scale of such changes can be transformational (wide-reaching, fundamental and significant affecting all or most parts of an organsiation) or transactional and incremental (small steps affecting some parts of the organisation) change.

Organisational development is a long-term strategic planned and systematic behavioural science approach to managing change in an organisation's individual-, group- and systems-levels for improved performance and overall sustained levels of effectiveness of a business.

Key Questions and Learning Activities

Question. 1 What are the key challenges in selling the change agenda in a change management initiative?

Question. 2 Change management is living in the shadow of OD.

Discuss the above statement and outline any differences that you believe exist between OD and change management as we know of today.

Question. 3 Building on your knowledge of HR professional competency frameworks wherein change management is identified as a key HR competency, what are the most important task(s) an HR practitioner must deliver a successful change management initiative.

Learning Activity: Managing Growth

> **Let's Grow Tomorrow**
> *Radhika Subramanian* and Vijayakumar Parameswaran Unnithan**.*
>
> ** Founder of Glow Worm Consulting, a Learning, Leadership and Organization Development Consulting firm.*

(continued)

** *Professor and the Chairperson of the Centre for Social and Organisational Leadership (CSOL) at Tata Institute of Social Sciences Mumbai, India*

Key words: Intercultural Development, Millennials, Unconscious Biases, Hofstede's Cultural Dimensions, High Context versus Low Context Cultures

Company Overview

John Bear and Sons (JBS) is an investment banking major, headquartered in New York, USA. An investment bank with a 30-year legacy, JBS now has offices in 14 countries around the world with four businesses – Investment Banking, Global Markets Trading, Wealth Management and Global Research. The company has been doing exceeding well in the last 7 years and has been steadily climbing the league tables to now have the number three ranking across Europe and the Americas. It has a revenue of over USD 3 billion and amongst the highest fees collections in the Mergers and Acquisitions (M&A) space.

While this growth is a consistent upward trend for JBS, their number one ranked competitor has net revenue of over USD 30 billion, clearly 10 times the number that JBS makes. For JBS, this is a huge gap in its plans to become a worthy competitor in the market and be able to win business over the bigger giants. All of JBS competitors have massive presence in the emerging markets of India, China and Africa, where JBS has none.

The India Story

The JBS leadership decides to start with India. Key reasons include: the presence of other investment banks, availability of English-speaking world-class talent, and a growing market for M&A and wealth management. Two senior bankers, Allan Blanc from Oil & Gas, a suave New Yorker and Timothy Williams from M&A, a short, stout African-American business wizard; are shipped off to Mumbai for interviews and picking the best talent in the local market for JBS.

Setting up in Mumbai was easy, other than everyone arriving late for the interview, "thanks to the traffic situation in the city", as they all repeated. Candidates practically spoke English as their first language, came from premier management education institutions with a major in Finance, had an investment banking background from their internships and were perfect hires for JBS. Though they had not heard much about JBS beyond what they found on a Google search, it was a potentially well paying opportunity. These millennial bankers, who had started out with local boutique firms, were thrilled about the opportunity of moving into a multinational firm.

(continued)

Within 6 months, JBS had a ready team of 17 people in Mumbai vis-à-vis a requirement of 14. Nine of them were bankers. Of these, one was a senior banker, to whom the others reported on a day-to-day basis. Beyond the banking teams, rest were support staff required to keep the machinery running smooth.

It's Complicated

The new team in Mumbai reported to Timothy Williams. Tim relocated to Mumbai and was now based out of the JBS Mumbai office. In his first month, he ensured that everyone had targets set for the year. He set up a weekly review with each individual banker so he could monitor progress against these targets.

The India experience was new to him and he wasn't enjoying it too much. People didn't seem very friendly outside work and at work, the unprofessional behavior he noticed during the interviews continued with more frequent tea, coffee and smoke breaks, personal conversations at work, coming late and sometimes staying late. It was his worst nightmare. He needed to become more and more prescriptive with the team every day. Until he gave specific instructions on what needed to get done, things never got done the way he wanted them to.

Timothy and the Mumbai team found working together difficult. The team disliked working with Tim and were irritated by "his high-handedness". They started complaining about the situation in their coffee breaks.

He gets all these fancy expat benefits. It's easy for him to say, "Be on time, it's basic professionalism"

Exactly. Like Harlem is the world's largest slum. And India is a hardship posting? Seriously?!

My point. He lives in a posh company funded accommodation, two lanes down the office and yet, gets a chauffeur driven car. We may be earning 15 lakhs but we live with roommates, 2 hours away from work and use public transport or drive to work ourselves.

I don't think he even wants to understand, high-handed as he is. I don't care anymore about what he says. At least the days Allan is here, work is fun

Tim felt his advice was being treated lightly on a regular basis. In meetings with him, the team always joined late and almost always seemed to have a disinterested body language. The team, on the other hand, felt a lot more comfortable with Allan, who not only stayed in touch with them but also had occasion to visit Mumbai a few times over the next two quarters. Tim was upset about Allan stepping into his space and taking over his team. Allan, on the other hand, found that the team was enthusiastic and bright, often coming up with great ideas on what new and better could be done to improve business in the region.

(continued)

Early Warning Signs

In a catch-up meeting with his reporting manager, Managing Director William Ross, Tim made his displeasure about Allan known to William. He established that William needed to step in to get things in order. William was taken aback at Tim's sharp reaction. After all, both Allan and Tim were senior bankers, had worked together several years and had the maturity to work these things out like adults. Though he gave Tim a patient hearing, he went away feeling that this was not something he needed to meddle with. From his discussions with Allan, William also knew that the Mumbai team was rather affronted by Tim's direct manner and perceived him to be rather aggressive in his approach with them. Allan was doing very well and his association with the Mumbai team was helping them do exceedingly well in the business.

Problems Begin

One year into the expansion for JBS:
- Tim had resigned and become the M&A head at a competitor
- 4 of 9 bankers in the Mumbai office had resigned and the JBS India business was grossly understaffed
- Allan was pulled in to replace Tim, finding himself stretched thin across his various roles

Discuss in Your Group
1. *Are these teething troubles of JBS's expansion plans?*
    a. *If yes, should these have been anticipated or planned for?*
    b. *If not, discuss what went wrong at JBS?*
2. *What do you think are some of the underlying dynamics at play in this situation?*
3. *What could have been done by whom to prevent key challenges or facilitate key outcomes?*

Bibliography

Burnes, B. (2004). *Managing change*. Essex: Pearson Education.
Burnes, B., & Jackson, P. (2011). Success and failure in organizational change: An exploration of the role of values. *Journal of Change Management, 11*(2), 133–162.
Caldwell, R. (2001). Champions, adapters, consultants and synergists: The new change agents in HRM. *Human Resource Management Journal, 11*(3), 39–53.
Caldwell, R. (2003). The changing roles of personnel managers. *Journal of Management Studies, 40*(4), 983–1004.

Child, J. (1997). Strategic choice in the analysis of action, structure, organizations and the environment: Retrospect and prospect. *Organization Studies, 18*(1), 43–76.

George, J., & Jones, G. (2001). Towards a process model of individual change in organizations. *Human Relations, 54*(4), 419–444.

Jick, T., & Peiperl, M. (2003). *Managing change: Cases and concepts.* New York: McGraw-Hill Higher Education.

Kotter, J. (1995, March–April). Leading change: Why transformation efforts fail. *Harvard Business Review, 73,* 59–67.

Malik, A. (2013). Post-GFC people management challenges: A study of India's information technology sector. *Asia Pacific Business Review, 19*(2), 230–246. https://doi.org/10.1080/13602381.2013.767638.

Malik, A. (2016). The role of HR strategies in change. In *Organizational change management strategies in modern business* (pp. 193–215). Hershey: IGI Global.

Malik, A. (2017). *Human resource management and the global financial crisis: Evidence from India's IT/BPO industry.* Abingdon: Routledge.

Nilakant, V., & Ramnarayan, S. (2006). *Change management: Altering mindsets in a global context.* New Delhi: Response Books.

Reynierse, J. H. (1994, January/February). Ten commandments for CEOs seeking organizational change. *Business Horizons, 37*(1), 40–45.

Ulrich, D. (1997). *Human resource champions.* Boston: Harvard University Press.

Wood, S., & de Menezes, L. (2011). High involvement management, high performance work systems and wellbeing. *International Journal of Human Resource Management, 22*(2), 1586–1610.

Worley, C., & Lawler, E., III. (2006). Designing organizations that are built to change. *Sloan Management Review, 48*(Fall), 19–23.

Strategic Compensation and Benefits Management

Ashish Malik

Key Learning Outcomes
At the end of this chapter, you should be able to:

- *Understand the multiple goals of strategic compensation and benefits*
- *Describe the dominant approaches to strategic compensation and benefits*
- *Analyse the relationship between of strategic compensation and benefits and performance*
- *Identify the theoretical bases for determining strategic compensation and benefits*

Introduction

This chapter focuses on the role of compensation and benefits for strategically managing the contribution employees make to an organisation. While compensation and benefits are critical aspects of keeping employees motivated and committed in their jobs, often the strategies implemented do not achieve the intended results. In some cases the 'M' factor in the AMO framework gets compromised by the 'O' or the opportunity that exists in the wider environment. Motivating employees is a core task of managers often through HR policy choices they exercise. The options range from meeting intrinsic to extrinsic motivational needs of employees. Different groups of employees desire different motivational bases and for some, a hybrid approach can indeed be very effective for motivating them and realizing their discretionary performance effort. Therefore, implementation matters a lot as does

A. Malik (✉)
Faculty of Business and Law, Central Coast Business School, The University of Newcastle, Ourimbah, Central Coast, NSW, Australia
e-mail: ashish.malik@newcastle.edu.au

communication and managing the expectations of employees when it comes to distributing discretionary aspects of compensation and benefits. HR practitioners must, in the first instance be mindful of the wider strategic context, a firm's business model and the ability of the firm to afford the disbursement of a given set of compensation and benefits. Typically, problems that occur during implementation often relate to feelings and perceptions of inequity and unfairness. This chapter briefly reviews popular functional approaches to compensation and benefits and then proposes some guidelines for its design and implementation for ensuring that strategic fit and employee expectations are met. The issue of 'appropriation' of value captured and realized through a firm's business model and the extent to which certain constituencies in an orgsnsiation perceive problems in the distributive and procedural justice aspects of rewards are vital aspects to attend to in a successful compensation and benefits program.

Strategic Compensation and Benefits Approaches

Martocchio (2006) suggests that strategic decisions must include activities in a functional area that allows a firm to differentiate itself from the marketplace. Armstrong (2007) highlights that the terrain of rewards and incentives should cover both internal and external factors such as business strategy, culture, technology, people, global trends, national demographic trends, local and industry norm, industrial relations, legislation and institutional factors. Based on a firm's strategic positioning in the market in terms of compensation and benefits, the next step focuses on tactical decisions such as determining the bases of pay (for example, HR managers can choose from a seniority versus merit-based approach; and incentive versus person-focused pay, which includes pay for skills and knowledge-based pay systems). Most individual-focused pay options include aspects such as piecework plans, behavioural rewards, referrals and so on. Differences in performance may also necessitate the design and implementation of group or team-based approaches such as those evident in gain-sharing plans, the Scanlon Plan, Lean Six Sigma, company-wide profit sharing, employee stock option and ownership plans (Martocchio 2006).

The second set of strategic and tactical decisions focus on deciding the guiding principles for determining the compensation and benefit systems. In this latter set of decisions, Stewart and Brown (2009) argue that rewards can take a transactional or a relational form and can be further provided in monetary and non-monetary reward forms. Transactional elements typically include direct and indirect forms of monetary and non-monetary rewards. Relational rewards on the other hand focus on intangibles such as provision of learning opportunities, employee and peer recognition, offering employment security, providing challenging learning tasks and work opportunities and so on. This latter aspect of design focuses on factors that appeal certain individuals intrinsically.

Objectives of Strategic Compensation and Benefits Program

Martocchio (2006) noted that from a strategic perspective, irrespective of the chosen bases for pay, firms must attempt to build (1) internally consistent compensation and market systems; (2) achieve strategic and internal /horizontal fit with other HR systems; (3) ensure that such pay systems are competitive in the market to prevent loss of talent; and (4) be able to continuously attract high quality talent. We know from the research on performance management and rewards is that typically there exists a distribution of performers ranging from outstanding and high performers to poor and average performers. An organisation must be able to offer some differentiation for these groups of employees to recognise high performing individual contributors. High performers may be offered market and performance loadings or some form of merit-based pay.

Building on the notion of workforce flexibility, firms must also differentiate different groups of workforce in its compensation and benefits approaches. An egalitarian and one size fits all approach may not be the best way forward as it may create different emotions amongst other groups of employees who are on permanent fulltime employment versus non-standard forms of employment. Additionally, consideration should be given to accommodate 'employee flexibility' in the design of both compensation and benefits. For example, this might include allowing benefits in terms of flexible scheduling and options such as working from home, a co-working place or a smart work hub (Malik et al. 2016). Similarly, an organisation must offer rewards and recognise their top talent from the rest of the staff to avoid losing them to competition.

Although there are a number of well-developed industry HR approaches for managing compensation and benefits, the Hayes method of job evaluation, for determining the relative worth of a job is well established. Annual wage and salary surveys also inform strategic choices in the design and implementation of compensation and benefits. Classical economics theories, for example, argue for the idea of *exchange* and *use value* as a sound basis for compensating employees in exchange of the services offered. Marginal productivity theory notes that employees are recompensed based on the 'use' value of their services expended. Similarly, as noted earlier, human capital theories have attempted to link pay with the associated increases in human capital and productivity. As a proxy for the quality of human capital, firms often rely on the level of education and the length of experience in determining the appropriate levels of compensation. Theories from the literature on organisational behaviour, such as motivation theories of equity theory, reinforcement theory, expectancy theory and agency theory are highly relevant in designing and implementing compensation and benefits. Equity theory provides guidance on the extent to which employees make assessments of whether the efforts they have expended at their workplace and the rewards they receive for their contribution is fair. Often these assessments are undertaken in relation to internal and external market relativities of occupations. Equity theory is also linked to the idea of procedural and distributive justice where, in instances of perceived inequity in rewards for the expended efforts, a sense of distributive injustice and unfair treatment sets in (Baron and Kreps 1999). Alternatively, the process through which rewards are offered for some employees relative to others can be cause for procedural unfairness (Baron and Kreps 1999).

As noted above, a firm must pay special attention to the principles of natural and distributive justice and we mustn't forget a firm's ability to pay. Ability to pay has been noted as a make or break point in a number of industries that are struggling under competitive pressures or operating in industries that have very inefficient resourcing models. Sometimes extremely generous reward schemes bargained by trade unions or indeed very high levels of executive compensation distributed by senior executives and top management teams can lead to the financial collapse of a business. Agency theory provides some discussion that is relevant in maintaining the balance between employee, shareholder and senior manager interests. According to agency theory (Jensen and Meckling 1976), the owners of an organisation (principals) recruit managers and leaders (agents) for carrying out the productive operations of an enterprise. As agents, they have an obligation to provide financial returns to the principal (and the shareholders) on the invested capital. The agents however also keep in mind ways in which they can maximise their returns. While the principal views the agents as costs and aims to minimise such costs, there is tension here as agents often look for ways to increase their income. In a bid to deal with this dilemma, the principal engages in profit sharing schemes, bonuses and pay for performance plans to manage the expectations of agents and at the same time ensuring a fair return for the principals. One can argue that there is a significant misalignment between the goals of the agency and principals that led, albeit partially, to the global financial crises of 2008–2009, as the incentives offered in the pay for performance to agents were disproportionate to the risks involved in the safe running of banks on a sustainable basis. As Boxall and Purcell (2011) caution that managing the problem of (politics) and (mis) appropriation is critical in maintaining the solvency of firms. In times of a slowdown or boom, there are plenty of examples where senior executives have come under direct media scrutiny for rewarding themselves in a selfish and often unjustified manner. Designing your own golden handshake, a practice that has been implemented by senior executives and noted in media reports, raises ethical issues. Therefore, not only is it critical, but it is also necessary to maintain transparency in design and implementation of executive compensation schemes. There are ethical dilemmas at work and several commercial-in-confidence issues that have brought disrepute to organisations due to the nature of their compensation and benefit schemes.

In relation to benefits, these can be broadly classified into: *legally mandated* – through legislation such as medical and work cover insurance, unemployment insurance, health and safety awards, and disability benefits; and *discretionary benefits* – for example, varying rates of superannuation contribution, union membership benefits, paid time-off, and purchase of car and computer and other goods lease plans.

Critical Reflections

Perceived inequity and unfair treatment are core issues that the practice of compensation and benefits is grappling with. There are numerous instances where a well-designed compensation and benefit system is not applied consistently due to either lack of understanding of how to administer rewards on part of the managers or by engaging in political behavior and deliberate and unethical conduct on part of senior managers. The problem is that often such deals are made in private and are generally brought to public knowledge when either the beneficiary or the person responsible for the decision have moved on. The issue of developing moral intensity is central here. This was covered earlier in chapter "SHRM & ER: Professionalism and Ethics" using the example of sexual harassment where a number of factors contribute to people not seeing a moral issue in an activity and hence engaging in immoral and unethical conduct. The likely consequences of such poor implementation is loss of key talent, expensive lawsuits and a damage of organizational reputation. In some extreme cases of misappropriation of value capture, this could lead to the demise of the entire organsiation or even a wider industrial, national or indeed global contagion, as was noted in the recent global financial crisis.

Illustrations and Skills Sandpit

Using the concepts from agency theory, design a system of incentives for lawyers in a large law firm who are specializing in medical compensation claims. Ensure you define who the agent and the principal is. What type of incentive system might be most appropriate here?

Concept Integration with Cases and Learning Activities

The case study by De Simone et al. entitled *Stressed and demotivated public servants...Looking for a motivational miracle at Paywell agency* provides a novel context of the public sector organisation where people seek membership of such an organisation driven primarily by a public service motivation (PSM) ethos. However, in an era of new public management, the concept of PSM gets challenged significantly with the ongoing change and demands posed on public servants leading to adverse employee outcomes. The case study by Bardoel titled *Work-life balance in an MNE* can also be explored for viewing work-life balance as a non-monetary benefit for employees.

Conclusion

To summarize, strategic rewards management must assess the impact of change (cultural, value, and external influences), fit design with business strategy and other HR systems for effective implementation and monitoring against pre-established measures and benchmarks. Further, managers need to make strategic choices about the nature and the degree to which strategic alignment with competitive strategies is necessary. Whether they want a market positioning stance to be seen as *leading* the market, remain as an organization offering compensation and benefits in the *median* range or be looked at as a *laggard* are critical choices. Implementation in terms of transparent communication, developing internally consistent policies, putting in place appeal and evaluation procedures and regularly reforecasting budgets is vital in a dynamic and fast changing environment. Irrespective of the choices and techniques followed, there are some desirable outcomes for all strategic rewards management systems. These include: equity, efficiency, quality, high performance, statutory compliance and customer focus (internal and external).

Glossary

Agent in relation to agency theory covered here typically refers to senior leaders of the executive team whom the principals have hired for day-to-day decisions of an organisation.

Principals are those who own and have invested a major equity stake in an organisation. Though this has now been widely interpreted and used to include other shareholders of an organsiation.

Public service motivation can be defined as a set of values and attitudes that motivates individuals involved in undertaking public service jobs that serve and benefit the wider society.

Work engagement refers to employees demonstrating high levels of involvement, dedication and energy in carrying out their work tasks. Often highly engaged employees tend to involve them so much in work that they are sometimes unable to balance their work-life balance but are still holding high levels of job satisfaction.

Work-related stress is a psychological state of mind that is caused by stressors at work such as the nature of job, excessive volume of work demands, little or no control over one's workflow, minimal levels of social support, lack of role clarity, high degree of work-related conflict, feelings of job insecurity, and harassment and violence at the workplace.

Key Questions and Learning Activities

Question. 1 What are the key sources of inequity and unfairness caused by compensation and benefits in an organsiation?

Question. 2 Provide an overview of the dominant theories of motivation that can be directly linked to the design and implementation of compensation and benefits in an organsiation.

Question. 3 What are the common consequences of a poorly designed compensation and benefits program?

Learning Activity: Analysing Your Personal Motivations at Work

Thinking of your key motivators at work, what would these be? Are these motivators available to you through your employing organisation's current rewards and benefits program? If yes, what aspects of the program would you like to change? If they are not offered, does your organisation offer other motivators? Are there voice mechanisms available to you? If so, how and who would you approach in the first instance for having a meaningful say in relation to your terms and conditions of employment and why?

Bibliography

Armstrong, M. (2007). *Employee reward*. London: Chartered Institute of Personnel Development.

Baron, J. N., & Kreps, D. (1999). *Strategic human resources: Frameworks for general managers.* New York: Wiley.

Boxall, P., & Purcell, J. (2011). *Strategy and human resource management.* Houndmills Basingstoke: Palgrave Macmillan.

Jensen, M. C., & Meckling, W. H. (1976). Theory of the firm: Managerial behavior, agency costs and ownership structure. *Journal of financial economics, 3*(4), 305–360.

Malik, A., Rosenberger, P. J., III, Fitzgerald, M., & Houlcroft, L. (2016). Factors affecting smart working: Evidence from Australia. *International Journal of Manpower, 37*(6), 1042–1066.

Martocchio, J. J. (2006). *Strategic compensation: A human resource management approach.* Hoboken: Pearson Education.

Stewart, G., & Brown, K. (2009). Motivating employees through compensation. In *Human resource management: Linking strategy to practice* (pp. 401–441). Hoboken: Wiley.

Additional Reading

Dulebohn, J., & Werling, S. (2007). Compensation research: Past present and future. *Human Resource Management Review, 17,* 191–207.

Dulebohn, J., Molloy, J., Pichler, S., & Murray, B. (2009). Employee benefits: Literature review and emerging issues. *Human Resource Management Review, 19,* 86–103.

Special Topics in SHRM & ER

Ashish Malik

Key Learning Outcomes
At the end of this chapter, you should be able to:

- *Define the terms ambidexterity and public service motivation*
- *Analyse the relationship between HRM practices, ambidexterity and innovation*
- *Analyse the impact of employee well-being on the HRM-performance link*
- *Identify the emerging trends in Green HRM*
- *Discuss the key approaches in managing people in times of a crisis*

Introduction

This final chapter focuses on the emerging trends and challenges faced by the field of strategic HRM and ER. This chapter therefore provides an overview of the topical areas of interest. The following topics are covered in brief: HRM in the public sector, innovation, ambidexterity and HRM, green HRM, HR offshoring, employee well-being and managing people in crisis. These special topics are vital areas of future research within the domain of strategic HRM and ER.

A. Malik (✉)
Faculty of Business and Law, Central Coast Business School, The University of Newcastle, Ourimbah, Central Coast, NSW, Australia
e-mail: ashish.malik@newcastle.edu.au

© Springer Nature Singapore Pte Ltd. 2018
A. Malik (ed.), *Strategic Human Resource Management and Employment Relations*, Springer Texts in Business and Economics,
https://doi.org/10.1007/978-981-13-0399-9_14

HRM in the Public Sector

The public sector (PS) represents a typical professional services bureaucracy (Daley 2012). As the term professional service would imply, the public sector also requires a specialist set of knowledge, skills and abilities in order to fully discharge the responsibility of public servants towards the wider community they intend to serve. PS employees are regarded as employees driven by public service motivation (PSM) rather than the typical economic and profit motives (Mann 2006). Mann (2006) further argues that the role of HRM in developing PSM is to ensure that PS employees commitment is high for making a difference in the delivery of what is essentially a public good. Mann notes that a problem with this view is that often HR managers are unable to quantify the nature of PSM and, as a result, the subsequent problems associated with designing and implementing HR practices for PS employees to deliver on the PSM ethos become evident. While in principle, one might offer some generic service delivery guidelines, the operationalisation of PSM construct is a little bit problematic. Presence of intrinsic motivation and non-tangible aspects of personal satisfaction in serving in PS roles remain the obvious ones, however, there is a potential for damaging these intrinsic drivers through the application of new public management HR approaches, which often rely upon using extrinsic rewards and a shorter-term focus. While typical strategic HRM and ER discourse centres around formal planning and alignment issues and delivering sustainable performance in the longer term, the application of such ideals is problematic in the traditional bureaucratic public sector models (Brown 2004; Daley 2012). Brown (2004) notes that the traditional bureaucratic PS model has always been rule-bound. More recently, it is witnessing a shift towards a new performance-based culture (Shim 2001) or what has been recently described as the 'New Public Management' (NPM) agenda. This latter agenda, Brown argues, is akin to what we find in the private sector–a focus on efficiency, effectiveness and quality of services. Within this neo-liberal and managerial agenda, the nature of HRM practices represent the need for a flexible workforce model and work processes that typify work undertaken in for-profit organisations. The whole ethos of PSM comes into question with such changes that are now widespread. NPM HRM has received significant critique in the form of deteriorating working conditions, mergers of multiple public sector entities to deliver on economic agendas of efficiency, effectiveness and high quality public service. Can one deliver a variety of social goods and services employing rational economic principles? This remains a key question among public sector employees.

Innovation, Ambidexterity and HRM

In pursuit of high growth, literatures on innovation and ambidexterity suggest firms that are able to innovate and be ambidextrous are more likely to offer sustained levels of growth. The literature on organisational ambidexterity suggests that firms that are able to *simultaneously* pursue exploratory and exploitative modes of learning or *ambidexterity*, are more likely to succeed and innovate (O'Reilly and Tushman

2008; Raisch and Birkinshaw 2008). O'Reilly and Tushman (2008), for example, define ambidexterity as firm's ability to manage the duality of simultaneous learning processes of experimentation and alignment with current goals, through refining, efficiency and well-developed routines. The underlying logic is that firms that are able to do both forms of learning simultaneously are able to successfully implement technological and administrative innovations. In this background, prior research examining the role of HRM practices in impacting innovation performance and ambidexterity is gradually becoming mainstream (Malik et al. 2017b, c; Prieto and Pilar Pérez Santana 2012; Shipton et al. 2006). The central argument of these studies is that HRM practices are antecedents in creating an ambidextrous context, which will ultimately lead to a range of innovation outcomes such as successful product and process innovations. Innovation outcomes can vary from work-design innovations, through process and product innovations to business model innovations (Malik et al. 2017a, c, 2018). Analysing the relationship between HRM and innovation, Seeck and Diehl (2016) found support for the impact of universalistic best-practice bundles or configurational approaches in the HRM–performance–innovation link. Several HRM practices have been identified in the literature that have an impact on innovation (Beugelsdijk 2008; Ceylan 2013) as well as in shaping ambidextrous learning (O'Reilly and Tushman 2008; Raisch and Birkinshaw 2008). For example, firms that are able to assimilate and apply new ideas at work are more likely to be innovative. The research points to HRM practices such as training, performance management, reward systems and a learning culture, which, if implemented collectively as a bundle is likely to generate innovation outcomes (Laursen and Foss 2003; Gupta and Singhal 1993). Others (Jiménez-Jiménez and Sanz-Valle 2008; Lau and Ngo 2004), also noted a bundle of HRM practices to positively impact innovation. The above links in well with the earlier discussion in chapters titled "HRM and ER: A Strategic Perspective" and "Strategic HRM&ER: Best-Practice Versus Best Fit" on best-practice schools.

HRM and Ambidexterity A recent review exploring the relationship between ambidexterity and HRM suggests there are numerous HRM and organisational practices that act as antecedents for the creation of an ambidextrous context conducive to innovation (Junni et al. 2015). Junni et al.'s (2015) review, identified the influences of employees, leaders and HRM practices, and how these variables interact with structure, culture and other contextual variables to create an ambidextrous context. More recently, high-involvement and high-performance work systems have been noted to create a social climate that supports an ambidextrous context through a number of ability-, motivation- and opportunity-enhancing HRM practices (Malik et al. 2017c; O'Reilly and Tushman 2011; Prieto and Pilar Pérez Santana 2012). Ahammad et al. (2015) found the influence of motivational practices in developing ambidexterity.

In their discussion of contextual ambidexterity, Gibson and Birkinshaw (2004) explain if employees that can simultaneously partition their time and behaviours to balance "alignment and adaptability", they are more likely to create new learning and routines. A contextual ambidextrous context advocates that employees engage simultaneously with exploitative and explorative learning in their day-to-day routines, and as a result, this helps in reducing the costs of coordination. This approach to ambidexterity assumes individuals decide on how to allocate time and resources so firms can manage the duality of the two learning modes (Tushman and O'Reilly 1996). This approach clearly places HR and people management approaches as a key antecedent in supporting organisational ambidexterity, managing dualities and achieving innovation outcomes (Malik et al. 2017a, b, c).

Green HRM

Research linking environmental failures with aspects of corporate social responsibility and HRM has led to discussions of Green HRM practices. Such an emergence of interest is understandable as there are massive environmental disasters that have occurred in major utility industry sectors such as oil and natural gas, coal-fired power generation stations, and highly hazardous chemical industries. Notable among these were Enron, Union Carbide, AEC and Shell to name a few. While a broad framework of reference is still emerging, some scholars have begun to map all the core processes of the employment life cycle with the idea of Green HRM (Renwick et al. 2008). These authors highlight the application of an environmental approach to all HRM core processes such as right from the time of developing job descriptions and person specifications through to recruitment and selection. Additional changes are also evident in employer-of-choice campaigns wherein, overall job-value proposition for potential employees is presented to those who value ideas of responsible business and have corporate social responsibility attitude towards the society. Similarly, followers of this approach want to ensure that there are conscious efforts made in the management of performance and administration of rewards that embrace such values and attitudes. Specialized training programs to support this approach are also becoming prevalent to increase awareness of the problems as well as suggesting common solutions. For example, programs focusing on reducing waste and environmental compliance training are quite common. A number of German car manufacturers and technology firms are embedding specialized training programs under the umbrella of Green HRM approach (Renwick et al. 2008). The approach also appears on the bargaining table at the time of putting forth a charter of claims with the unions for finalizing the collective employment agreements. Specific projects, for example, focus on reducing pollution and disposal of waste for creating a healthy and safe work environment. Indeed as an extension of this idea, firms such as DuPont, Nordstrom and 3M have implemented incentive and reward schemes for minimising emissions and providing positive reinforcements for favorable environmental climate. Its increasing proliferation is also evident in Special Issues dedicated to the topic. For example, in *Human Resource Management* in 2012, *Journal of Organizational Behavior* in 2013 and more recently, the *International Journal of Human Resource Management* (2016) have all ran special issues on Green HRM. Rendwick et al. (2016) map the current developments in

Green HRM and note that additional research on this topic is needed in relation to the desired type of HR systems and employee behaviours that are conducive to supporting a Green HRM ideology.

The theory of planned behaviour, AMO, attribution theory, stakeholder theory and corporate social responsibility are among the commonly used theoretical frames for situating and conducting Green HRM research. Further research is needed in developing a holistic theory of Green HRM, its causes, consequences and the core values and behaviours of employees and managers to support its adoption and proliferation.

HR Offshoring

As part of the wider phenomenon of offshore outsourcing, HR offshoring is not immune to outsourcing of HR processes to overseas locations such as India and the Philippines (Cooke and Budhwar 2009; Pereira and Anderson 2012). The modularisation of transaction processing services to offshore locations was expedited by the high levels of service excellence and maturity experienced in the call-centre and back office outsourcing industry. Realising the ability of services providers to successfully deliver and operate on complex processes such as HR has triggered its widespread diffusion. While the earlier stages saw the offshoring of locally outsourced activities such as pay, training and recruitment process outsourcing. The rationale, although initially, was driven by labour cost arbitrage and efficiency seeking motives. Subsequently, the rationale changed to accessing high quality competencies and capabilities in HR at these offshore service providers who had accumulated, through their experience of working with a range of clients, spanning diverse industry sectors. The decision rules suggested by Atkinson regarding the 'core and periphery' activities of a business have also contributed to the thinking that certain non-core HR activities can and should be outsourced. However, with an increasing strength of capabilities of the service providers, it is not surprising to see a shift from low-end to high-end strategic HR processes outsourcing in the form of consulting advisories, as well as designing the entire architecture of HR systems for medium to large organisations. Cooke and Budhwar (2009) note that often in relation to major decisions in HR offshore outsourcing, HR practitioners are not consulted. The Chartered Institute of Personnel Development (CIPD), UK survey (2006) revealed that 70% of HR practiotioners felt they should be involved in the decision to make the HR offshoring actually work for the business. A related aspect of the phenomenon is managing the relationship between a client firm and third-party service provider. Again, to the point above, in the absence of HR's involvement in the first instance, HR practitioners are left to manage the relationship with service providers and ensure their quality of services delivered. This often results in poor employee well-being outcomes and failed relationship management with third party service providers.

Employee Well-being

In increasingly competitive and uncertain times, the concepts of employee resilience and subjective wellbeing have come to the fore. Developing employees' psychological states so they can effectively discharge their work through their resilience and subjective well-being has been a widely researched topic in the field of industrial and organisational psychology. More recently, we have seen detailed literature reviews within management and HRM (see e.g. Van De Voorde et al. 2012). Such reviews throw light on a number of aspects such as why this concept is important to researchers and firms and its direct and indirect impacts on, for example, employee satisfaction at work. Studies of HRM exploring this area fall into two broad categories. The first group of studies note that the mutuality of purpose is important. Both parties must benefit through the implementation high performance HRM bundles, or in other words, theorists in this group argue for a 'win-win' outcome: HRM practices should make employees *happy* and at the same strive to achieve sustained high performance (e.g., Appelbaum et al. 2000). The second group of studies in HRM do not find adequate support for realizing positive health and well-being outcomes through the logic of high performance HRM. The underpinning logic of this approach is that a disproportionate focus on strategic goals and alignment with a firm's objectives for achieving high performance comes at a cost and often leads to work intensification, higher levels of stress and fatigue at work (e.g., Godard 2001; Peccei 2004). This eventually leads to poor employee health and well-being outcomes. The important point to consider is how employees perceive the managerial *intent* and how well managers balance the excessive focus on performance and alignment with opportunities with work and life in a way that it does not result in major spill-overs from one domain to the other. Often the problem lies in having unrealistic expectation from people, which then translates into poor health and well-being outcomes.

Managing People in Crisis–Credibility of HR in Today's Times

I conclude this final chapter with a discussion on one of the most pressing topics: managing people during a crisis and the deteriorating credibility of HR in today's uncertain times. Are we back to the drawing board and asking where to from here? Our societies have witnessed 16 major economic crises between 1720 and 2013 (Warner 2013), six of which occurred since the 1997–1998s Asian Crisis and include: the dotcom bubble burst, Wall street crisis, Islandic Banking crisis, global financial crisis, global recession and the Eurozone crisis. More recently, we have witnessed other forms of cash crises such as noted in India's demonetization efforts in 2016. Crises can be natural or man-made. What is interesting is that the latter type of crises are increasing in its incidence and intensity and we are most likely to witness more of the same as we are still part of a neoliberal agenda, which, some would argue caused the 2008 global financial crisis (GFC) in the first place. Typically, a small group of people design most human-engineered crises. However, their actions have far-reaching consequences, as was noted in the case of the GFC, which spread like a contagion to almost all parts of the globe, affecting, even those who had nothing to do with the US financial system or who had no understanding of what it is like investing in stock markets, let alone financial derivatives. These groups of people were severely affected and were often also people living on the fringe with minimum wage protections. Where was HR in managing such human engineered disasters? Can HR play a role? How can it prevent organisational psychopaths from engaging in such behavior, again? In the events that followed the GFC, why did HR play the role of a stooge of management and an implementer of their neoliberalist agendas? Could HR have saved some jobs? Should HR challenge the dominant coalition of stakeholders in making decisions that affected the source of livelihood of thousands of people? Unfortunately, there is mounting evidence that HR has clearly lost its credibility in living up to its role as an *employee champion,* a key role espoused by Ulrich in some of the earlier work on HR tasks. The issue of professional ethics and personal values were constantly challenged in an environment where the only way to stand up for a cause would have meant losing your own source of livelihood. In such conditions, have we lost hope in HR and the widespread neoliberal order? Are institutional forces so strong that people have little choice and leeway to exercise alternate strategic choices through their human agency? The answer to this question, in short is yes. Nevertheless, all hope is not lost and we must not undermine the critical role *human agency* can play by politically navigating through, and negotiating with, the key stakeholders to change the dominant logic and explore alternate solutions to overcoming the problem. Aspects of this were evident in recent research on the GFC (Malik 2017). And yes, there are other studies in HRM (see for example, Boon et al. 2009) that have highlighted the role active developmental (innovative) human agency can play in dealing with institutional forces by creating an innovative fit and expanding the degrees of leeway available to people in a given environment. Even in a post-GFC era Malik (2013) noted that a number of firms adopted different approaches in solving the same problems in a post-GFC environment. While all providers had the pressure to undertake job cuts to stay afloat, the study found diversity in HRM practices and ideologies, suggesting that firms implemented different strategic choices in dealing with environmental and institutional pressures, in this case, managing the excesses imposed by the GFC on firms in the Indian IT industry. Building on this work, Malik (2017) undertook further research in a post-GFC period in the Indian IT industry, as well as other industries, from selected international contexts. The research found that while the wider institutional environment imposes constraints on the extent of strategic choices that leaders and managers can exercise, these constraints can be manipulated through political and power processes, which enhances the degree of leeway and choice managers have in implementing and exploring different solutions. Malik (2017) argues that through active developmental and innovative human agency, a number of leaders in the Indian IT industry and indeed other industry and national contexts, explored additional opportunities by re-negotiating with stakeholders alternate revenue paths to minimize, and in some cases, avoid total job losses. In part, the ability to deliver on their promises was also contingent upon the concomitant investments these firms made to certain HRM practices and organisational capabilities, which allowed them to deliver on the re-negotiated opportunities to their stakeholders.

Critical Reflections

Not all is lost. There is hope. All this requires courage and adopting a higher level of moral standpoint for upholding the core values and maintaining HR's credibility. The task however is not easy in what is largely a capitalist system. HR managers are perceived, in the main, as agents of the principal rather than as professionals who are also tasked with playing the role of *employee champions*. Cultural, institutional and value differences may well explain alternate paths leaders may embark upon to balance their businesses' economic interests with employee interests. In the case of offshore outsourcing, while it was business interest that led managers to navigate through, and negotiate with, key stakeholders to commit to the offshore outsourcing decision, evidence from the literature suggests that several offshore service providers also went under, following the GFC. Raising the threshold and baseline of *equity* and *voice* is a good place to start if one were to balance it with efficiency. Through international and national platforms and strengthening moral intensity of managers and leaders, we might lead them to explore the path of innovative and developmental human agency rather than succumbing to conformist pressures.

Illustrations and Skills Sandpit

The examples from the GFC, Christchurch earthquake disasters, bushfires and several other natural and man-made disasters have time and again proven that humans are resilient and capable of adaptation and change and have in many instances be able to minimise the impact of, and in some cases even turn the course of the tide around. Such major events often require collaboration and cooperation between the affected parties. Adopting a competitive model might not be the best way forward.

Concept Integration with Cases and Learning Activities

The case study by Tasoulis and Progoulaki entitled *Crisis, internationalization and HRM in Project-based organisations: The tale of SOFMAN* covers a number of the above aspects on managing in a post-crisis context. Additionally the case study titled *Gender Inclusive Leadership for Innovation and Change –an HR Head's reflections* also provides a good account of how to manage innovation and change through HR.

Conclusion

This final chapter highlighted the central role played by a number of HRM practices in supporting innovation, creating an ambidextrous context and managing people in crisis through the exercise of developmental and innovative use of human agency. Learning and development can support in the development of agile and flexible leaders who are willing to challenge the status quo and navigate or re-negotiate opportunities with the dominant coalition of stakeholders. As a result, this will lead to longer-term commitment and loyalty of employees and possibly help HR regain its credibility. While this approach is evident in a number of contexts, the path taken is not easy and requires courage, it does, however, offer some hope for people and organisations in the wake of adversity. In a highly turbulent and disruptive world that we live in today, there is hope and we need to rethink and institute processes, which, in the first place prevent such crisis from occurring. Second, we must think of a cooperative and collaborative, rather than competitive approach to HRM. Firms and people in firms must be viewed as collectives of capacities and capabilities. Potential collaborators from both within and between a network of firms must come together to fully deal with the excesses imposed by natural and manmade crises. Being mindful of resources that go against the spirit of cooperation and collaboration, efforts must be made to make people aware of the unimaginable harm their neglect and deliberate actions might cause. This might sound like performing the first task of change and will require a special kind of cognition and action for dealing with such major events. People will need to engage in emancipatory frames of learning to come up with novel solutions to what is becoming a common and pervasive problem.

Glossary

Ambidexterity is a firm's ability to manage the duality of simultaneously engaging in learning processes of experimentation and exploration of new ideas with alignment to current goals, refining, efficiency and working on well-established routines.

Contextual ambidexterity occurs when individuals in a firm are able to partition their time and learning for simultaneously exploring and exploiting new and existing learning for achieving sustained levels of performance.

Key Questions and Learning Activities

Question. 1 What are the key HRM practices that support innovation at work? Discuss.

Question. 2 Which aspect of human agency is most conducive to managing people in times of a crisis? Discuss with examples.

Question. 3 What is the relationship between high-performance work practices and employee well-being? Provide a critical discussion.

Learning Activity: The Secret Ingredient

The Secret Ingredient
Radhika Subramanian* and Vijayakumar Parameswaran Unnithan**

* Founder of Glow Worm Consulting, a Learning, Leadership and Organization Development Consulting firm.
** Professor and the Chairperson of the Centre for Social and Organisational Leadership (C SOL) at Tata Institute of Social Sciences Mumbai, India.

Key words: *Organization structures; family-run businesses; Leadership; Ambidexterity*

Company Overview

Globe Build is a 20-year old, family-owned construction company. It started out with building small residential buildings, and with time, it has grown into a developer of large commercial estates, especially in Special Economic Zones or Tech-Parks as they are colloquially called, in Bangalore – the Silicon Valley of India. Kariappa Reddy is the founder and CEO of the company. A capable man under whose leadership the company has grown to USD 250 million in market value of property and a name in construction in India to reckon with.

The Leadership

Reddy is the family patriarch. He is now 58 years old and proudly declares himself a "self-made-man". He came from tough times, the oldest of 4 sons, in family where the parents passed away when the children were still of a school-going age. Inheriting just the old family home on the outskirts of the city, Reddy had to start working odd jobs to sustain his siblings and educate them. That's how he found himself in the construction business. Working his

(continued)

way up from brick laying and concrete pouring, Reddy found an opportunity in real-estate when salaried city dwellers started investing in "holiday homes" for weekends away from the city. He refurbished their family home and sold it for a massive profit. Reinvesting the proceeds into, smaller but prime, land purchases within city limits. And the rest, as they say is history. A stern, demanding yet generous man, Reddy is considered a father-figure of the Globe Build family, treating every one of his staff like his children, patronizing them when they make a mistake and pampering them when they do well. He runs Globe Build like a tightly run ship, taking quick, firm decisions on matters. This gives the company a competitive edge in the form of lightning speed decision making and very low bureaucracy.

Reddy has a son and a daughter, both of whom are now involved in the business. His son Arjun, who is a Civil Engineer has been supporting in key construction projects for the last 7 years, while his daughter Avni, who is a Chartered Accountant, is now helping out with the finance function for the past 3 years. Prior to the children entering the family business, Reddy was supported by some of his childhood friends and early career associates, who continue to remain his trusted aides and members of his company's board.

The Staff

Globe Build has about 150 full-time office staff, managing business operations including architecture and construction, and support functions such as finance, procurement, marketing and HR. Ninety are business staff spread across the 5 key construction sites in Bangalore and 3 sites outside of Bangalore in the country. The remaining 60 are support staff working out of the corporate office.

All staff have a direct line of communication with Reddy and he gives direct orders when he needs things done. Of course, his closest aides and family members also manage the staff and ensure they work on getting things done immediately and as required by Reddy to support the rapidly expanding business.

About 30% of the staff have been around 5 years or more and are used to the inner workings of the company. They know how to work with Reddy and deal with his tempers. They know how to prioritize when different people give opposing instructions. But some staff are new in the system, a few about 2 years and majority, with less than a year. With the rate at which things are moving in the company and the limited number of seasoned people in the company, they are struggling to cope. One of the new procurement hires, Seema, asked one of her seniors, why they were placing an order from a vendor who was decidedly more expensive than several more popular options in the market. The answer she got was, "If Reddy Sir says that's what he wants, that's what we must do." When Seema shared her experience over lunch with

(continued)

a few other colleagues from different functions, everyone had a similar view of not questioning management and doing as they are told.

The Transformation

After his almost 4-decade-long career and running Globe Build, Reddy feels like he now wants to step back and put himself in a more relaxed position where he can enjoy the fruits of his labor and when required, guide the company to grow. He knows where he wants to take the company in 5 years before stepping back and he feels like his people are stuck in every day operations. They are too caught up in the moment to appreciate his vision for the company and work towards the future. In the past year alone, he has fired at least 15 staff himself, where he has observed that they haven't been able to deliver at the pace and standards at which he needs work done.

To strengthen his leadership, Reddy has also recently roped in a professional sales manager, along with his son-in-law who is an attorney and his daughter-in-law who is an architect to support the business. He believes everyone must support the business at a critical time like this.

The Challenge

Two years into his 5-year plan, Reddy is faced with some tough challenges:

- 3 out of 8 projects have overshot time and budget plans upsetting projected company revenues
- Reddy's aides and his family members have become two groups clearly opposing each other and fighting for decision making authority and possible succession to the business
- Increasing errors across key processes has put Globe Build at a compliance risk that now needs to be reactively addressed since it is stalling active projects.

Discussion Questions
- What are some risks for Globe Build's business right now?
- What should be Reddy's key current priorities to create a transition / retirement plan for himself?
- How can Globe Build start to deliver on current requirements while also being prepared for the future?
- Who else beyond Reddy must have a role to play in Globe Build's transformation? And what should be some of their key focus areas?

Bibliography

Ahammad, M. F., Lee, S. M., Malul, M., & Shoham, A. (2015). Behavioural ambidexterity – The impact of financial incentives on employee motivation, productivity and performance of commercial bank. *Human Resource Management.* https://doi.org/10.1002/hrm.21668.

Appelbaum, E., Bailey, T., Berg, P., & Kalleberg, A. (2000). *Manufacturing advantage: Why high performance work systems pay off.* New York: Cornell University Press.

Beugelsdijk, S. (2008). Strategic human resource practices and product innovation. *Organisation Studies, 29*(6), 821–847.

Boon, C., Paauwe, J., Boselie, P., & Den Hartog, D. (2009). Institutional pressures and HRM: Developing institutional fit. *Personnel Review, 38*(5), 492–508.

Brown, K. (2004). Human resource management in the public sector. *Public management review, 6*(3), 303–309.

Caniëls, M. C. J., & Veld, M. (2016). Employee ambidexterity, high performance work systems and innovative work behaviour: How much balance do we need? *International Journal of Human Resource Management.* https://doi.org/10.1080/09585192.2016.1216881.

Ceylan, C. (2013). Commitment-based HR practices, different types of innovation activities and firm innovation performance. *The International Journal of Human Resource Management, 24*(1), 208–226.

CIPD (Chartered Institute of Personnel and Development). (2006). *Offshoring and the role of HR: Survey report.* London: CIPD.

Cooke, F. L., & Budhwar, P. (2009). HR offshoring and outsourcing: Research issues for IHRM. *Handbook of International Human Resource Management: Integrating People, Process, and Context, 5*, 341.

Daley, D. M. (2012). Strategic human resources management. *Public Personnel Management,* 120–125.

Gibson, C. B., & Birkinshaw, J. (2004). The antecedents, consequences, and mediating role of organizational ambidexterity. *Academy of Management Journal, 47*(2), 209–226.

Godard, J. (2001). Beyond the high-performance paradigm? An analysis of variation in Canadian managerial perceptions of reform programme effectiveness. *British Journal of Industrial Relations, 39*, 25–52.

Gupta, A. K., & Singhal, A. (1993). Managing human resources for innovation and creativity. *Research Technology Management, 36*, 41–48.

Jiang, J., Wang, S., & Zhao, S. (2012). Does HRM facilitate employee creativity and organizational innovation? A study of Chinese firms. *The International Journal of Human Resource Management, 23*, 4025–4047.

Jimenez-Jimenez, D., & Sanz-Valle, R. (2008). Could HRM support organizational innovation? *The International Journal of Human Resource Management, 19*(7), 1208–1221.

Junni, P., Sarala, R., Tarba, S. Y., Liu, Y., & Cooper, C. (2015). The role of human resources and organizational factors in ambidexterity. *Human Resource Management, 54*(S1), 1–28.

Lau, C. M., & Ngo, H. Y. (2004). The HR system, organizational culture, and product innovation. *International Business Review, 13*, 685–703.

Laursen, K., & Foss, N. J. (2003). New human resource management practices, complementarities and the impact on innovative performance. *Cambridge Journal of Economics, 27*, 243–263.

Malik, A. (2013). Post-GFC people management challenges: A study of India's information technology sector. *Asia Pacific Business Review, 19*(2), 230–246.

Malik, A. (2017). *Human resource management and the global financial crisis: Evidence from India's IT/BPO industry.* London: Routledge.

Malik, A., Mitchell, R., & Boyle, B. (2017a). Contextual ambidexterity and innovation in healthcare in India: The role of HRM. *Personnel Review, 46*, 1358.

Malik, A., Sinha, P., Pereira, V., & Rowley, C. (2017b). Implementing global-local strategies in a post-GFC era: Creating an ambidextrous context through strategic choice and HRM. *Journal of Business Research.* https://doi.org/10.1016/j.jbusres.2017.09.052.

Malik, A., Pereira, V., & Tarba, S. (2017c). The role of HRM practices in product development: Contextual ambidexterity in a US MNC's subsidiary in India. *The International Journal of Human Resource Management*, 1–29. https://doi.org/10.1080/09585192.2017.1325388

Malik, A., Pereira, V., & Budhwar, P. (2018). Value creation and capture through human resource management practices: Gazing through the business model lens. *Organisational Dynamics*, 1–9. https://doi.org/10.1016/j.orgdyn.2017.09.002.

Mann, G. A. (2006). A motive to serve: Public service motivation in human resource management and the role of PSM in the nonprofit sector. *Personnel Administration*, 35(1), 33–48.

O'Reilly, C. A., III, & Tushman, M. (2008). Ambidexterity as a dynamic capability: Resolving the innovator's dilemma. *Research in Organizational Behavior*, 28, 185–206.

O'Reilly, C. A., III, & Tushman, M. L. (2011). Organizational ambidexterity in action: How managers explore and exploit. *California Management Review*, 53(4), 5–22.

Peccei, R. (2004). *Human resource management and the search for the happy workplace. Inaugural address*. Rotterdam: Erasmus Research Institute of Management.

Pereira, V., & Anderson, V. (2012). A longitudinal examination of HRM in a human resources offshoring (HRO) organization operating from India. *Journal of World Business*, 47(2), 223–231.

Prieto, I. M., & Pilar Pérez Santana, M. (2012). Building ambidexterity: The role of human resource practices in the performance of firms from Spain. *Human Resource Management*, 51(2), 189–211.

Raisch, S., & Birkinshaw, J. (2008). Organizational ambidexterity: Antecedents, outcomes, and moderators. *Journal of Management*, 34(3), 375–409.

Raisch, S., Birkinshaw, J., Probst, G., & Tushman, M. L. (2009). Organizational ambidexterity: Balancing exploitation and exploration for sustained performance. *Organization Science*, 20(4), 685–695.

Renwick, D., Redman, T., & Maguire, S. (2008). Green HRM: A review, process model, and research agenda. *University of Sheffield Management School Discussion Paper*, 2008(1), 1–46.

Renwick, D. W. S., Charbel Jabbour, J. C., Muller-Camen, M., Redman, T., & Wilkinson, A. (2016). Contemporary developments in green (environmental) HRM scholarship. *International Journal of Human Resource Management*, 27(2), 114–128.

Seeck, H., & Diehl, M. R. (2016). A literature review on HRM and innovation–taking stock and future directions. *The International Journal of Human Resource Management*, 28, 1–32. https://doi.org/10.1080/09585192.2016.1143862.

Shim, D. (2001). Recent Human Resources Developments in OECD Member Countries. *Public Personnel Management*, 30(3), 323–347.

Shipton, H., West, M. A., Dawson, J., Birdi, K., & Patterson, M. (2006). HRM as a predictor of innovation. *Human Resource Management Journal*, 16(1), 3–27.

Tushman, M. L., & O'Reilly, C. A., III. (1996). Ambidextrous organizations: Managing evolutionary and revolutionary change. *California management review*, 38(4), 8–29.

VanDe Voorde, K., Paauwe, J., & Van Veldhoven, M. (2012). Employee well-being and the HRM–organizational performance relationship: A review of quantitative studies. *International Journal of Management Reviews*, 14(4), 391–407.

Warner, M. (2013). The global economy in crisis: Towards a new paradigm? *Asia Pacific Business Review*, 19(2), 157–161.

Part III

Cases

Case 1: To Cyber-Vet or Not to Cyber-Vet: An Ethics Question for HRM

Peter Holland and Debora Jeske

New Information Challenges

The rapid change in technology which is the hallmark of the workplace in the twenty-first century has given rise to unique challenges to Human Resource (HR) Management, not least in the frontline interaction with the outside world such as recruitment and selection. Applicant vetting may go beyond a reference check as technology now gives professionals access to much more information than ever before. For example, as prospective employees as well as applicants often have both personal and professional social network accounts, HR practice has to be expanded from what is possible to what is ethically and morally appropriate – especially when the law is one step behind these rapid changes. In other words, the amount and accuracy of the information that is submitted for the position by applicants is not the main issue anymore. An important concern regards the extent to which HR professionals and other individuals involved in recruitment and selection seek out information online to obtain further information via means (such as websites and social media) that cross both legitimate and ethical boundaries. The following overview and learning exercise provides an opportunity for students to learn and reflect on these issues. We conclude the sections with two lists, one for references cited in the overview and another that includes additional reading suggestions.

P. Holland (✉)
Monash University, Melbourne, Australia
e-mail: peter.holland@monash.edu

D. Jeske
University College Cork, Cork, Republic of Ireland

© Springer Nature Singapore Pte Ltd. 2018
A. Malik (ed.), *Strategic Human Resource Management and Employment Relations*, Springer Texts in Business and Economics,
https://doi.org/10.1007/978-981-13-0399-9_15

Ethics Guidelines and Professional Integrity

The capacity of Human Resource Information Systems (HRIS) and online tools to gather information on prospective candidates for employment has increased dramatically, in part due to the greater connectedness of databases as well as people's engagement with social media and online platforms. Worryingly, technological affordances have come to dominate certain information gathering processes. These developments have the potential to move the focus on gathering data to what is possible rather than validated. New tools such as search engines and interconnected databases make it even easier to retrieve personal information about applicants. This then creates a conundrum where, in the search for more data legally defensible ethical practice may be side-lined. How to navigate this potentially treacherous path towards information has become an ethical dilemma and new challenge for HRM professionals. The key therefore is to consider the moral ambiguity that may further perpetuate the situation of having so much (not necessarily validated) information at one's finger tips. Moral ambiguity refers to a situation where no moral or legal frameworks can be delineated, and individuals are left to decide what is appropriate based on their own moral values and prior experience with such situations. In this vacuum managers may adopt a number of different moral standpoints on what is and is not acceptable practice when seeking information, specifically in recruitment and selection. Two different perspectives might therefore influence which decisions HR professionals will make when facing this information challenge. Taking a consequentialist or utilitarian perspective it could be argued that the establishment of a holistic framework would be best practice, acknowledging that potentially problematic processes (from a legal or ethical perspective on cyber-vetting) will uncover a varied list of contextual as well as clear information about the candidate. The assumption here is that all contextual factors which have no relevance to the job should be ignored so as to minimise harm to the decision-making approach, while relevant information should be considered to increase the likelihood of recruiting the best candidate for the job. Equally, many organisations are concerned about corporate social responsibility and the on-going 'organisational fit' of the candidate. It is increasingly difficult to determine now, what are the relevant future skills for the job, in an increasingly dynamic environment (noting the 1 in 5 jobs today did not exits 15 years ago). This makes it even more challenging to draw a line between what kind of (social media) activity and information are relevant to the role itself and a successful appointment.

From a deontological perspective, HR professionals will often focus on their obligation and responsibility for the employing organisation. This perspective draws on the work by Immanuel Kant, specifically his respect-for-persons principle. Here, this principle and notions are applied to organisations. The idea here is that an organisation "must treat its stakeholders as rational beings with a right to pursue their own interests without undue interference" (Greenwood and de Cieri 2005, p. 5). Professionals holding this view ensure that the candidate is the right fit for the organisation, arguing that it is appropriate to collect and explore all information readily available. An argument supporting this would be the fact that the candidate would put information on the Internet knowing that it may be viewed in a public forum. This argument is often used as a defence for utilising such information (Hedenus and Backman 2016), for example professional websites such as LinkedIn. In gathering and using this type of information, the applicants' right to privacy may be infringed as well as this information (which may not be accurate) can influence the decision-making process, it can be difficult for a third party to identify the veracity of all information in this medium. This perspective then, while well intentioned, can be undermined by the questionable accuracy of information. These two perspectives exemplify the importance of a clear framework for HR professionals and managers. The reliance on 'good judgement' alone leaves HR managers vulnerable when dealing with these complex, dynamic and varied issues on their own. Debating behavioural integrity and morals without guidance is not a desirable situation from a professional, ethical and, increasingly, a legal perspective. The absence of such guidelines moreover shows that decision-makers within an organisation are not fully aware of the complexities HR professionals face in their role and the often (enticing but potentially unethical) opportunities afforded by social media and other technologies. Only in the presence of clear guidance will HR and managers be able to make effective, defensible, and valid decisions.

Addressing the Challenge

It is clear therefore, these issues have several legal, ethical and moral implications (see Berkelaar and Buzzanell 2014). An important way forward in addressing the challenge is to develop a code of conduct that helps guide HR professionals in times of uncertainty. This code of conduct should be linked to clear standards in HR practice and serve as a beacon for good managerial practice and appropriate staff training.

So What Is a Code of Conduct?

Codes of conduct are basically a set of ethical and/or professional guidelines and recommendations that reduce the reliance on individual judgement and morals. In its simplest form, codes of conduct are policies that stipulate acceptable standards of behaviour by employees at work and when representing their organisation. It can also relate to a set of professional standards or practices that guide management decision-making. The code of conduct provides rules and boundaries that all employees are guided by (including management) and that employers can refer to for appropriate or accepted ethical, professional or disciplinary behaviours.

Value of Codes of Conduct to Organisations and Employees

A well-structured and thought-through code of conduct can provide a fair, consistent and valuable signal to all in the organisation (employers and employees) of the core values of an organisation as well as what is considered acceptable practice.

Codes of conduct also provide clear reference frameworks when the organisation is facing a difficult a decision. It can also provide the foundation for a decision above and beyond stakeholder (public) pressure. An example of this was the high-profile enactment of a code of conduct with the termination of the BBC presenter Jeremy Clarkson for verbally and physically abusing another colleague at work. In this particular case, Clarkson was sacked because he had clearly breached the code of conduct. It is clear therefore that a code of conduct needs to be ethical and underpinned by integrity, and as this high profile case illustrates, provide clear and fair guidelines for behaviour and on how decision-making should be undertaken in the workplace. In such a context you would not expect such policies to breach employment law.

Recommendations

Professional bodies such as the Society for Human Resource Management have produced guidance on social media policy which may be an important element of codes for conduct in this emerging area of work. If you are looking to develop a set of quality codes of conduct, you may wish to consider these existing guidance. However, here are a number of additional suggestions when you are tasked with developing a code for conduct. Firstly, identify and involve all stakeholders, especially employees, in the process. HR experts and employment lawyers are appropriate and knowledgeable authorities that need to be consulted and should sign off on any guidance produced. Secondly, link the code of conduct to training. Whilst code of conducts may exist, few of these are actually linked to induction training upon hiring or promotion. Education is key. The mere existence of social media policies is unlikely to be effective (Pallarito 2014; Roberts and Sambrook 2014). These concerns are only fostered when we review evidence about the lack of guidance within organisations. For example, the Society of Human Resource Management reported that over 40% of respondents in surveys conducted in 2013 had no formal or informal policy on applicant screening. However, even training is unlikely to reduce discriminatory practices if the training is not complemented by good management practice, open discussion around inclusion versus discrimination. Having organisational resources to educate employees and managers is an important additional step, especially for HR professionals advising staff (useful resources include the work by Appel 2015). Third, review and update this code on a regular basis, and involve all stakeholders in the revision. Technology is continuously evolving, and so are the possibilities (e.g., for cyber-vetting) for ethical pitfalls (see Smith 2016).

Learning Exercise

Consider the following background scenario: You are the incoming HR manager for a new retail organisation. You are tasked with recruiting a new store-based sales team that will interact face-to-face with a diverse set of customers. In addition, the new team members will also use a store-specific social media account to respond to queries from customers. In line with these developments, you have to develop a code of conduct to prepare for the upcoming recruitment and selection processes. Here are the specifics: The code for conduct has to cover aspects relevant to recruitment and selection. The code has to be relevant to everyday use of social media at work - not just by HR professionals, but also line managers. And finally, the code has to be written so it is readily accessible and understandable to all current and new employees, but also potentially new applicants (so it needs to be general enough to be informative for those who are not part of or familiar with the organisation).

In order to tackle this learning exercise, please consider the following steps. First, search for existing guidance and code of conduct examples provided by organisations to get a sense of how social media codes of conduct may vary in style and content. You may also wish to consider what inspired these codes of conduct (as they are often the result of previous social media disasters; see Cotton-on in Australia (Holland 2015) and Sainsbury's in the UK). Second, together with your colleagues, review these examples of code of conducts, identifying the strengths and weaknesses of each. Third, outline the key criteria you think may be relevant for the new code of conduct. Pay particular attention to the use of and access to information on social media.

Additional Considerations in Your Design of the Code and Policy May Include Seeking Answers to the Following Questions

1. Does the policy and code of conduct state who will have to comply with it?
2. Does the policy provide clear guidance on what happens if an employee violates the code of conduct?
3. Does it make reference to data security practice and how and where the data is securely stored?
4. Does the code suggest how long data is kept and who has access?
5. Is it clear what happens if an employee violates the policy?

References

Appel, E. J. (2015). *Cybervetting: Internet searches for vetting, investigations, and open-source intelligence* (2nd ed.). Boca Raton: CRC Press/Taylor & Francis Group.

Berkelaar, B. L., & Buzzanell, P. M. (2014). Cybervetting, person–environment fit, and personnel selection: Employers' surveillance and sensemaking of job applicants' online information. *Journal of Applied Communication Research, 42*(4), 456–476. https://doi.org/10.1080/00909882.2014.954595.

Greenwood, M., & de Cieri, H. (2005, July). *Stakeholder theory and the ethics of Human Resource Management* (Monash University Working Paper 47/05). Department of Management Working Paper Series, 1–17.

Hedenus, A., & Backman, C. (2016, April 20–23). *Explaining your data double: Confessions honesty and trust in job requirements*. Proceedings of the 7th Biannual Surveillance and Society Conference, Barcelona, Spain. Available at: http://www.ssn2016.net/?page_id=1383. Accessed 10 June 2016.

Holland, P. (2015). *Codes of conduct: making things clear is better than 'keeping it real: The conversation*, 24th April.

Pallarito, K. (2014). *Training for social situations; Educate workers on social media advantages, pitfalls*. Post published on April 14th on Business Insurance, 48, p. 0016.

Roberts, G., & Sambrook, S. (2014). Social networking and HRD. *Human Resource Development International, 17*, 577–587. https://doi.org/10.1080/13678868.2014.969504.

Smith, A. (2016). *Old Chipotle social media policy was unlawfully vague*. Blog post published on August 26th on SHRM. Available at: https://www.shrm.org/resourcesandtools/hr-topics/labor-relations/pages/chipotle-outdated-policy-vague.aspx

Wright, A. D. (2016). *Fired for facebooking: Nasty political posts could cost employees their jobs*. Blog post published on September 26th on SHRM. Available at: https://www.shrm.org/ResourcesAndTools/hr-topics/technology/Pages/Fired-for-Facebooking-Nasty-Political-Posts-Could-Cost-Employees-Their-Jobs.aspx

Further Student Reading on Ethical and Moral Dilemmas in the HR Domain

Acikgoz, Y., & Bergman, S. M. (2016). Social media and employee recruitment: Chasing the runaway bandwagon. In B. R. Landers & G. B. Schmidt (Eds.), *Social media in employee selection and recruitment. Theory, practice, and current challenges* (pp. 175–195). Cham: Springer International Publishing.

Bazerman, M. H., & Sezer, O. (2016). Bounded awareness: Implications for ethical decision making. *Organizational Behavior and Human Decision Processes, 136*, 95–105. https://doi.org/10.1016/j.obhdp.2015.11.004.

Black, S. L., Stone, D. L., & Johnson, A. F. (2015). Use of social networking websites on applicants' privacy. *Employee Responsibilities and Rights Journal, 27*, 115–159. https://doi.org/10.1007/s10672-014-9245-2.

Kang, S. K., DeCelles, K. A., Tilcsik, A., & Jun, S. (2016). Whitened résumés: Race and self-presentation in the labor market. *Administrative Science Quarterly, 61*(3), 469–502. https://doi.org/10.1007/s10672-014-9245-2.

Linehan, C., & O'Brien, E. (2016). From tell-tale signs to irreconcilable struggles: The value of emotion in exploring the ethical dilemmas of human resource professionals. *Journal of Business Ethics, ePub., 141*, 763. https://doi.org/10.1007/s10551-016-3040-y.

Schneider, T. J., Goffin, R. D., & Daljeet, K. N. (2015). "Give us your social networking site passwords": Implications for personnel selection and personality. *Personality and Individual Differences, 73*, 78–83. https://doi.org/10.1016/j.paid.2014.09.026.

Slovensky, R., & Ross, W. H. (2012). Should human resource managers use social media to screen job applicants? Managerial and legal issues in the USA. *Info, 14*, 55–69. https://doi.org/10.1108/14636691211196941.

Vaast, E., & Levina, N. (2016). Speaking as one but not speaking up: Dealing with new moral taint in an occupational online community. *Information & Organization, 25*(2), 73–96. https://doi.org/10.1016/j.infoandorg.2015.02.001.

Waring, R. L., & Buchanan, F. R. (2010). Social networking web sites: The legal and ethical aspects of pre-employment screening and employee surveillance. *Journal of Human Resources Education, 4*(2), 14–23.

Case 2: Work-Life Balance in an MNE Context

Anne Bardoel

Global work-life initiatives present unique challenges for HR departments in multinational enterprises (MNEs) because of the complexity of implementing policies that require sensitivity to local issues such as cultural traditions and legislation (e.g., Bardoel and De Cieri 2007; Scullion et al. 2007; Sumelius et al. 2008). However, discussion specific to work-life management in a global context is limited (e.g., Allen et al. 2010; Lewis et al. 2007). Amid unprecedented levels of global mergers, acquisitions and international growth, the challenge for HR professionals working in multinational enterprises is to define a global work/life strategy that establishes shared guidelines while allowing for local differences. Although there are a number of common issues faced by working women and men and their families, a global work-life strategy needs to reflect a course of action that is appropriate to the local environment. According to Spinks (2003) an effective family friendly strategy requires managers to be cognizant of a number of local factors that influence employees' work and personal lives. These factors include the culture and tradition, the role of key stake-holders, public policies, community resources and infrastructure, and workplace practices and demo-graphics (Bardoel and De Cieri 2007).

Work-life management practices refer to those practices in organizations introduced to facilitate the integration of employees' work and non-work demands (McCarthy et al. 2010). Work-life policies include flexible working conditions, leave options (e.g. parental, adult care, bereavement etc.), and child and dependant care (e.g. childcare centers, afterschool care support etc.) (Smeaton et al. 2014). Various studies have also linked work-life practices to improved employee

A. Bardoel (✉)
Swinburne University of Technology, Melbourne, VIC, Australia
e-mail: abardoel@swin.edu.au

© Springer Nature Singapore Pte Ltd. 2018
A. Malik (ed.), *Strategic Human Resource Management and Employment Relations*, Springer Texts in Business and Economics,
https://doi.org/10.1007/978-981-13-0399-9_16

commitment (Muse et al. 2008; Richman et al. 2008), employee performance and organizational citizenship behavior (Lambert 2000; Muse et al. 2008), enhanced recruitment efforts (Christensen and Schneider 2010) better employee health and well-being (Grzywacz et al. 2008) and, increased job satisfaction (Grandey et al. 2007; Muse et al. 2008).

Corporate promotion of work-life balance (WLB) has attracted interest globally because of the potential role of these efforts in fostering effective recruitment, retention and productivity among employees (Christensen and Schneider 2010). From a strategic HRM perspective, WLB promotion among multi-national enterprises (MNEs) can be understood using the tensions theoretical framework provided in Bardoel (2016). This case study provides an example of WLB efforts around lesbian, gay, bi-sexual and transexual (LGBT) employees, and uses the tensions framework to understand likely complexities and resolutions to those difficulties around LBGT issues. The tensions framework, as the name suggests, is designed to surface and respond to sources of conflict and contradiction. Applying that approach, LBGT issues provide an ideal topic given they have been and remain controversial. In the U.S., major corporations moved from having a strong aversion to so much as discussing the topic to a strong public embrace of marriage equality for gays and lesbians in only two decades (Socarides 2015). Indeed, 199 of the Fortune 500 corporations in the U.S. achieved a perfect equity index rating from the Human Rights Campaign by 2017, with strong majorities of the Fortune 500 including "sexual orientation" and "gender identity" anti-discrimination policies, and half providing transgender health care benefits, such as surgical procedures (Human Rights Campaign 2017). This movement stands in stark contrast to the absence of housing or employment protections for LGBT employees in the U.S. (Ibid.), suggesting that tensions remain. Many of the Fortune 500 are also MNEs, and IBM stands out as one that has diffused its WLB policies across its global operations (Hill et al. 2006), including its LGBT policies (Mahtani and Vernon 2010). Bardoel located relevant difficulties in an interview with a diversity manager working in Singapore for an anonymous IT MNE:

> … [T]he gay, lesbian, bi-sexual and transgender constituency … is also a group where we look into ensuring that the workplace is conducive for employees. So yes we have these challenges … trying to introduce the same kind of initiatives that we have in the US… International Women's Day is celebrated 8 March every year … in all the countries we have posters put up, communication notes going out to employees …. But LGBT is not celebrated in the same way. In fact the posters are not put up in all locations, it's definitely not in Malaysia or Indonesia because they're Muslim countries … (Bardoel 2016, p. 1697).

Bardoel (2016) places organizational tensions along three axes: strategic or policy vs. operational concerns, centralization vs. decentralization, and contextual or institutional vs. organizational objectives and constraints. The quote above highlights each of these. As a strategic or policy objective, the MNE seeks to make the workplace inclusive of LGBT employees, but doing so explicitly with posters may interfere with day-to-day operations. Similarly, the MNE acted in a centralized fashion with the provision of the posters and expectation that they will appear in the workplace, while the manager acted in a decentralized fashion. Finally, the reason for the manager ignoring corporate policy lay in the Muslim context of employees living in Malaysia and Indonesia, and interference with religious beliefs and practices may be unwise. Indeed, the manager implies that the appearance of the posters would create conflict, and perhaps reduce productivity and make the recruitment and retention of talented employees more difficult, which is counter to the overarching objective of WLB and LGBT programs and policies.

Behind the issue of the posters per se lie several related issues which are sources of organizational tensions. In the Asian operations, managers undoubtedly have LGBT employees, but if posters are not put up, the likelihood of LGBT employees feeling comfortable about coming out, much less using same-sex partner benefits in terms of health or retirement benefits, or benefits supporting sex-change procedures, is very low. And if those policies cannot be accessed, then any prospective benefits from these policies in terms of recruitment, retention or productivity are lost (Eaton 2003). It might even be the case that operations would suffer if MNE LGBT policies, such as same-sex partner benefits, were known at all, again highlighting the tension between strategy or policies and operations. Further, this conflict calls up questions of centralization vs. decentralization, and particularly whether the manager feels comfortable informing higher-ups of the decision to keep the posters hidden or not put up at all, or ask that exceptions be included in corporate policy. Again, institutions and context come into play because the manager requires close knowledge of those in order to accurately assess the consequences of putting up the posters, or informing employees of LGBT policies. Conflicts need not be limited to overseas operations. If the home nation of the MNE is the U.S., there is likely to be conflict stemming from strong corporate support for LGBT employees in the U.S. opposing practices in overseas operations. For example, if the MNE has a practice of rotating promising young managers through various overseas assignments, should it place LGBT employees from the U.S. or Australia in a location where their sexual orientation or gender identity would undercut their authority and ability to function effectively? Again, the three axes of conflict are relevant (application is left to the reader).

Bardoel (2016) provides five types of organizational responses to tensions. These involve: no recognition, opposition, spatial separation, temporal separation, and synthesis. The first, no recognition, is not strategic and may lead to contradictions surfacing in unexpected and unproductive ways. For example, if the manager does not feel comfortable informing headquarters that the LGBT posters are hidden in some workplaces, then headquarters cannot recognize that a problem exists. If a promising and out LGBT manager were to rotate through one of these operations, he or she might be unpleasantly surprised by the likely negative reception he or she would receive. The second, opposition approach, is indeed strategic, as it involves explicit recognition of the tensions, and a strategic decision to let sleeping dogs lie; in other words, sometimes the costs would outweigh the benefits of explicitly resolving a tension. In this case, the local manager would have informed headquarters that the posters are not consistently utilized, and headquarters might leave corporate policies in place while recognizing that they are not uniformly applied.

Managers at headquarters might further either not rotate LGBT employees through operations where they would not be welcome, or at least inform them ahead of time of the local context. The third, spatial separation, involves strategically applying different policies to different locations depending upon context and institutions or, relatedly, separating local from corporate policies. In this case, corporate LGBT policy could either be written to include exceptions for local conditions, or policy development and metrics to measure success could be pushed down to the regional or local level; in the latter case, corporate policy might include support for LGBT employees as an objective, with methods for doing so determined at the local level, pressing regional managers to use their contextual and institutional knowledge to move forward where and in ways such that the benefits outweigh the costs. The fourth, temporal separation, involves taking time into account. For example, LGBT policies might be trialed in nations that are relatively less discriminatory, such as the U.S., with evaluation and further policy development prior to global implementation. By extension, the policies might be implemented over time as local conditions warrant. In this case, headquarters might have made use of the posters optional, and similarly spread LGBT policies only gradually across operations in diverse locations. The fifth, synthesis, refers to the development of new terms or concepts to resolve tensions. One well-known case of synthesis appeared in the mid-1990s, when HRM practitioners and researchers shifted from the relatively exclusionary term, "work-family," to the more inclusive term, "work-life" (Harrington 2007). Not incidentally, it seems unlikely that LGBT issues would have entered WLB policy discussions absent this shift. A related example of synthesis, pioneered by IBM, involved casting WLB initiatives as part-and-parcel of broader diversity initiatives (Childs 2005). In the present case, applying the approach might have involved communications targeting diversity across many lines, including, gender, ethnicity or race, age, and religion, with LGBT diversity as only one part.

As Bardoel (2016) notes, responses to tensions are not necessarily mutually exclusive. For example, the examples of temporal and spatial separation regarding LGBT policies provided above, could both be utilized while the MNE works both at headquarters and globally towards an effective synthesis approach.

More concretely, Mahtani and Vernon (2010) analyze LGBT issues for employers in Hong Kong, and particularly for MNEs, and expand upon many of the tensions surfaced here. They provide a list of eight types of recommended policies and practices, including: equal opportunity policies, diversity training, diversity structure, benefits, corporate culture, market positioning, monitoring, and community and advocacy. Without detailing specific policies, it is important to note that these policies are designed for a community where LGBT acceptance if not rights has expanded markedly in recent years, and case studies are provided where each type of policy or practice has already been implemented in Hong Kong (Ibid.). Note further that implementation of these policies might use the tensions resolution approach outlined here. Opposition might involve MNE policies and practices along the lines of the eight types suggested that are only implemented in part or not at all depending upon the specific workforce involved. Spatial separation might involve applying different sets of policies in, e.g., manufacturing and financial services or communications operations. By extension, temporal separation might involve starting with one or several of the eight policy and practice recommendations, evaluating the results, and proceeding to implement further recommendations depending upon the results achieved. Finally, given the cultural baggage around LGBT people carried by many employees in Hong Kong and elsewhere (including the U.S.), the development of a synthesis approach, perhaps via the active involvement of frontline employees (Rapoport et al. 2002) might be valuable.

Case Study Questions

Following the above case study and relying on the key resource stated below, your task is to:

1. Analyse three generic sources of tensions are identified in the management of global work-life issues.
2. Evaluate various resolutions that could apply to MNEs in relation LGBT employees.
3. Decide which strategy do you think would be most effective in the case study MNE?
4. Comment should this MNE have a global LGBT policy? Why/ why not?

Key Resource Bardoel, E.A. (2016). *Work-life management tensions in multinational enterprises (MNEs). International Journal of Human Resource Management, 27, 1681–1709.*

References

Allen, T. D., Shockley, K. M., & Biga, A. (2010). Work and family in a global context. In K. Lundby & J. Jolton (Eds.), *Going global: Practical applications and recommendations for HR and OD professionals in the global workplace* (pp. 377–401). San Francisco: Jossey-Bass.

Bardoel, E. A. (2016). Work-life management tensions in multinational enterprises (MNEs). *International Journal of Human Resource Management, 27,* 1681–1709.

Bardoel, E. A., & De Cieri, H. (2007). Reconciling work and family responsibilities: A global perspective, Anima. *Indonesian Psychological Journal, 23*(1), 17–23.

Childs, J. T., Jr. (2005). Workforce diversity: A global HR topic that has arrived. In M. Losey, S. Meisinger, & D. Ulrich (Eds.), *The future of human resource management* (pp. 110–118). Hoboken: Wiley.

Christensen, K., & Schneider, B. (Eds.). (2010). *Workplace flexibility: Realigning 20th-century jobs for a 21st-century workforce*. Ithaca: ILR Press.

Eaton, S. (2003). If you can use them: Flexibility policies, organizational commitment, and perceived performance. *Industrial Relations, 42,* 145–167.

Grandey, A. A., Cordeiro, B. L., & Michael, J. H. (2007). Work-family supportiveness organizational perceptions: Important for the well-being of make blue-collar hourly workers? *Journal of Vocational Behavior, 71,* 460–478.

Grzywacz, J. G., Carlson, D. S., & Shulkin, S. (2008). Schedule flexibility and stress: Linking formal flexible arrangements and perceived flexibility to employee health. *Community, Work & Family, 11*, 199–214.

Harrington, B. (2007). *The work-life evolution study*. Boston: Boston College Center for Work & Family.

Hill, E. J., Jackson, A. D., & Martinengo, G. (2006). Twenty years of work and family at International Business Machines Corporation. *American Behavioral Scientist, 49*, 1165–1183.

Human Rights Campaign. (2017). *Corporate equality index 2017*. Washington, DC: Human Rights Campaign.

Lambert, S. J. (2000). Added benefits: The link between work-life benefits and organizational citizenship behavior. *Academy of Management Journal, 43*, 801–815.

Lewis, S., Gambles, R., & Rapoport, R. (2007). The constraints of a 'work-life balance' approach: An international perspective. *The International Journal of Human Resource Management, 18*, 360–373.

Mahtani, S., & Vernon, K. (2010). *Creating inclusive workplaces for LGBT employees: A resource guide for employers in Hong Kong. Report*. Hong Kong: Community Business.

McCarthy, A., Darcy, C., & Grady, G. (2010). Work-life balance policy and practice: Understanding line manager attitudes and behaviors. *Human Resource Management Review, 20*, 158–167.

Muse, L., Harris, S. G., Giles, W. F., & Field, H. S. (2008). Work-life benefits and positive organizational behavior: is there a connection? *Journal of Organizational Behavior, 29*, 171–192.

Rapoport, R., Bailyn, L., Fletcher, J. K., & Pruitt, B. H. (2002). *Beyond work-family balance: Advancing gender equity and workplace performance*. San Francisco: Jossey-Bass.

Richman, A. L., Civian, J. T., Shannon, L. L., Hill, J. E., & Brennan, R. T. (2008). The relationship of perceived flexibility, supportive work-life policies, and use of formal flexible arrangements and occasional flexibility to employee engagement and expected retention. *Community, Work & Family, 11*, 183–197.

Scullion, H., Collings, D. G., & Gunnigle, P. (2007). International human resource management in the 21st century: emerging themes and contemporary debates. *Human Resource Management Journal, 17*, 309–319.

Smeaton, D., Ray, K., & Knight, G. (2014). *Costs and benefits to business of adopting work life balance working practices: A literature review*. UK: Department for Business and Innovation Skills (gov.uk).

Socarides, R. (2015). Corporate America's evolution on L.G.B.T. rights. *The New Yorker*, April 27. http://www.newyorker.com/business/currency/corporate-americas-evolution-on-l-g-b-t-rights

Spinks, N. 2003. *Work/life around the world (Building a global work-life strategy)*. Paper presented at the Designing the Future, 7th Annual Work/Life Conference, Orlando, Florida.

Sumelius, J., Bjorkman, I., & Smale, A. (2008). The influence of internal and external social networks on HRM capabilities in MNC subsidiaries in China. *The International Journal of Human Resource Management, 19*(12), 2294–2310.

Case 3: Crisis and IHRM

Crisis, Internationalisation and HRM in Project-Based Organisations: The Tale of SOFMAN

Konstantinos Tasoulis and Maria Progoulaki

"I was following Abu and Mohammed in the jungle, under the hot sun and with great humidity, unaware of where we were going. They said they had the solution for me. Behind some tall branches hiding our view, we stepped to a place from where we could see a quarry. Abu personally knew the local workers who agreed to make the spare part for me in 2 days for 10 $, 1/100 of the shipping cost from Greece". If not because of loyalty and a sense of engagement, then why assist a foreign "boss" save time and money?

Company Background

Elefsina is the birthplace of Aeschylus and the site of the ancient Eleusinian mysteries revolving around issues of life after death. In modern times, it hosts a major industrial center, few kilometers away from Athens, Greece. Elefsina is also home to SOFMAN S.A., a small-medium sized firm operating in the steel and mechanical structures industry. SOFMAN was established in 2000, following the merger of two steel and mechanical structures firms with 30 years of experience. The firm designs, produces and installs steel structures in a tailor-made fashion, such as heavy industrial constructions, bridges, steel buildings and architectural projects (SOFMAN company website n.d.). SOFMAN uses the latest CAD-DAM manufacturing technology in the design of steel structures, and owns two fabrication plants. The main plant is used for most of its production operations (e.g. cutting, welding, assembling) while the second, developed in 2012, is dedicated to painting. The firm has earned a number of international and European certifications related to quality of its

---

K. Tasoulis (✉) · M. Progoulaki
ALBA Graduate Business School & Deree School of Business, The American College of Greece, Athens, Greece
e-mail: ktasoulis@alba.acg.edu; mprogoulaki@acg.edu

engineering operations. Today, the firm employs 75 full time employees; approximately 2/3 work in the fabrication plants and 1/3 in the administrative and design functions. Led by the two sons of the founders, Michalis Sofras, Chief Executive Officer (CEO), and Nikos Mandras, Managing Director (MD), this family run firm has contributed to landmark construction sites in Greece, including the Acropolis Museum, the Athens International Airport, and the Stavros Niarchos Foundation Cultural Centre.

SOFMAN's values include: safety, quality, innovation, flexibility, and people development, underlined by a traditional, family culture. This is manifested in very low labour turnover rates and a large proportion of skilled technical staff who has worked with the firm for decades. In some cases, workers' children have also been hired and internally developed by the company.

In terms of HRM practices, recruitment appears to be challenging in case of attracting highly-skilled individuals, especially in technical jobs which are not as popular in the labour market as in the past (e.g. assemblers, welders, fitters, painters). Although the company lacks a formal human resources (HR) department, common in small-medium enterprises (SMEs; Curran 2006), people development is emphasised through on- and off-the job training. For example, SOFMAN recently conducted an extensive development programme for engineers on leadership and management skills, while technical staff participated in craft-specific seminars, involving theory and practice. Nonetheless, training needs are identified on an ad-hoc basis, such as when new equipment and machinery is introduced in the production.

The Greek Crisis and SOFMAN's Strategic Response

The financial crisis tormenting the country since 2010, has played a key role in the evolution of SOFMAN's business activities. In Greece, the crisis affected SMEs more than large multinational firms, while construction activity was one of the sectors most severely affected (OECD 2016). Faced with a very difficult macroeconomic and industry environment with few inland construction opportunities, top management decided to embark upon an internationalisation process for the first time in the firm's history, initially seeking for opportunities to export. Figure 1 illustrates evidence of SOFMAN's growth in international operations, during a period that the home market was shrinking.

Through networking with Greek entrepreneurs and using personal contacts, a crucial theme for SMEs (Širec and Brada 2009), SOFMAN managed to earn its first international project as a contractor of a Greek-owned firm in Nigeria in 2010. This involved fabricating a sugar process refinery building and shipping it from Athens to Lagos. Word-of mouth and further networking enabled SOFMAN to secure 42 additional contracts in Nigeria, worth of € 12 million. *"We were successful because of our quality standards and our ability to find innovative solutions to problems in very difficult circumstances; our small size provides us the flexibility to adjust and be responsive to customer needs"*, says Mr. Sofras, CEO. As the firm acquired more experience and confidence operating in an international setting, it expanded its

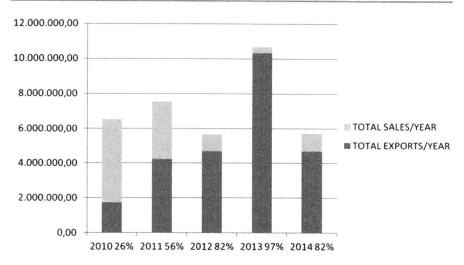

Fig. 1 SOFMAN sales and exporting activity during the crisis in Greece. (Source: SOFMAN, SA. Internal document, Note: Amounts are in €)

services to offer on-site installations. A € 4 million milestone project in the firm's history involved the fabrication of a bioethanol and power generation plant in Greece and its installation in Ebola-stricken Sierra Leone, using SOFMAN's own lifting equipment. Sierra Leone was not a desirable destination for most competitors given the unfavourable circumstances in the country, discussed below. However, to survive and compete with larger European multinational construction firms in the steel industry, *"we had to go to places where others wouldn't"*.

In parallel to projects in Africa, the firm became a subcontractor of large construction firms managing projects in Central and Eastern Europe. Following a € 10 million contract for fabricating a refinery project in Bulgaria, SOFMAN was subcontracted to produce steel structures in Greece (e.g. pipe racks, shelters) and install them in Slovakia and Czechia (formerly Czech Republic).

The Project in Sierra Leone: Leadership & HRM Issues

While the manufacturing of the customised steel structure in Greece seemed business as usual, transportation and installation in the middle of the jungle was certainly not an ordinary activity. The CEO led the team in the initial stages of the project in Free Town, the capital of Sierra Leone, where machinery and the steel structures were shipped, and subsequently, at the construction site in Makeni. The project involved the management of several difficulties first and foremost, health and safety conditions in an underdeveloped country, where some regions were suffering a humanitarian crisis due to Ebola, leading to the death of an estimated 3955 people ("Ebola in Africa" 2016). Poor infrastructure was also an impediment, such as the low quality of roads affecting the transportation of heavy machinery from the port to remote rural areas. Low quality of institutions (e.g. banking), theft, and generally low levels of security posed significant risks that had to be managed by the CEO and the project team, in collaboration with the Elefsina office. On top of these, cross-cultural differences were another major challenge.

The installation project team in Sierra Leone comprised a leading project manager and highly skilled construction workers, in charge of the erection of facilities. The team's manager was an experienced SOFMAN engineer who conducted on-site management, and communicated with the leadership team in Athens almost on a daily basis, particularly in the first stages of the project. Skilled construction workers were supplied by a subcontractor in Greece. SOFMAN took the latter decision concerning the supply of construction staff in order to manage risk and control the costs of the operation, as well as to obtain access to technicians quickly and effectively, from a known and trusted firm. Technicians were selected following careful evaluation and discussions between the leadership teams of SOFMAN and their subcontractor, reflecting the importance of team member selection in such projects (Anyanwu 2013). The client mandated that the project team was assisted by a group of low skilled workers, who were supplied by a sub-contractor from Sierra Leone, introducing an element of national diversity in the team.

A key challenge for SOFMAN was to enable the project team to work as a cohesive unit. The CEO and the Greek project team of expatriates lived together in the best possible accommodation at Makeni, which became the home of the project team for several months to follow. During this period, the CEO set team norms and bonded the project team through discussions and shared activities such as cooking meals, treating all members as part of a unit representing SOFMAN, and setting three priorities: a) strict focus on health and safety practices inside and outside the construction site, b) strong quality orientation, encouraging team members to readily report problems when they occur, and c) efficiency in all levels of operations.

In terms of the collaboration with local unskilled workers, SOFMAN's CEO attempted to integrate these workers to the team as well as improve their competencies by transferring technical know-how in fundamental areas. However, cross-cultural differences posed a significant challenge. Locals were perceived as friendly and warm but professionally unreliable, with a different work ethic and a laxed orientation when it came to timing. *"Tomorrow could mean next week in Sierra Leone, so we had to adjust to the culture and be proactive in our planning. Also, despite our efforts to upskill local workers and transfer some of our knowledge, I learned the lesson that some people unfortunately are reluctant to learn."* Nonetheless, in many cases locals contributed to troubleshooting and offered out-of-the box solutions. For example, when a hydraulic part was needed in order to fix a crane, locals guided SOFMAN employees to a quarry whereby such materials were available, saving money and the time that would have been required to ship the items from Greece. Some of these locals became integrated to SOFMAN's culture and felt part of the project team, otherwise they would have not contributed. The CEO was collecting the fruits of his personal leadership and care to his workers. SOFMAN successfully completed the project and identified additional business opportunities, such as renting their own materials and equipment to other international firms operating in the country. The firm still continues operations in Sierra Leone and nearby regions, having developed a joint venture in steel construction services with a local company specialising in logistics.

Project Management in Central and Eastern Europe

SOFMAN entered the European market as a fabrication subcontractor in 2012. In 2016, it was contracted to manufacture and install steel pipe racks, process buildings and shelters in Slovakia. In comparison to Sierra Leone, this was a larger scale project with more demanding technical requirements. Nonetheless, the project team structure remained similar in many respects. This team consisted of a project manager, a SOFMAN engineer in charge of the supervision of the project and four engineers specialising in specific functions (e.g. surveying, safety, quality); the latter were leased from specialized firms in Greece. Additionally, 30 skilled workers in charge of the installation were also sourced through subcontractors based in Greece and Slovakia and offered their services for the specific project. Such a structure enabled SOFMAN to control the project through the site engineer, but also attain flexibility and control costs. Simultaneously, SOFMAN opened an office in Slovakia in order to facilitate its business operations in the country, hiring two local employees for administration and accounting purposes. Overall, the approach followed and team synthesis reflect a gradual strategic move from a home-based ethnocentric approach, to a polycentric perspective, utilising an increasing amount of host-country human resources (Perlmutter 1969).

Following the same recipe, the CEO aimed to establish norms and increase the cohesion of this nationally diverse project team, so that they would all work with the culture and quality standards of the firm. After all, SOFMAN was eventually accountable for the project. In addition to training offered to all employees on various issues (e.g. health and safety, quality), SOFMAN incentivises employees through a performance-based reward scheme for all employees, including those leased by the Greek and Slovak subcontractors. Additionally, rewards and strict penalties were set based on workers' compliance to health and safety project standards.

Working with locals provided a number of benefits and solutions to SOFMAN. For example, the local administrator helped the site manager identify and communicate with local suppliers who provided items required in steel panels. In some cases, however, new cross-cultural differences became relevant, which were in sharp contrast to those experienced in Africa. In Slovakia, Greeks perceived locals as punctual, accountable and having a good work ethic, yet quite strict, introverted and distrustful towards foreigners. Such cross-cultural problems were managed by the interventions and site visits of the CEO, who used various methods to increase the sense of identity and unity in the team. Relying on its well-established production capabilities in Greece as well as project-based, culturally diverse teams seems to have worked well for SOFMAN. Flexible teams comprising of a core SOFMAN manager, engineers and workers from home and host country subcontractors, enabled the firm to respond to customer needs on a project basis, without having to increase the size of its workforce in the long-run. This would have been a risk with significant cost implications, given the high levels of volatility and uncertainty in the construction market of the home country.

Future Prospects

During the Greek crisis, SOFMAN gained unique experience on managing construction projects in the sub-Saharan Africa and Europe. Pursuing international business opportunities involving fabrication and on-site installation, as well as expansion to other geographical areas reflect the growing confidence of top executives in SOFMAN's ability to compete internationally. As the firm was successful in its endeavors in both continents, SOFMAN intends to expand its operations in Greece and abroad. It is currently licensing a third plant in Greece, which is expected to double its annual output. It is also in the process of setting up a subsidiary office in Europe, which is expected to enable the firm to identify further business development opportunities, as well as increase its ability to manage international projects. While the state of the Greek economy could have inspired Aeschylean dramaturgy, SOFMAN's gradual but bold internationalisation steps are paying off, signaling a promising future for the firm.

Case Study Questions

1. Discuss SOFMAN's response to the changing external environment since 2009/10. Examine the key factors underlying SOFMAN's strategic choices and critically evaluate the internationalisation strategy.
2. Critically evaluate SOFMAN's HRM practices in the process of internationalisation and offer suggestions for improvement.

References and Recommended Readings

Anyanwu, C. I. (2013). The role of building construction project team members in building projects delivery. *Journal of Business and Management, 14*(1), 30–34.

Curran, J. (2006). "Specificity" and "denaturing" the small business. *International Small Business Journal, 24*(2), 205–210.

Ebola in Africa: The end of tragedy? (2016, January). *The economist*. Retrieved from http://www.economist.com/blogs/graphicdetail/2016/01/daily-chart-12

OECD. (2016). *OECD economic survey: Greece 2016*. Paris: OECD Publishing. Retrieved from https://doi.org/https://doi.org/10.1787/eco_surveys-grc-2016-en

Perlmutter, H. (1969). The tortuous evolution of multinational enterprises. *Columbia Journal of World Business, 4*(1), 9–18.

Širec, K., & Brada, B. (2009). How does networking Impact the SMEs growth? *Organizacija, 42*(2), 59–66. https://doi.org/10.2478/v10051-009-0003-4. Retrieved from http://www.dlib.si/stream/URN:NBN:SI:DOC-ZOIJLL28/d5d9100c-fe12-46a9-b2c8-cc4da618b32e/PDF.

SOFMAN company website. (n.d.). Our projects. Retrieved from www.sofman.gr.

Case 4: Japanese Cross Border M&A and German Target Employee Alienation Issues

Ralf Bebenroth and Roman Bartnik

Introduction to M&A

Mergers and Acquisitions (M&A) occur frequently all over the world and about 70% are categorized as cross-border deals with the aim of multinational firms to undertake investments in foreign countries (Peng 2008). There is evidence that cross border deals are more difficult to successfully realize than domestic deals because employees not only experience a different organizational culture but also have to interact with a different national culture (Chung et al. 2014). The rule of thumb is that integrations become increasingly difficult as cultural distance and differences increases between the bidder and the target in a M&A context. Most of the studies take it for granted that employees are heavily affected by direct involvement in a cross border acquisition (e.g. Chung et al. 2014; Nemanich and Keller 2007). Yet, indirect effects of social identification can also affect the lack of direct interaction between employees from both parties (the acquirer and the acquired). This case study deals about a Japanese steelmaker who overtook a German engineering firm specializing in waste disposal business. Challenges in the post-merger integration and especially between the expatriated Japanese managers to the German subsidiary and the German employees are discussed.

R. Bebenroth (✉)
Kobe University, Kobe, Japan
e-mail: rbeben@rieb.kobe-u.ac.jp

R. Bartnik
Cologne Business School, Cologne, Germany

Alienation Issues

Integration can be more difficult when the merging firms differ strongly in a number of aspects such as language, culture, cultural distance and so on. Research literature offers evidence that a sense of continuity plays an important role in employees' feelings about the post-merger process, e.g. see Jetten et al. (2002) and Bartels et al. (2006). In this context, it is important for target employees to fully understand the intentions of the bidder. Recent studies have focused on differences in culture and the impact of buyer firm's status. (Björkman et al. 2007; Yildiz 2016). Bauer et al. (2015) look at the role of cultural similarity as a moderator and find beneficial effects of cultural similarity for innovation-driven M&As. Relatedly, Ahammad et al. (2014) find that cultural similarity mediates the relationship between knowledge transfer and performance. Regarding the effect of status, Yildiz (2016) finds that similarity between buyer and target firm promotes benevolence-based trust, whereas higher status of the acquiring firm promotes competence-based trust and out-group favoritism. The present case study sheds light on a cross border acquisition and focuses on the effects of rather less involved employees. We present here an in-depth study on the dyad of buyer-target firms. Notably, the bidder firm is very hesitant to directly impact operations at the target. The target firm employees thus have a rather weak bond with the bidder firm (Bartels et al. 2006).

Social Identity Theory

Our case study is partly grounded in the Social Identify Theory advanced by Tajfel and Turner (1986). It starts from the presumption that a (social) group membership is important in the creation of a self-concept of people (Bartels et al. 2006). People perceive themselves as sharing the same fate with other people in their organization (Mael and Ashforth 1992). That means they identify with their organization. Meal and Ashforth defined it as: "perception of oneness with or belongingness to an organization, where the individual defines him- or herself in terms of the organizations(s) in which he or she is a member" (p. 104). Social identity theory offers an explanation of why employees often react so negatively to organizational changes such as I mergers or acquisitions. Employees affected by a M&A feel threatened because their stability and continuation is endangered (Hogg and Terry 2000; Bartels et al. 2006). However, some of the employees would be part of the in-group and supporters while others would be in the out-group facing difficulties and not having support from the new firm.

Japanese Steel Maker and German Engineering Firm: Case Study

The present M&A case study involves one of the biggest Japanese steel makers in the world. In December 2014 a medium sized German firm in the waste energy power plant production industry with 195 employees in Duisburg was taken over by the Japanese firm. The deal can be considered as a horizontal integration in nature, which means that the Japanese bidder has experience in the same field of business (besides producing steel). Positive about a horizontal acquisition, the Japanese bidder can support the target in strategic ways and with its knowledge. In a negative sense, sometimes the bidders have to let go of employees of the target firm as some jobs become redundant. It is also to mention, that before the Japanese investor overtook the firm, it was previously held for many years by several European financial investors. With the acquisition, the German target's management intended to realize several benefits. It aimed of becoming more globalized as a result of the deal. There is a steadily increase in competition in the European market for engineering solutions in waste disposal industry and for the establishment of waste energy power plants from biomass and gas. In spite of attractive (new) markets in Asia, the German small firm could not bid by themselves as they lacked human resources necessary. One of the German managers was quoted saying: "we could not make it to China without any support from outside. We just did not have anyone to introduce us to these markets".

The Japanese bidder side was interested in competing with the German technology of waste disposal energy power plants in Asia. In contrast, the German target firm thought of receiving Asian market access for their energy plant engineering solutions provided by the Japanese side. In this context, the technical leadership of the German target for waste energy power plant was a trigger for challenges from the overtaking the firm. Another German manager, Schmidt is quoted as: "They took our technology and we (the Germans) are left out". Interviews with German top management showed that the German management intended to receive bigger projects with a financially and more solid ground by the Japanese investors. For this, the Japanese investor were seen by the German target management as strong financial parent to be able to compete for bigger projects in Asia. Furthermore, it was attractive for the German firm to have Japanese engineers with especially experience and language skills in other Asian countries. After about a year, German management sees themselves as being almost wrongly informed. "They (the Japanese contact of the bidder firm) told us at the beginning that we go together to China to sell our (German) solutions; now they go by themselves". Also, even the Japanese headquarter gave the German target firm high autonomy for the European market. However, many business changes decided at the Japanese headquarters and the Germans then only had to run it. A surprise was that the Japanese headquarter asked the Germans themselves to come up with ideas to implement synergies. Besides strategic issues, communication issues were also mentioned to be a source of problems faced by the German managers.

Communication Difficulties

After the acquisition was done, the Japanese bidder firm moved their 20 Japanese employees from other European cities to the target firm. Aim was to establish the new European headquarter at the target firm location. However, even after 6 months, there was virtually no contact between the Japanese managers and target employees as all Japanese were located in the building next to the German firm – and even the dining hall for employees is separate (for Germans and Japanese) so that there is hardly any communication possible.

Mr. Meier from the German side: "I never see any Japanese around. For what did they take us over?" Also, at interviews (6 month after the acquisition), German top managers complained about a lack of communication from the Japanese bidder to the German target. Mr. Schulz (from the German side): "The Japanese was talking last week to all of us here in this room (where the interview took place), but I have the feeling no one understood what he was telling us (the Germans).

Japanese Expatriates to German Target Firm

Expatriates are managers sent to foreign subsidiaries for a limited time. This strategy is a common way for multinational firms to internationalize all over the world. Also the Japanese steel maker sent two additional (English speaking) Japanese managers form the Japanese headquarters to the target. These two managers even share their office at the same floor of the German target top management (in contrast to all the others who stay at the neighboring building). However, target management still complains that there is not enough information flow. Feeling at the target top management is that the Japanese bidder uses their technology in the Asian market – without any exchange given to them in return. Mr. Yamamoto (Japanese sent top manager) was asked about the speech he gave a week earlier to the Germans (mentioned above). He is quoted as: "I clearly told the German managers what my (Japanese) headquarter wants them to do".

It is clear that it is not only the language but also the behavior of people what brings frictions and problems. Japanese managers were satisfied with their information flow to the new venture. Mr. Yamamoto: "I gave all German managers lots of information." He admits at the same time: "The problem is that I am just transferring what the head office tells me. That means, decisions are taken in Tokyo – and I tell this to the German managers." The German managers on the other end hand, however, want to be more involved in decision making, and want to know in detail who the decisions took at the headquarters.

Due Diligence

A successful acquisition depends on a careful ex-ante investigation about chances and weaknesses of the target firm. This investigation is called "due diligence". Common are due diligences in different areas, e.g. in finance, in environment and in human resource (Hassan et al. 2016). Hassan et al. (2016) look at one potential reason for M&A failure: the business evaluation process. How do the components involved in this process influence the outcome of M&As? The authors find that careful assessment and selection of target firms can improve M&A performance.

Interestingly, the German managers mention that target firms are often not reasonably assessed due to acquiring firms reluctance to use professional outsiders for this and the vague definition of valuation parameters. Moreover, literature finds that "the professionalism [of the evaluation] has also been tailored to suit the excitement of the management to enter into the M&A transaction." (Hassan et al. 2016).

In this case study, the due diligence process was conducted by a professional law firm, but only lasting a few weeks in time. The German top management was surprised by this action because lawyers from big consulting firms are not familiar with peculiarities of the given industry (in this case, of waste disposal plants). Mr. Meier: "They did a due diligence with us in a week – and did not even ask about what we have in our (product) pipeline!" That means synergies were not satisfactorily investigated at all. Also, just a handful of target managers were involved into the deal. No others, even team leaders did not know anything about the deal before until it was signed.

What was seen as an efficient way to conduct business (by the Japanese management) at the first glance, turned out to become a more serious problem after the deal was done. In the first few months after the deal, the German management wondered what the Japanese want them to do. Mr. Schulz: "I have no glue what they want us to do in the future". There is no clear concept offered yet by the Japanese side, of how synergies should be realized. In this, German managers feel frustration because Japanese side does not tell them where and when they want them to go and how that future is to be shaped.

Case Study Questions

1. How autonomous should the target be left after the merger deal?
2. Why are problems expected to increase in case the target employees have a low contact with the bidder firm?
3. To what extent should the Japanese business system be adopted to suit the German business context?
4. Identify the difficulties in communication between bidder managers and target employees that are apparent in the case study?
5. How fast should bidder managers move into the target?
6. What expatriate behavior is best for Japanese managers who are sent to Germany?

Publication Bibliography

Ahammad, M. F., Tarba, S. Y., Liu, Y., & Glaister, K. W. (2014). Knowledge transfer and cross-border acquisition performance: The impact of cultural distance and employee retention. *International Business Review, 25*(1), 66–75.

Bartels, J., Douwes, R., Jong, M., & Pruyn, A. (2006). Organizational identification during a merger: Determinants of employees' expected identification with the new organization*. *British Journal of Management, 17*(S1), S49.

Bauer, F., Matzler, K., & Wolf, S. (2015). M&A and innovation: The role of integration and cultural differences—A central European targets perspective. *International Business Review, 25*(1). https://doi.org/10.1016/j.ibusrev.2014.07.010.

Björkman, I., Stahl, G. K., & Vaara, E. (2007). Cultural differences and capability transfer in cross-border acquisitions: The mediating roles of capability complementarity, absorptive capacity, and social integration. *Journal of International Business Studies, 38*(4), 658–672.

Brannen, M. Y., & Peterson, M. F. (2008). Merging without alienating: interventions promoting cross-cultural organizational integration and their limitations. *Journal of International Business Studies, 40*(3), 468–489. https://doi.org/10.1057/jibs.2008.80.

Chung, G. H., Du, J., & Choi, J. N. (2014). How do employees adapt to organizational change driven by cross-border M&As? A case in China. *Journal of World Business, 49*(1), 78–86. https://doi.org/10.1016/j.jwb.2013.01.001.

Hassan, I., Chidlow, A., & Romero-Martínez, A. M. (2016). Selection, valuation and performance assessment: Are these truly inter-linked within the M&A transactions? *International Business Review, 25*(1), 255–266.

Hogg, M. A., & Terry, D. J. (2000). Social identity and self-categorization processes in organizational contexts. *The Academy of Management Review, 25*(1), 121–140. https://doi.org/10.2307/259266.

Jetten, J., O'Brien, A., & Trindall, N. (2002). Changing identity: Predicting adjustment to organizational restructure as a function of subgroup and superordinate identification. *The British Journal of Social Psychology/The British Psychological Society, 41*(Pt 2), 281–297.

Mael, F., & Ashforth, B. E. (1992). Alumni and their alma mater: A partial test of the reformulated model of organizational identification. *Journal of Organizational Behavior, 13*(2), 103–123.

Mael, F., & Ashforth, B. E. (1995). Loyal from day one: Biodata, organizational identification, and turnover among newcomers. *Personnel Psychology, 48*(2), 309–333. https://doi.org/10.1111/j.1744-6570.1995.tb01759.x.

Nemanich, L. A., & Keller, R. T. (2007). Transformational leadership in an acquisition: A field study of employees. *The Leadership Quarterly, 18*(1), 49–68.

Peng, M. W. (2008). *Global business*. Mason: Cengage Learning/South Western.

Tajfel, H., & Turner, J. C. (1986). The social identity theory of inter-group behavior. In S. Worchel & L. W. Austin (Eds.), *Psychology of intergroup relations*. Chicago: Nelson-Hall.

Yildiz, H. E. (2016). "Us vs. them" or "us over them"? On the roles of similarity and status in M&As. *International Business Review, 25*(1), 51–65.

Case 5: Dorian LPG's Rapid Fleet Growth: A Story of Maritime HR Planning and People Management

Maria Progoulaki and Konstantinos Tasoulis

It was another Friday evening at the office, when Dimitris was looking at the view of Piraeus port, thinking some words from the last meeting: *"We need to do what needs to be done, in order to be fully compliant, over and above regulations, industry standards and principals' requirements. Our commitment to compliance 'by-the-book' is our way of doing business, and money should be spent for this concept"*. Dimitris is the Chief Operating Officer (COO) of Dorian LPG Management Corporation, the wholly owned subsidiary of Dorian LPG Ltd. Dorian is tasked with the technical management of the fleet owned by the parent company. Dimitris has been also a member of the shore technical management team since 2004, when the shipping company was a small one, with three owned ships on the water (plus two under management from other owners), manned with less than 80 seafarers and 17 people ashore. The Chairman and CEO John Hadjipateras, holding a long experience on tanker vessels management, had announced the new strategy of the company. He envisioned his 200-year-old family shipping company running in a niche market, that of Liquefied Petroleum Gas (LPG) carriers. LPG was considered one of the energy resources of the future, and at that time (2001), there were very few ships in the world, specialised to carry this dangerous, liquid commodity. The number of competitors in the LPG market was limited. Entry barriers were high, due to stringent regulations and industry standards. Clients were also few, and already known to the management team, as the same oil majors were chartering Dorian tanker vessels for decades. The option to buy second-hand ships was not even considered, as the characteristics of the existing fleet (in terms of ship age, capacity, technology) did not match to Dorian's strategy which would focus on modern, fuel efficient ships with clear advantages over the existing ones.

M. Progoulaki (✉) · K. Tasoulis
ALBA Graduate Business School & Deree School of Business, The American College of Greece, Athens, Greece
e-mail: mprogoulaki@acg.edu

The company managed to raise funds from Norway and USA markets, and invested in building new, high specification LPG ships. The original order book of Mr. Hadjipateras to two world-class shipyards in Korea with the best know-how for this type of vessel included six LPG ships. In 2013, Dorian purchased the newbuilding contracts of Scorpio Tankers Inc. Scorpio, an emerging competitor with a different strategy and operational approach. Deliveries started in July 2014, with 16 new ships being delivered only in 2015, and 19 by February 2016, the company had more than tripled its fleet within a period of less than 2 years.

The rapid fleet expansion raised a great people management challenge. A vessel needs people to navigate her.[1] Consequently, an extensive Human Resources (HR) planning for both sea and shore based personnel was required. Considering the clients' demanding standards, the limited sources of qualified and experienced seafarers for the specialised fleet of Dorian, and the limited time for running the expansion and strategic HR Planning programme, the *'Dorians'* knew they were facing a storm ahead. Today Dorian manages a fleet of 22 Very Large Petroleum Gas (VLPG) carriers, with an original purchase price for the whole fleet of US$ 1.35 billion. The Dorian fleet represents 10% of the world Very Large Gas Carrier (VLGC) LPG fleet and holds the 2nd position globally.

About Dorian

Constantine Hadjipateras, the great grandfather of today's company Chairman, John, was born in the small island of Oinousses on the east side of Greece. The family shares a ship managing tradition dating back more than 200 years. The company was named after the Dorians (in Greek: Δωριεῖς, pronunciation in English: Dōrieis), one of the four major ethnic groups in Greece during 2000 BC. The founder highly valued his family's reputation, on which trust with business partners and industry stakeholders was built and fructified throughout the years. The company's philosophy is based on five key values: (i) respect for the customer, (ii) commitment to quality, (iii) appreciation of each and every worker, (iv) contribution to community and environmental sensitivity, (v) tradition of hard work and modesty. The company is committed to safety; *"safety does not merely happen- it is the reward of good management, good housekeeping and good procedures"* ("Dorian LPG- Health, Safety, Environment and Quality", n.d.). Dorian S.A. was established in 1973. The Hadjipateras family holds experience and expertise on managing tanker vessels for the transportation of crude oil, which later expanded to the management of LPG ships. In 2000, the company owned a fleet of three LPG vessels, managed by third parties. Dorian started to manage its own LPG ships in 2002. The forward thinking strategic decision to focus on the LPG market was based on the belief that LPG energy fuel production and consumption would increase in the future, as the world increasingly looks for cleaner energy. Thus, the LPG market was evaluated as an attractive and profit-promising segment in the shipping industry, with entry barriers

---

[1] The use of the pronoun 'she' to refer to a ship is a common practice in the shipping industry.

feasible for Dorian to surpass. Competition back in 2000 when Dorian entered the LPG market was limited with very few players. Nowadays major global competitors in the VLGC market that Dorian operates include BW Gas, Exmar, Avance Gas, Astomos Energy and others.

Today Dorian provides in-house commercial and technical management services for its fleet, including its vessels participating in the Helios Pool LPG (Helios Pool) (Singapore). The company operates a fleet of 22 modern VLGCs, including 19 new fuel-efficient 84,000 cbm^2 ECO-class^3 (eco-) VLGCs and 3, 82,000 cbm VLGCs (the latter built between 2006 and 2008). The fleet has a total carrying capacity of approximately 1.8 million cubic meters and an average age of 2.8 years (as of April 30, 2017). The company has offices in Stamford, Connecticut (USA) where the headquarters are located, London (UK) and Athens (Greece). Corporate and financial management is operated by the Stamford office. Marine operations, technical management, Health, Safety & Environmental Management (HSE), supplies and accounting activities are run from the Athens office, while chartering, legal and commercial operations are conducted in London. Crewing (management of the seagoing personnel) is conducted by the Athens office, in collaboration with Magsaysay Inc. (Magsaysay) (the Philippines) and Pasat Ltd. (Pasat) (Croatia).

Timeline

In the first months of 2014, the executives' team had already started work in crafting of and executing a large fleet expansion programme. At that time, the team had to create a plan, seize its existing resources and needs, and be prepared for carrying out a complex and difficult project. A year earlier (July 2013) the company had managed to raise capital from the Norwegian Over The Counter Market (NOTC), which offered low liquidity, but whose players are familiar to the dynamics and conditions of the shipping industry. In February 2014, Dorian announced that it managed to complete a US$ 100 million Private Placement (with a plan to use the proceeds for the partial finance of the eco-class VLGCs under construction and for general corporate purposes including working capital and transaction costs (Dorian LPG 2014). Dorian closed its initial public offering on May 13, 2014 at an offer price of US$ 19 per share, and successfully stepped in the public domain on the New York Stock Exchange market (NYSE: LPG). In October 2013 Dorian announced that it has successfully come to an agreement with Scorpio to acquire its VLGC newbuilding contracts, associated deposits of US$ 83.1 million, and a cash contribution of US$ 1.9 million in exchange for US$ 39.9 million newly issued Dorian shares representing 30% of the Company's pro-forma outstanding shares. Concurrently with the completion of the transaction between Dorian and Scorpio, Dorian has also declared the

---

^{2}cbm: cubic meter (m^3), a measurement of volume that an ocean freight shipment can take, equal to space of 1 m wide, 1 m long and 1 m high.
^{3}ECO-class: ECO design of ship ensures improved fuel efficiency through incorporating hull optimisation, engine features and technical specifications.

two options that were acquired from Scorpio increasing its fleet to 16 'sister'[4] eco-VLGC with deliveries in 2014 and 2015 from Hyundai Heavy Industries Co. Ltd. (HHI) and Daewoo Shipbuilding & Marine Engineering Co. (DSME) (Dorian LPG 2013a, b). After the first few months of 2014, the enormous restructuring programme concerning the operation and HR management of Dorian in Greece began to take shape.

The company's ship newbuilding plan relied on the construction experience and expertise of HHI and DSME. Ships were designed to meet future international environmental regulations and deliver economic performance (ECO-class) with low fuel consumption engines and optimised hulls. The first two new built eco-ships were delivered in 2014, followed by a mass delivery of 16 in 2015. The last eco-VLGC was delivered in 2016, completing the fleet of 22 (including three regular VLGCs). On April 1, 2015, Dorian and Phoenix Tankers Pre Ltd. (Phoenix) began operations of the Helios Pool, a commercial pool of VLGCs whereby revenues and expenses are shared. The intention of Dorian is to pursue a balanced chartering strategy by employing its vessels on a mix of multi-year time charters, some of which may include a profit-sharing component, shorter-term time charters,[5] spot market voyages[6] and Contracts of Affreightment[7] (COAs) (Dorian LPG 2017). Dorian's major clients include: Exxon Mobil Corp., China International United Petroleum & Chemicals Co. Ltd., Royal Dutch Shell plc, and other oil and gas producing companies. Also, commodity traders (Itochu Corp., Vitol Group), and importers (E1 Corp., Indian Oil Corp.) form an important part of its business.

The Market of LPG Transport

Liquefied Petroleum Gas (LPG) is mainly a fossil fuel, which can be manufactured during the refining of petroleum (crude oil) or extracted from petroleum or natural gas streams emerging from the ground. LPG energy source, commonly known as propane or butane, is flammable but non-toxic gas, with multi-purpose applications in commercial business, transportation, production, farming, power generation, heating and cooking. LPG is transported in bulk via specialised ships or pipelines. The gas (propane, butane or in a blend of two) is carried in forms of ambient

---

[4] Sister vessels: ships that are of the same class or of virtually identical design; can be easily chartered under COA.

[5] Time charter: type of chartering where a merchant (charterer) hires the ship for a specific period of time, which may vary from days, weeks, months or years.

[6] Spot market voyage: type of chartering where the ship is chartered to carry an agreed quantity of cargo from port A to port B (voyage). The spot market is highly volatile, because commodities are traded immediately ('on the spot') and ships are employed voyage by voyage.

[7] Contract of Affreightment (COA): a contract according to which the shipowner agrees to carry goods for the charterer in the ship, or to give the charterer the use of the whole or part of the ship's cargo carrying space for the carriage of goods on a specified voyage or voyages or for a specified time. Under this chartering type, the agreement is usually on a consecutive voyage basis, and multiple vessels may be involved.

temperature under pressure, or insulated tanks at liquefaction temperature (-5 °C to -45 °C, depending on the gas mixture) under atmospheric pressure, or in combination of liquefaction temperature under pressure. Thus, the gas in an LPG tank is squeezed and occupies 274 times less space as a liquid, compared to the actual amount of energy contained. Demand for LPG has been steadily increasing the last few years (UNCTAD 2012). As of July 1, 2016, 234 fully refrigerated VLPG carriers were in service globally, and 52 on order (Corkhill 2016). The main trading route in this industry has been traditionally from the Arabian Gulf to Asia. With the emergence of Houston as a major LPG export hub and the 2017 initiated new locks of the Expanded Panama Canal, the US Gulf to Asia has become a faster, thus a more busy, trade route (from 45 to 25-day voyage).

Following Porter's (2008) five forces industry analysis model, Hokroh (2014) assessed the bargaining power of specific groups of stakeholders. In terms of competition, the international seaborne LPG transportation services are generally provided by two types of operators: LPG distributors and traders, and independent ship managers like Dorian. Vessels in the LPG market are operated under time, bareboat[8] or spot charters, or alternatively under COA. LPG distributors and traders use their fleets not only to transport their own LPG, but also to transport LPG for third-party charterers in direct competition with independent LPG shipowners/operators (Dorian LPG 2017). The buyers of transportation via sea are oil and gas companies, including several states of the Organisation of the Petroleum Exporting Countries (OPEC) and members of the Oil Companies International Marine Forum (OCIMF) (e.g. Saudi Aramco, Pemex, PdVSA, Petrobas, Statoil), and international oil companies (ExxonMobil, Royal Dutch Shell, BP, Chevron and others); the latter known as 'Big Oil' ('Oil Majors' in the past). The market is generally considered concentrated, while since 2014 a large number of investors were attracted to the biggest publicly traded oil companies (Rapier 2016). OPEC's decisions play a major part in pricing, because the OPEC countries produce the largest percentage of the world's oil supply.

The oil and gas industry has specific key entry barriers, affecting the decision to invest in this market: large initial capital requirements, patents of technology and innovation, ownership of resources, huge fixed costs of setting up a fully integrated operation, government regulations, predatory behaviour by cartels and relationships with governments (Gupta 2016; Jones et al. 1978; Llewellyn Consulting and Puma Energy 2013). Several market experts predict that new entrants will put negative pressure on spot freight rates as more vessels compete for same cargoes. The unprecedented levels of LPG produced for export in 2015, in combination with a balanced VLGC fleet drove spot rates for such vessels to near record highs of US$ 3.7 million per month by July 2015. A tonnage influx equating to a 30% increase in the VLGC fleet in 2016, had driven VLGC spot rates down to US$ 1.7 million a month by January and as low as US$ 405,000 a month by July 2016 (Corkhill

---

[8] Bareboat chartering: type of chartering agreement wherein administrative and technical assistance is not provided by the shipowner. The charterer is responsible for providing crew, operating expenses, insurance and port expenses.

2016). Yet, the LPG market has a much more mature spot market than other gas markets (e.g. LNG); it is not as big project-based as LNG. This allows Dorian to exploit the advantages of a multiple chartering strategy and the benefits of joining the Helios Pool, where the majority of its fleet is chartered in the spot market.

Strategic HR Planning and People Management

Considering the time schedule of the new ships' delivery, Dorian executives' team decided to craft a maritime HR planning and people management programme and execute it alone, without involving external consultants. Utilising the experience in managing and manning a fleet of six vessels (two oil tankers and four LPG), the challenge of HR planning was now linked to the company's fleet expansion strategy, thus the order of initially three, then six more, followed by the acquisition of 13, ending with 19 new VLGCs, and a fleet of 22 in total. The greatest challenge was to be prepared for the mass delivery of the new vessels in a very short span of time (about 18 months from first to last vessel delivery). The aim was to man the soon to-be-delivered vessels and enhance the staff ashore for the effective and safe operation of the fleet. The management team knew that due to the complexity of the rapid fleet expansion project in such a specialised market, the strict clients' requirements concerning Dorian employees' profile and the limited sources of available and appropriate seafarers, the cost for people management would increase enormously. However, the relative cost was taken as an investment in people, not a waste of money and a necessary element for the success of the whole project. The profitable market at that time did not require from the company forced economising; on the contrary, the conditions of the project allowed the executives team to proceed to operational actions needed for the future fleet to be managed effectively. The Big Oils clientele of Dorian had specific requirements for the qualifications and experience of the staff. Based on Tanker Management Self-Assessment (TMSA) programme, issued by OCIMF, vessel operators are encouraged to assess their safety management systems, measure them against listed key performance indicators (KPIs) and improve them based on the provided best practice guide. Oil companies exercise due diligence in selecting well-maintained and well-managed ships for charter (OCIMF 2008); part of their auditing process focused on the recruitment and management of the shore-based and vessel personnel.

The special conditions of Dorian's rapid fleet expansion dictated a difficult and complex people management system for the seagoing and the shore-based personnel. In the case of the office in Greece, the organisational structure of the company has been evaluated, and after analysing the workload, possibilities of merging departments and other options, the organisational structure remained the same during and after the fleet expansion; only the people flow increased significantly. The offices in Greece, UK and the USA managed recruitment (i.e. advertising job posts, receiving CVs, short-listing, interviews, selection and hiring) on their own under the approved plan, but all key hirings (i.e. manager level) were being individually approved by the Stamford office too. The number of Dorian shore- staff in Greece grew from 17 in 2002 to 47 people in 2017. Its sea staff strength grew from approximately 100 in 2002 to around 1000 in 2017, including stand-by seafarers. The pool of seafarers is managed by Dorian through a crew department in Greece (with a team of five), and the two manning outsourcers (Pasat and Magsaysay). Concerning the shore-based staff, an HR Coordinator manages administrative issues (hiring process, screening, short listing candidates), while key HR decisions (identifying the needs, setting the criteria, interviewing and approving candidates) are taken by the company's top executives.

For the office in Greece, the management's desire was to hire people ready to take on duty immediately. This led to headhunting and lateral moves of professionals for positions ashore, and luring with attractive remunerations, crew rotation and regular employment for the seagoing personnel. Dorian's low turnover for both sea and office personnel was a goal, due to TMSA's requirements for monitoring the retention rate. The retention rate was 97% for the sea staff and even higher for the shore staff. Although this can be generally linked to personnel's loyalty and job satisfaction, the management team understood that they had to question whether high retention rates ensure extremely high quality of employees. The clients' external auditors have highlighted the risk of very high retention rates, as this may hide retention of less effective workers.

Dorian's special recruitment, training and compensation people management programme (further discussed below) cost about US$ 5 million, for training the additional crew alone to meet the market's stringent standards. Today Dimitris confesses that

> *the high cost of implementing the maritime HR planning and people management programme was worth it; in fact, essential in our opinion. The company's principals communicated the need for such a people management cost to the shareholders immediately and very clearly, everything was transparent, and most importantly, logically justified. The HR cost was budgeted in the overall fleet expansion project, because it was needed to make the fleet operational at the standards we had built our market reputation on. Everyone, and critically our executive team and shareholders, understood and acknowledged that need signing off the necessary investment early on.*

Sea-Going People Management

The complicated fleet expansion project relied heavily on the careful crew planning, so as to ensure that within a year the company would have adequate number of fully qualified and experienced officers to lead the new fleet. TMSA aimed to ensure that all vessels in the fleet have competent crew who fully understand their roles and responsibilities, and who are capable of working as effective teams. Further, the clients' requirements emphasised on the qualifications and experience of the top four heads in the ship's hierarchy,[9] i.e. senior officers. The biggest challenge in the

---

[9] Ship's hierarchy and ranks: ship's staff is divided by the deck, engine, steward department and other. The captain (or master) is the ship's highest responsible person on board, acting on behalf of

hiring process was linked to the level of skills required per rank and the years of experience needed both on the specific ship type and the specific company's management system. Recruitment specifications were determined by Crew Requirements Matrices, slightly different among the Big Oil principals. In order to satisfy these complicated and demanding restrictions, Dorian decided to follow the stricter matrix. The main problem came from the *"time in the same type of tanker"* requirement. In the case of Dorian, this meant LPG ships, and more importantly similar LPGs to the ones Dorian was building (i.e. VLGC, the largest available size). This requirement narrowed the pool of available officers significantly. For this, *"the only remedy was to accept LPG qualified officers from different LPG types and sizes, and train them on the existing LPG fleet during the same period (four months in total, two times of two months each)"*. The COO explained that in terms of the required seagoing personnel it was extremely difficult to manage compliance to the customers' requirements if not rotating the top four senior officers more frequently and training on board the new-joining senior officers. The crew rotation plan was developed to ensure not only principals' requirements, but also satisfy crew's desire for a work- life balance. The idea was to identify the actual number of seafarers required in order to fulfil a position on board, depending on seafarer vacation (or employment) duration ratio.

The most difficult requirement during the expansion was the *"time with operator"* part of the matrix, which necessitated the company to go with the training programme. Until the fleet enlargement the company was also employing Croatian cadets (i.e. junior officer trainees on board). This development programme was ceased for 1.5 year, due to the urgency to train new fully qualified, certified and experienced officers. Each available cabin on board had to be utilised for the urgent training programme. The onboard employment was following the ship type's safe manning[10] restriction of minimum 22 (plus two cadets) while a few other vacant cabins existed. The cabins occupied by cadets were given to new trainees while 2 or 3 vacant ones (depending on the ship) were also reclaimed. A policy of maximum 5 trainees were imposed to ensure their training did not overwhelm the existing crew. It is worth noting that all new comers were senior officers, thus fully qualified and active professional sailors, being asked to be trained by the same-ranked colleagues on the specific ship type (i.e. VLGC) and the specific company's Safety Management System (SMS).

To assist on the speedy induction of the new entrants on board, Dorian developed in-house a web-based familiarisation programme that was offered before sign-on; the Dorian Training System (DOTS). While the company has been using third-party

---

the shipowner. The main ranks on board are: Senior officers (i.e. captain, chief officer/mate, chief engineer and second engineer), officers (or junior officers, i.e. third, fourth assistant engineers), and ratings (lower level crew of mariners without a certificate of competence). Cadet captain and engineer are unlicensed trainees that may also be part of the crew.

[10] Safe manning: describes the minimum number of duly certified deck officers and engineers, as well as overall personnel that every vessel must carry on board. The manning scales depend on the type and size of vessel, the trade in which she is engaged, and other factors (see IMO 2011).

independent training providers for the sea staff, they found out that the web-based training was mitigating the burden to group seafarers and train them in-class. The familiarisation training programme, mandatory by international regulations, describes the company's safety, quality and environmental protection policies and procedures. For other training programmes, Dorian appoints independent training providers per occasion. In terms of the cultural synthesis of the crew, the top management team believed that there was no time for testing; thus, decided to retain the known crewing companies for outsourcing foreign crew. Pasat and Magsaysay were already supplying the company with Croatian officers and Filipino ratings. The previous experience of the company with the employment of Croatian seafarers was utilised. Dorian's order to its officers' supplier Pasat was clear: *"The fleet expansion does not allow us to be dependent on a single country for the provision of senior officers"*. In order to reduce the cultural shock, the supplier targeted countries that have similar or close cultural profile to the Croatian and compatibility to the Filipino culture for matching to the commonly used cultural mix on board. Since the market of Croatian senior officers with experience on LPG ship operation was saturated, Pasat was directed to turn for LPG officers in Latvia, Russia and Ukraine; these countries are the ones recognised for the seafarers' expertise on LPG ships, along with India. The two main concerns in the selection of the seagoing labour sources were: the manning cost being influenced by the average market wages, along with the cultural synthesis of the crew per ship. For instance, a mixed nationality crew of Croatian officers and Filipino crew was less costly than a single nationality Croatian or Indian crew.

The compensation function of the seagoing personnel has been also affected by the fleet expansion and the maritime HR planning programme. The competition in the LPG market has long introduced a complex and expensive compensation system, comprising a base salary [way over the minimum wage of the seafarer collective bargaining agreement (CBA) as per International Transport Workers Federation (ITF)], owners' bonus and stand-by wages. Dorian aimed at developing an overall pay package that would attract experienced officers without resulting to an unsustainable crewing cost structure. Seniority bonuses (recognising serving time with the company) and pay allowance for time spent under shore training were some of the key benefits, apart from the basic salary and owner's bonus, that were adjusted for each rank individually to achieve that goal. All pre-existing benefits were honoured despite sometimes being not of insignificant cost. Other factors considered in the design of the compensation package, included: market perceptions towards the expertise of the seafarers of certain education and training, attractiveness of the salary in the targeted labour markets, competition with other shipping companies, cost of living in the source countries. On another point, stand-by wages represent a common practice in the tanker and gas market, as a way to retain an officer available for the company, while the sailor is off duty (not sailing). The free-lancing character of the seafaring profession has been a common problem for many shipping companies in the tanker shipping sector struggling to find appropriate quantity and quality of seafarers to man their fleet; offering attractive financial perks has been widely used as an attraction tool (Progoulaki and Theotokas 2010). Stand-by wages may be of the same or reduced level of a working salary, but represent an important element of the overall pay package.

The big investment of the company to new recruits, training, compensation and rewards was very much linked to the need for ensuring a high retention rate of the sea personnel. Retention can be a difficult task in a market where seafarers are freelancers (Progoulaki 2012). Apart from the stand-by wages, the company had to apply a working scheme (as agreed in the seafarers contracts) that would satisfy the need of the seafarers for sufficient time ashore to spend with their family and friends. The contract scheme that applies today varies: 3 months on board and 2 or 3 months ashore.

The crew planning and rotation was received by the investors and shareholders of Dorian as a proof of commitment and 'by-the-book' focused management aiming at retaining high quality at all levels. However, the existing seafarers felt threatened by the new comers on board and the company's expanded pool. It was the personal intervention and declaration of Dimitris and other managers (i.e. Crew Manager) in conferences and officers meetings explaining and communicating the company's strategic plan and clarifying that future jobs were to be ensured, that eased their concerns.

Shore-Based People Management

In the case of the office in Greece where the technical, operation and crew key ship management functions are taking place, the team of the shore-based personnel had to be enhanced. Hirings ashore have been taking place in parallel to the normal ship management operations and the recruitment of the seagoing personnel. Similar to the sea staff, the job description for all shore-based positions followed the requirements of the TMSA (OCIMF 2008). The aim of the TMSA is to ensure that the fleet is supported by key staff that is competent to carry out the full range of responsibilities and tasks. Thus, the recruiters of the company should check and verify validity of the new recruits' qualifications, offer a formal familiarisation, and identify any training needs. Moreover, the ship operator monitors the job retention rate, encourages and supports additional and higher education courses, and promotes appropriate interpersonal skills training.

Under the fleet expansion project, the shore staff recruitment strategy was to hire experienced and ready-to-work maritime professionals so as to enhance the existing teams and cover the extreme workload of operating the existing and expected new fleet, especially the 16 new vessels to be delivered all within 2015. The number of people ashore more than tripled; since there was no room for the new comers, the Greek branch moved to new premises in Athens, in order to facilitate the enlarged shore-based operations. The recruitment and selection process was done using regular tools, like advertisements, screening of applications, and multiple interviews. For key positions, attractive remuneration schemes were offered to professionals being employed elsewhere. The single HR Coordinator was in charge of the process, while the executives' team conducted all interviews and the Stamford office approved the hirings, especially of new managers. Some additional rewards like private insurance, company mobile phone and laptop are also provided today.

With regards to the cultural synthesis ashore, almost all of the people working in Athens were and are Greeks, while in the UK the majority is local nationals, with limited presence of foreigners (i.e. a Greek, an Indian, and two Danes). The Stamford team generally comprises Americans with a couple of Indians too. In terms of turnover, there have been only two resignations due to promotions not being offered internally, thus career stepping up was offered from other companies. Overall, retention rate was extremely high for the shore staff. The main challenge that the executives' team had to deal with when increasing the number of people in the Athens office, was related to the varying corporate cultural values, working practices, professional behaviours and perceptions of the new entrants, when mixed to the old Dorian team. The new entrants were joining Dorian, coming from small or big tanker management companies. They were carrying knowledge and experience of the strict regulatory framework and the tanker industry standards, but also a different working culture - sometimes more laxed, more cost- prioritising or less quality-oriented culture. As Dimitris noted, *"we managed this by clearly communicating from the very beginning the strategic priorities and expectations of the company, not simply with regard to the execution of the fleet expansion project, but mostly on how we want things to be done. The 'by-the-book' mentality towards safety and quality is in all our procedures and had to be followed by all employees, since deviations, alterations and of course, non-compliance is non-acceptable because it will ruin the reputation of the Dorian brand. This is extremely important for a NYSE-listed company"*.

The term "Dorianisation" of the new staff, either onboard or ashore, was coined internally to describe this process of getting all those new people on the same values and operating principles that Dorian had been working on to that point and intended to preserve going forward – its culture.

The Outlook

"With the delivery of the CARAVELLE [ship] and the sale of the GRENDON [ship], our fleet is comprised solely of VLGCs and firmly positions us as a leading operator of modern eco- VLGCs focused on providing safe, reliable and trouble-free transportation" –John Hadjipateras' words in 2016 signalled the successful completion of the fleet expansion programme. Dorian's main source of strategic competitive advantage is indeed, its large, modern, young eco-class VLGC fleet. In terms of future goals, Dorian is still in a growth mood, continuing to consider strategic opportunities, including the acquisition of additional vessels through joint ventures or business acquisitions and repurchases of its own securities (Dorian LPG 2017). While Dimitris, the COO and an ex-seafarer himself, emphasizes on the importance of a strict vessel maintenance programme, he also underlines the humans' role, both on board, and from shore: *"The truth is that anyone can order tomorrow a ship*

exactly the same like yours, if money allows. So, the only potential advantage can derive from the management of the fleet, which means, management of people that man the fleet or direct the crew from ashore. The expertise, experience of the seagoing personnel, the effective utilisation of these people, their learning ability, monitoring when the process has reached a plateau... people is the only thing that can make a difference in the long-run".

Case Study Questions

1. Discuss the key people management challenges that Dorian faced.
2. Examine the links between Dorian's business strategy, organisational culture and its people management system.
3. Analyse and critically Evaluate Dorian executives' decisions concerning the selection of crew, by examining the cultural compatibility.

References

Corkhill, M. (2016, August 12). *LPG shipping retains strong fundamentals. LNG world shipping.* Retrieved from http://www.lngworldshipping.com/news/view,lpg-shipping-retains-strong-fundamentals_44130.htm.

Dorian LPG (2013a, October 28). *Dorian LPG Ltd. Announces agreement with Scorpio Tankers Inc. to acquire its VLGC fleet.* Retrieved from http://www.dorianlpg.com/news-and-media/press-release-details/2013/Dorian-LPG-Ltd-Announces-Agreement-with-Scorpio-Tankers-Inc-to-Acquire-its-VLGC-Fleet/default.aspx

Dorian LPG (2013b, November 26). *Dorian LPG Ltd. announces completion of acquisition of Scorpio Tankers Inc. VLGC fleet and $250 million private placement and declaration of 2 options.* Retrieved from http://www.dorianlpg.com/news-and-media/press-release-details/2013/Dorian-LPG-Ltd-Announces-Completion-of-Acquisition-of-Scorpio-Tankers-Inc-VLGC-Fleet-and-250-Million-Private-Placement-and-Declaration-of-2-Options/default.aspx

Dorian LPG (2014, February 27). *Dorian LPG Ltd. announces completion of $100 million private placement.* Retrieved from http://www.dorianlpg.com/news-and-media/press-release-details/2014/Dorian-LPG-Ltd-Announces-Completion-Of-100-Million-Private-Placement/default.aspx

Dorian LPG (2017). *Dorian LPG Ltd. Quarterly Report pursuant to S13 or S15(d) of the US Securities Exchange Act, for the quarterly period ended December 31, 2016.* Retrieved from http://www.dorianlpg.com/investor-center/financial-information/default.aspx?section=quarterlyreports

Gupta, K. (2016). Oil price shocks, competition, and oil & gas stock returns- global evidence. *Energy Economics, 57,* 140–153. https://doi.org/10.1016/j.eneco.2016.04.019.

Health, Safety, Environment and Quality. (n.d.). Retrieved from http://www.dorianlpg.com/operations/hseq/default.aspx

Hokroh, M. A. (2014). An analysis of the oil and gas industry's competitiveness using Porter's five forces framework. *Global Journal of Commerce and Management Perspective, 3*(2), 76–82. https://doi.org/10.24105/gjcmp.

International Maritime Organisation (IMO) (2011, November 30). *Principles of minimum safe manning*, Resolution A.1047(27). Retrieved from http://www.imo.org/en/OurWork/HumanElement/VisionPrinciplesGoals/Documents/1047(27).pdf

Jones, R. O., Mead, W. J., & Sorensen, P. E. (1978). Free entry into crude oil and gas production and competition in the U.S. oil industry. *Natural Resources Journal, 18*(1), 859–876.

Llewellyn Consulting, Puma Energy (2013). *The changing face of the oil industry*. White Paper. UK, Switzerland. Retrieved from http://www.trafigura.com/media/1362/changing-face-oil-industry.pdf

OCIMF. (2008). *Tanker management and self- assessment, a best-practice guide for vessel operators* (2nd ed.). London: Oil Companies International Marine Forum.

Porter, M. E. (2008). The five competitive forces that shape strategy. *Harvard Business Review, 86*(1), 78–93.

Progoulaki, M. (2012). The choice of seafaring profession. In T. Pawlik (Ed.), *Handbook of container shipping management: Volume 3- Human element in container shipping* (pp. 11–38). Bremen: Institute of Shipping, Economics & Logistics (ISL).

Progoulaki, M., & Theotokas, I. (2010). Human resource management and competitive advantage: An application of resource-based view in the shipping industry. *Marine Policy, 34*(3), 575–582. https://doi.org/10.1016/j.marpol.2009.11.004.

Rapier, R. (2016, March 30). *The 25 biggest oil and gas companies in the world*. Forbes Retrieved from https://www.forbes.com/sites/rrapier/2016/03/30/the-worlds-largest-public-oil-and-gas-companies/#20fe6d731733

UNCTAD (2012). *Review of Maritime Transport 2012*. United Nations Conference on Trade and Development. New York/Geneva: United Nations. Retrieved from http://unctad.org/en/PublicationsLibrary/rmt2012_en.pdf

Case 6: Appraisal at Systel Technologies

Mathew J. Manimala, Malavika Desai, and Divisha Agrawal

Part-I: Appraisal at Systel – Review and Diagnosis

Systel Technologies is an embedded telecom solutions company that helps businesses across the telecom value chain to accelerate product development life cycles. It was established in 1989 and currently employs about 2400 people at offices in India, Canada, China, Germany, Japan, Sweden, the UK and the US. Among its clients are Fortune 500 companies such as Nortel, Nokia & Motorola. The company was born in a small garage in San Francisco. The founding team consisted of four partners, all of whom were software technologists working in US companies. They invested $200,000 to set up Systel in 1989. The company later relocated its headquarters to Bangalore in 1991. Systel's history can be divided into three phases. In phase one the company was just founded and the emphasis was on building technical competence. This was followed by a second phase, in which there was a sustained thrust on marketing. This was done through setting up of basic marketing infrastructure by recruiting marketing professionals and also modernizing the company website. During the third phase of its growth, Systel decided to restructure the organization into market-centric Strategic Business Units (SBUs). Accordingly they reorganized themselves into three divisions, namely, the semiconductor division, the terminal equipment division and the networking services division. They are also in the process of establishing a new SBU for the service-provider market to focus on wireless LAN technology.

M. J. Manimala (✉)
Indian institute of Management, Bangalore, India

M. Desai
King's College, Kathmandu, Nepal

D. Agrawal
University of Allahabad, Allahabad, India

© Springer Nature Singapore Pte Ltd. 2018
A. Malik (ed.), *Strategic Human Resource Management and Employment Relations*, Springer Texts in Business and Economics,
https://doi.org/10.1007/978-981-13-0399-9_20

Systel is a very organic type of organisation, with very few hierarchical levels in the work place. The total number of levels in the organization including the CEO is only five. The company is known in the software industry for its work culture and innovative human resource policies. One such well-known policy of Systel is to differentiate people only on the basis of performance, and nothing else. Hence it was a top priority for Systel to have a frank and fair system of performance appraisal. As it is almost impossible to have a perfect appraisal system, there has to be periodic review of the system itself with a view to improving it. The system in place was in operation for a few years and therefore the management thought that it is time for a comprehensive review. For this purpose they recruited a specialist, Mr Nitin Parekh, to head their HRD department with a special mandate for reviewing the performance appraisal system as one of his immediate tasks.

Nitin Parekh is a graduate of the Xavier Labor Relations Institute (XLRI), Jamshedpur. While at XLRI he specialized in the HR stream and joined a banking organization in Delhi on graduation. He spent close to 5 years working in this organization, where his job was mainly to assist the senior professionals of the HR department. His initial job was to help the HR team of the organization in developing a set of guidelines for customer interactions of the bank's employees. Over the course of his 5 years with the bank, Nitin handled many responsibilities, in various capacities in the HR department, including employee recruitment, training and assessment. At the end of 5 years, he left the organization to move to his hometown of Bangalore, and took up a HR job in a software firm. He stayed with this organization for a period of 3 years and was working as the HR manager, with the special responsibility of the performance management system of the organization.

At this point in his career he was offered the job as the HR head of Systel Technologies in Bangalore. Before accepting this job, he wanted to have an idea of the HR policies of the company, and he obtained the following information. As mentioned above, Systel is a performance-driven organization. Such organizations require very good measurement systems and incentive schemes to identify and encourage good performers. Their efforts in this direction have led to innovations by their HR department in their systems and practices. These innovative, employee-oriented, human resource practices resulted in Systel receiving a Lifetime HRD Excellence Award from the National Human Resource Development (NHRD) Network. Systel's corporate credo, "People First", focuses on the importance it gives to its employees. They are what make or break an organization. This approach was successful at Systel where an atmosphere of mutual trust and respect exists, and the employees are motivated to work hard. Finally he found out that Systel was rated as one of the 'Best Employers to Work for' in a Hewitt Study in 2001, first in 'The Best companies To Work For In India', as well as first in terms of 'Employee Perception'. Systel was also a SEI Level 5 Company as of March 2002. In view of such positive features of the company's HR practices he decided to accept the offer. On joining the organization, the first thing that Nitin decided to do was to examine the Performance Management System, as this is perhaps the most important HR function in an organization, and as he had good experience in this area. His own views on the characteristics of an effective performance management system were as follows:

- The system should incorporate measurable characteristics.
- The system should not be susceptible to manipulation.
- Data on all aspects of the assessment as well as on the employee and his job should be easily available.
- Feedback should be provided periodically over the course of the evaluation period.
- Feedback should be provided on both individual and team performance.
- The system should enhance the effectiveness and efficiency of the deliverables.

The reason behind Nitin's decision to examine the entire Performance Management System was to see whether or not it was adequate for an organization of Systel's size and stature. The existing appraisal process starts with a self assessment by the concerned employees of their own abilities and performance, both on the job and in their individual capacities. This was then considered by the manager, and he gave his own inputs to the subordinate. The evaluation is deemed to be complete only when an agreement on performance and goals is reached by both the manager and the employee. Nitin's examination of the system revealed some deficiencies. One of the biggest deficiencies he noted was the fact that only the manager to whom the employee was assigned was allowed to assess him. In a software company, especially a large one like Systel with a matrix structure, employees work in dynamic and virtual teams and do not always work under the same manager. There is a lot of movement between teams, especially when there are important deadlines to be met and work needs to be done quickly. Also when employees worked on-site in different offices, cities or even countries, it would not be possible to report to one specific manager in a different location. It was hence difficult for that manager to gauge the employee's performance accurately and objectively.

Nitin felt that there is a need to improve transparency and to give clearer information on the reasons for fixing certain targets and goals. Another important problem he identified was that there was no system of normalization of the differences in the ratings given by different managers that is, one manager rating good performance as 8/10 while another rating the same level as 7/10. In other words, there was no system in place to counteract errors of leniency or severity on the part of the manager in rating an employee's performance. Besides, there were also issues of central tendency errors.

Noticing these deficiencies, Nitin decided to conduct an organization wide survey on the employees' views about the system. The study brought out some concerns of the employees. The major issues raised by them were as follows:

- The roles and expectations for the period of assessment had to be clearly defined.
- The existing process focused more on the deadlines rather than the quality of the jobs.
- Standardized benchmarks for evaluation have to be identified.
- There should be a standard format for the assessment.
- The present system did not allow for incorporation of changes based on the specialized nature of some jobs.
- There has to be a centralized 'storage' system that contains all the information regarding the assessment system, and also all details of an employee's performance in the organization.

Nitin was shocked by the responses of the employees. When he had found some discrepancies on his own, he felt that he was being overly critical of an organization known for its highly professional HR practices. Such unexpected responses on the part of the employees led Nitin to decide on changing the Performance Management System in the organization.

Part-II: Appraisal at Systel – Comprehensive Reforms

In his mission to improve the performance appraisal system at Systel, the first step taken by Nitin was to evaluate the present system of self assessment that has prevailed in the company for over 10 years. Nitin felt that the present system was ideal for a company like Systel where employees were given the first priority, leading to employee empowerment, mutual trust and respect. Self-evaluation was also the ideal approach for a company that has accepted the people-oriented philosophies, such as Total Quality Management, in an effort to improve organizational performance. He believed that self assessment allows the employees to asses their own performance and to come to conclusions about their performance levels and act on those to create a plan for developing and furthering themselves in the organization. Self assessment allows the managers to check their own assessment of their subordinates in terms of objective data.

Nitin strongly believed that self assessment results in a significant increase in the levels of commitment among employees and also ensures that the employee is an active participant in the appraisal process, not just a passive recipient of the evaluation. It internalizes the need for change in the employee and encourages him/her to take responsibility for his/her actions. This results in motivation coming from within, as opposed to external inducements. Another reason for Nitin's support for the self assessment system was his belief that the employee is the best judge of his/her performance and has the best idea about the work and the thought put into it.

The self assessment system also facilitates a high degree of involvement from the managers at Systel in evaluating their employees. They play a major role in assisting the employee formulate his goals and also in identifying the developmental needs for the employee based on the appraisal. Another important factor that made self assessment the ideal tool for Systel was that employees often had to work on their own and that it was difficult to be observed by others. In this scenario, self assessment is the ideal tool to provide an additional perspective on the employee's performance. Nitin also felt that, as the self assessment system had been in place at Systel for a considerable period of time, the employees were used to the concept. He did not want to bring in a completely new system, as the potential fallout might be harmful to the company. Besides, the practice of self assessment was highly appreciated by the employees in the survey that he conducted. Nitin concluded that the self assessment system was the ideal option for Systel, but realized that the way it was being implemented could be the source of problems. He then decided to delve deeper into the actual implementation of the system and the practices followed for evaluating an employee. He considered each of the major points of dissent that were raised by the employees and decided to tackle them in his own way.

Performance Measures

A major concern expressed by the employees in the survey was about the lack of quality in the performance measures. The most important part of a performance management process is to establish realistic and challenging and yet attainable performance expectations and standards. Nitin decided that a proper framework of performance measures that looked at all aspects of employees' performance was necessary. He wanted to implement a system that evaluated performance based on the employee's traits, behavior and achievements, thereby ensuring an all-round evaluation. At the same time, he wanted to stick to the five vital characteristics that any performance expectation or standard should possess. In effect, all the performance standards that he implements should pass the **SMART** Test (**S**pecific, **M**easurable, **A**chievable, **R**elevant and **T**imely). So he decided to implement a KPA cluster approach at Systel. KPA stands for 'Key Performance Area', which stems from the job description and is result-focused. A cluster can be defined as a 'grouping of similar things'. In the context of 'KPA Cluster' it refers to the grouping of KPAs with a related focus. Nitin identified the following KPA clusters to be used as performance evaluation criteria for Systel.

(i) ***Project Cluster:*** This refers to the goals that are to be achieved for the business to grow. They give a standard framework of what is expected of an individual. E.g. Requirement Analysis, Project Management, Innovation (For Business Units); and Vendor Payments/Quality Certification, Sustenance/Space Management & Contract Updating/Salary-Revision/Anti-Virus Management/ DBA (For Corporate Functions).

(ii) ***Process Cluster:*** These are KPAs which concentrate on the means to accomplish the project KPAs mentioned above. They guide the employees on how they need to perform and give them the means of accomplishing their goals. They refer to adherence to software engineering and organizational processes as well as tailoring the existing processes or defining new processes. E.g. Process Adherence, Process Definition.

(iii) **People Cluster:** These KPAs deal with the people skills of employees, their functioning in teams, and their customer interactions. E.g. Mentoring, Customer-centricity.
(iv) **Developmental Cluster:** These KPAs refer to enhancing the existing set of competencies or acquiring new ones through formal/informal ways, which help in the personal growth of employees and improves their participation in organizational initiatives, leading to greater organizational effectiveness of the company. E.g. Self-Development, Participating in Organizational Initiatives.

Nitin devised a system where the factors of each cluster of the KPAs are chosen and are assigned weightages according to the job profile of the employees and the time these employees spend on specific tasks. For example, a lower level programmer would have lesser weightage for the people cluster than for the project cluster so as to suit his job profile.

Goal-Setting

The next step was to tackle the problem regarding the transparency and openness in setting of goals by employees and managers. In the existing performance management system, employees and their managers set goals for the coming time period, one quarter, which were agreed upon by both parties. The problem that existed in this case is that while the manager knew what his goals were for the next quarter and could allocate work to his subordinates based on that, the subordinate did not know what part he played in achieving his manager's targets. Thus he did not have a clear picture of what he was doing and how it benefited the organization in terms of achieving its goals. This scenario percolated throughout the company from the CEO down to the newest recruit from an engineering college. This has created a situation where the employees worked to meet only their individual goals and paid very little attention to the overall organizational objectives. The general atmosphere therefore was not conducive to promote collective efforts by the employees to achieve the growth of the company.

In isolation, a performance appraisal system is just a procedure which involves the assessment of an individual's performance on a regular basis. But Nitin felt that it has to go much deeper. Performance appraisal lies at the heart of good business practice and it can effectively function only if the company has a clear picture of where it is heading, and has taken the necessary steps to ensure that it is taking its workforce along. Nitin decided to correct this situation by providing a more transparent system of goal setting and responsibility formulation for the next quarter. The first thing that struck Nitin on examining the system was that without a clear definition of the CEO's goals in the organization for the coming quarter, employees working directly under him would assume them without correctly knowing what these goals were, and hence fail to tailor their goals to meet them. Then the CEO would modify these according to his own thought process. In this exercise there was no dialogue which could clarify these assumptions. The same situation occurred at every level in the organization. Nitin proposed the following seven stage framework for goal-setting, hoping to remove the need for assumptions, thus bringing in transparency and clarity into the goal setting exercise.

- Planning: Employees plan their individual KPAs.
- Plan Forwarded: Employees forward the planned KPAs to the managers for approval.
- Plan Approved: Forwarded KPAs approved by manager.
- Plan Rejected: Forwarded KPAs rejected by manager, and alternatives discussed and agreed.
- Assessment Forwarded: Self-assessment completed and forwarded to the manager.
- Ratings Forwarded: Manager's assessment completed and forwarded to the employee.
- Accepted & Forwarded to HR: Ratings are accepted by the employee and forwarded to HR.

The advantages of this method are that the employees are allowed to question their manager's decision on their KPA's and then, depending on why they were approved/rejected, reset these goals. If there is still a disagreement regarding the goals between the employee and the manager, then the HR steps in and a compromise amenable to both sides is worked out. Another change brought in by Nitin was to make available to all employees the set KPAs of all superiors, right up to the CEO, so that they would be able to see the way goals have been set down the hierarchy and hence know his place in the fulfillment of the organization's goals. This would make it easier for the parties concerned, managers and employees, to set goals agreed upon by both parties.

Leniency, Severity and Central Tendency Errors

In any organization, the criteria to judge the effectiveness of the performance management system are essentially the same. These are Validity, Reliability, Freedom from bias, and Practicality. However, certain errors can creep into this system, and they can undermine the effectiveness of the performance management exercise, which would have an adverse impact on employee motivation. It takes a sizable amount of time, money and organizational effort to develop, implement and use a performance assessment system. The benefits of using such a system must outweigh the costs of organizing it. Moreover, the system should be easy to use, and should be widely perceived by both employees and management to be fair and free from any biases. There are two underlying issues that need to be considered in this regard.

Legal Issues of Fairness
An appraisal system would be free from legal problems if it is fair to all employees regardless of their race, sex, national origin, religion, etc. This is especially important for Systel, which has a presence in six countries. Nitin has therefore decided to adopt a uniform, company-wide HR metric, measuring all employees in the same

manner, regardless of their designation or location, along the same four dimensions of People, Project, Process and Development. This information was made freely available on the company intranet.

Freedom from Rating Errors

Ratings may be biased, either positively or negatively. Such biases may be intentional or unintentional. Nitin has identified a few such common biases; Leniency Errors: Employees receive ratings higher than what they deserve; Severity Errors: Employees are rated more unfavorably than they deserve; Central Tendency Errors: The evaluator rates all his employees close to the mid-point of a rating scale, so that it is difficult to differentiate between good and bad performers; and 'Halo/Horns-Efffect' Errors: This is the tendency of raters to allow their performance judgments influenced by a good or bad impression (incident) about the employee.

In order to counter these errors, Nitin decided to implement a standard seven-point scale with descriptions of achievement for each point, by which to judge employee performance across the board. Additionaly he introduced a rigorous normalization methodology for reducing the impact of such errors. For example, if a particular rater gives a maximum of 80 on a 100-point scale, and another gives a maximum of 60, the two groups of rating are brought under normal curves to enable a valid comparison between the two groups (where the value of 80 and 60 are equated and other scores adjusted accordingly).

The Rating

In order to tackle the problem of benchmarks in rating, Nitin decided to introduce a standardized system of assessment with which each factor of the KPA can be evaluated by the manger. So he implemented a rating system with seven stages on a scale ranging from 1 to 4, where each stage clearly defines the level of achievement of the KPA for the corresponding score. The following table shows the rating scale he introduced.

Score	Rating point explanation
1.0	Results not met the expectations and no efforts towards meeting them.
1.5	Results not met the expectations and inconsistent efforts made.
2.0	Results not met the expectations despite the consistent efforts.
2.5	Results met some of the expectations.
3.0	Results met all the expectations.
3.5	Results have exceeded the expectations.
4.0	Unique & exceptional achievement of results.

The managers and employees are expected to map the respective 'Performance Standards' against a performance measure defined in the KPAs to the ratings detailed above. Nitin also clarified that a minimum score of 2.4 is necessary for the performance to be rated as satisfactory. Employees who score below 2.4 are to be classified as low performing employees. But Nitin instituted a system of monitoring these employees and giving them sufficient opportunities to improve themselves before taking any action. He also decided to increase the frequency of appraisal to help monitor their progress better.

Standardization and Customization

Nitin noticed that even though the existing Performance Management System had a certain structure, this was not standardized, and differences cropped up when comparing scores across the organization. He also noticed that certain employees had to perform different roles at different points in the evaluation period of one quarter. This aspect was not recordable in the existing system and due to this a fair appraisal of those employees was not possible as certain aspects of their jobs were not included. Another point missing in the present system, as mentioned earlier, was the lack of a methodology by which employees working under different managers in Systel could be appraised by all the concerned managers. Taking all these points into account, Nitin decided on the KPA cluster as a standardized tool for evaluations. Within this tool, Nitin incorporated the possibility of recording scenarios where more than one job could be added into an employee's evaluation, and more than one manager could do the rating. Thus the evaluation was not complete for any employee until each role handled was assessed, and each manager evaluated the employee and agreed upon the ratings. Thus, he made sure that the problems of the employee working under different managers, in different locations, or in more than one role with differing responsibilities are taken care of by an objective system which gives fair evaluations of all that an employee has done.

Comprehensive Portal

On examining the employees' request for an all-encompassing system of data retrieval and evaluation, Nitin realized that such a system would make it easier for managers to access all the required information regarding an employee's performance and also come to a fair assessment quicker and in a more relaxed manner. Thus, as a logistical issue alone, it was appealing. Taking into account the added advantages for the performance evaluations, he felt it was worthwhile, and developed a system which would thus grant access to all aspects of an employee's job, as requested by them in the survey conducted.

Part-III : Appraisal at Systel – The Reform and the aftermath

About a year after Nitin implemented these changes into the Performance Management System at Systel Technologies, he wanted a survey done on whether or not they were successful, both from the employees' and the managers' points of view. Since the changes in the system were internally initiated, Nitin wanted an unbiased external agency to conduct the survey and analyze the data collected. In order to achieve this objective Nitin took the help of a professional HR consultant. The consultant prepared a questionnaire taking into account the changes made by Nitin, and adding some questions regarding any other changes the employees of Systel might want. This questionnaire was handed out to a wide cross-section of employees, right from the top management to freshly recruited engineers. Their responses were tabulated and an average score was computed for each question, which are reported in Table 1.

From the responses obtained to these questions the consultant arrived at the following conclusions regarding the changes implemented by Nitin. The scores obtained on the first three questions were all higher than 3.80. This indicated a strong agreement of Systel employees on the matter of percolation of company goals through the hierarchy, suggesting that the changes implemented by Nitin in this regard were successful and yielded good results. The employees also expressed a high degree of agreement to question number twelve, regarding their ability to accept, modify or reject the evaluation done by their managers. This shows that the appraisal system implemented by Nitin was flexible and respected the appraisees' inputs. For question nineteen the employees answered with a very high average score of 3.65. This indicated a strong agreement on the part of Systel employees that they were now properly evaluated by managers, even if working in different locations and under different managers. This was one of the main aims of the changes implemented by Nitin and has been a great success. For question sixteen, the average score obtained was 3.58. This tells us that any errors of leniency, severity or central tendency have been successfully reduced by the implementation of a scheme of normalization in the ratings given by various managers. In addition to these conclusions arrived at by the consultant, he also made some recommendations, based on the findings of the survey.

360-Degree Appraisal

The survey registered a 3.97 score favoring a peer evaluation in addition to the existing system. So, the consultant recommended that Systel should implement a 360–Degree Appraisal System. This is a system of appraisal where performance assessment is made using various sources of feedback that would be relevant to the assessment. As Systel's current performance evaluation system uses the feedback from employees and their superiors, the consultant reasoned that adding subordinates and peers to the list will help in increasing the effectiveness of the system. The open and participative culture of Systel would make it an ideal environment to implement the new system. The consultant recommended that the system be implemented with a focus on development so as to avoid apprehensions among the participating groups about a win/lose attitude that so often accompanies promotion and compensation decisions.

Table 1 Survey results

Q. no.	Items	Average score out of 5
1.	Every employee understands where the management is trying to take the company (The long term goals of the company)	3.81
2.	Your department's goal relates to the above mentioned goal of Systel.	3.86
3.	You understand how your job contributes to the overall department and company goals	4.11
4.	Your training and development needs are reviewed regularly, to ensure that you continue to have the skills needed on the job.	3.14
5.	The appraisal presents a true reflection of your work.	3.36
6.	You would like the current appraisal system to be changed in some ways.	3.58
7.	The appraisal system adequately covers all areas of your strengths and weaknesses.	3.14
8.	You are happy with the quality and frequency of feedback that you receive from your supervisors/managers.	3.47
9.	You would like to increase (5)/decrease (1) this frequency.	3.58
10.	You are told areas in which improvement is expected as a result of the appraisal process.	3.50
11.	You agree with your supervisors/managers on what is expected from you, as a result of the appraisal process.	3.50
12.	The current system enables you to reject/modify the appraisal in some way after your manager's evaluation.	3.92
13.	The goals, objectives and action plans are clearly laid out in the performance appraisal system.	3.47
14.	Adequate follow up actions have been taken with regard to past appraisals.	2.83
15.	The system is subject to leniency (5)/severity (1) errors. (Leniency/Severity of manager on employee's performance)	3.18
16.	The appraisal system is objective (managers' personal feelings/biases are not brought into it).	3.58
17.	The system allows work done under other managers/departments to be included.	3.34
18.	Innovation gets priority in the appraisal.	3.44
19.	The performance appraisal system used is effective even if you and your manager are working in different locations. (On-site assignments)	3.66
20.	You are happy with the compensation/advancement decisions made on the basis of your appraisal.	2.57
21.	The client (for whom work is being done) should also have a certain role to play in the evaluation and appraisal process.	3.56
22.	The appraisal captures any new skills/competencies acquired outside of, but related to, your work environment.	3.36
23.	The feedback covers sharing of new/acquired experience or special knowledge.	3.25
24.	You undergo training for your role in the appraisal process.	2.97
25.	You prefer a comprehensive peer review at the end of a team assignment to assess individual contribution, enthusiasm and teamwork in addition to the existing system.	3.97

1 = strongly disagree; 2 = disagree; 3 = neither agree nor disagree; 4 = agree; 5 = strongly agree

Adequate Follow-Up

It was found from the survey that the employees registered a score of 2.83 on item 14, which shows a feeling that there was not enough follow-up on the previous appraisals. The consultant made it clear that performance appraisal is not an end in and of itself – it is just a means to an end. It is only a part of an ongoing performance management process that starts with planning and identification of the goals and objectives of the organization and ends with the training and counseling given to the employees to improve their performance based on the results of the appraisal. After discussions with the employees and managers, the consultant discovered that the initial feedback mechanism was designed when the organization was in its early years and was following a linear structure. However, after the restructuring of the organization into various Strategic Business Units (SBUs), the needs and requirements of the performance management system are now much broader than before, because of the inherent differences in the type of work done and roles played by the various employees in the different SBUs. It was thus obvious that the performance management should capture this difference in the new organization structure. The consultant recommended that the employees undergo training programs as identified in the appraisals to enable them adapt better to the changing environment as mentioned above. These training programs are to be coordinated with each training cycle in the organization such that the employees are trained in whatever skills they are lacking in.

Appraisal Training

The survey results showed that the employees scored an average of 2.97 on item 24 regarding appraisal training, which shows that they were not being properly trained to participate in the appraisal process. Any appraisal process will prove to be effective only when it is performed correctly with the evaluators giving reliable and accurate ratings. This can be ensured by providing adequate training to the employees on how to participate in the appraisal process and what is required from them. So the consultant recommended that appraisal training should also be included in the training package for employees on a more regular basis, along with the follow-up training.

Compensation

The employees showed a strong disapproval for the way appraisal was used for making was compensation decisions, as is evident from an average score of 2.57 on item 20, which is the lowest among the 25 items. This might have been partly due to the fact that the timing of the questionnaire coincided with the announcing of a policy change regarding compensation. But the figure is significantly low to be a cause of concern. This issue cannot be just looked upon as a HR issue, as it involves

Case 6: Appraisal at Systel Technologies   207

other broader issues of company policy. So the consultant recommended that the Board of Directors sit with the HR department and review the compensation system in place and make the required changes in line with the organization's policies and goals.

Questions for Discussion

1. Distinguish between performance appraisal and performance management.
2. Discuss the feasibility and desirability of fixing and periodically reviewing the KPAs for each employee. Would it be better to do this exercise for job-categories rather than for each individual employee?
3. While trying to bring about transparency in the appraisal system and processes, is there a risk of violating confidentiality? How should Nitin bring in transparency without violating confidentiality?
4. Which method of appraisal do you think is the best for ensuring fairness and objectivity? Is it possible to completely eliminate subjectivity from appraisals?
5. What should Systel do with the appraisal outcomes? Should they be used only for giving feedback to employees? Or, should they be used for identifying training needs, improving performance, and/or deciding on increments and promotions?
6. Do you think it was appropriate on the part of Nitin to enlist the services of a consultant to review the appraisal system? What are the relative merits and demerits of engaging consultants for such reviews as against doing it internally?
7. Comment on the recommendation of the consultant to replace the present system with 360-degree appraisal. What other degrees (like: 90, 180, 270, 540, and 720 degrees) could be considered in the case of Systel and why? What are the cultural and operational barriers of implementing 360-degree appraisal system in Indian organizations?
8. Based on a review of literature on appraisal, examine the rationale and legitimacy of different systems of appraisal. Which one would you recommend for Systel?

Case 7: Patanjali: The Black Swan

Shashwat Shukla

When one of India's foremost news magazine puts you on their front page then you have certainly arrived. However, when the issue is closely read by stock market analysts who are understanding the dynamics of Indian stock market then there is something happening which is disruptive to say the least and a black swan to say the most. The person in question is Ramdev Baba of Patanjali, the most dynamic businessman in India, who continues to create a complex supply chain of products based on his learnings not from Havard but Haridwar, a pilgrimage site in the foothills of Himalayas. So why are the investors and consumers putting their bets behind this monk, fondly called Baba Ramdev by his followers? And here we enter the heart of the paradox. At one level he is a sadhu, an aesthetic, a monk and as a monk he has to leave his family, adopt a new name, and live a frugal life in a monastery or ashram as it is called in India. In these Ashrams the monks are usually engaged in religious practices, reciting hymns, offering prayers, doing rituals, doing meditation and reading religious scriptures. Ashrams have Hindu devotees coming to them for listening to religious discourses of the monks and conduct religious activities. Baba Ramdev has done all this and continues to do so, yet paradoxically, surprisingly and astonishingly he has been able to use the ethos and working principles of ashram ecosystem to create Indias's most ruthless, ambitious and expansive business organization with global ambitions. He himself is one the richest men in India.

It is this paradox which has added to his leadership style. He was asked this question in a recent interview (http://indiatoday.intoday.in/story/baba-ramdev-patanjali-yoga/1/714332.html) as to *"why is a self-proclaimed renunciate selling shampoo, toothpaste, detergent and anti-ageing cream?"* The answer is as follows, *"When I went to the Himalayas in my youth, I saw many sadhus who had given up the materialistic life. But what were they doing? Nothing for the welfare of mankind. That cannot be the purpose of life. In India, it's believed that sadhus can't do anything;*

S. Shukla (✉)
University of Allahabad, Allahabad, India

they are supposed to live on donations. It hurt me. The real goal of a sadhu is not to attain moksha for himself but to serve the masses. My business is not for profit but to spread wellness," Some indication that he is bringing in a new leadership mix to business organization. Black swan indeed!

Follower – Leader Interaction

Leadership in an organizational context can be viewed as an interaction between leader and followers. The premise is that leader and followers exchange certain psychological and social goods between each other. In Patanjali's case there was a pattern of communication choices exercised by the leaders in framing their business organization and engaging with the wider customer base. The next section focuses on the communication patterns by the leaders.

Communication: Use of Symbols and Sub Lingual

When leaders and followers communicate effectively amongst themselves it may lead to formation of a trusting relationship. It is this relationship which is the bedrock of effective leadership. Thus, one of the significant indicators of quality leadership may be the creation of trust between leaders and followers. The followers trust the leader's capability to lead them. The trust may broadly have two levels namely competence and intent. The followers should be able to trust that the leader is competent to lead them. The follower's perception of leader's competency is based on the past performance of leader. The issue of intent is more nuanced and is based on the observations of the conduct and mannerism of the leader. The two merge to create a shared opinion among the followers which may influence their trust on the leader. Thus the ability of the leader to communicate his competency and intent with the follower is very critical. In today's management scenario performance criteria are very complex. Thus the leader is faced with a huge challenge to establish his competency. He may do it by elaborating his past performance but since performance at senior management level is based on number of factors it becomes difficult to communicate them. Often we find leaders indulging in monologues in order to elaborate on their performances however instead of creating trust it leads to feeling of confusion and ambiguity amongst the followers. This defeats the very purpose of communicating about their competencies to create trust among followers. Another issue which emerges is that leaders are hard pressed for time and have limited opportunities to communicate with employees. The shortage of time also places constrains on the leader's ability to establish trust. Effective leaders have used symbols and sub lingual methods to communicate with their followers. The use of symbols simplifies the core message and does not place too much time burden on the leader. Effective organizational leaders have used powerful, symbols to establish their credentials. Some of the symbols which are used are as follows.

Education

The educational qualification of the leader is one very powerful symbol which the leaders can use. Generally the employees of an organization enter in the organization based upon their qualifications. Thus they tend to hold educational qualifications in high esteem. If the leader has superior education in respect to its employees then it helps the leader to garner the trust of the employees. Therefore it is common to find leaders in organization holding qualification from very prestigious institutes which are universally accepted as centers of excellence. If we look at the Indian scenario we find the use of education as a symbol is very extensive. Of the top 500 companies which are listed on the Bombay Stock Exchange nearly a quarter have CEO's who have educational qualification as MBA (http://www.livemint.com/Opinion/p2yxs2wI4dvdp0ouMDWRmK/The-Bschool-education-of-top-Indian-CEOs.html). A half of this number went to Ivy League B Schools in US and Europe. Of the people who received education in India one out of every seven CEOs calls IIM Ahemadabad as its alma mater. IIM Ahemadabad is the most sought after and prestigious center of excellence of management in India and was mentored by Harvard Business School in its initial years. This group of CEOs also includes many family run businesses that would have got the leadership position as a matter of inheritance. Therefore education has not only given business leaders intellectual depth but also legitimacy to hold leadership positions. They have been able to use their education as symbols of competence in order to establish their competence with the followers. The symbolism build around education is further strengthened by membership of educational bodies, professional associations and tieups with professional institutes. To use a specific example let us take the example of The Aditya Birla Group which is an Indian multinational conglomerate named after Aditya Vikram Birla, headquartered in the Aditya Birla Centre in Worli, Mumbai, India. Established in 1857 in the tiny village of Pilani, Rajasthan, the Aditya Birla Group took shape when Seth Shiv Narayan Birla ventured into cotton trading. Today, with operations across 36 countries revenues of US$41 billion, the Group is a leading player in aluminum, cement manufacturing, viscose staple fiber, chemicals, copper, insurance services, telecom, branded apparels, fertilisers, software, viscose staple yarn, carbon black and insulators. Aditya Birla Group's CEO Mr. Kumar Mangalam Birla, a much respected figure in Indian Business and Policy circles has adopted leadership choices that are distinct. Some excerpts of the publically available description from the Aditya Birla Group website is being put Exhibits 1 and 2 to highlight our above point (http://adityabirla.com/about/kumar-mangalam).

The key points which emerge from the above description are as follows: (1) Education has been given a prominent place in the description; (2) Even though Mr. Birla is inheritor of the Birla Group and acquires legitimacy on grounds of his shareholding, the symbolic value of education has not been overlooked. It is pertinent to note that Mr. Birla already had a credible education degree as he was a qualified chartered accountant yet he chose to get a qualification from London School of Business; (3) He has continued his association with academics in various forms in order to renew the strength of his education symbols; and (4) The description uses other symbols such as business performance to establish credibility. However business performance of an organization is a cumulative effort. If the leader tries to usurp the whole credit or is perceived that he is doing so then such an attempt will be counterproductive. Thus a business performance symbol is accompanied by education symbol. In using education as a symbol the individual performance can be highlighted and given more prominence. Thus, one may surmise that in today's knowledge economy where intellectual property is a very critical resource leaders have an incentive to use education as a symbol in order to communicate with their followers. The followers are likely to trust a leader whom they feel is competent. At the same time, it is interesting to note it is not merely the fact that the leader must be qualified, but also that his education in terms of prestige should have universal recognition for it to be used as a symbol.

Compensation

While the earlier section highlights how education of a leader can be used as symbol to establish trust of followers in shaping the competency of a leader. Another key symbol is related to the intent of the leader. The definition of a leader embodies the fact that leader is one who the followers look up to as benchmark for conduct and commitment. This brings in the issue of the ethical component of leadership. An ethically astute leader will have an equitable profit sharing arrangement in his organization. His/her compensation package should not be more than 50 times the median salary. In a specialized organizational framework the final output should be viewed as a cumulative of individual performances. It is generally very difficult to justify that one role would be attracting compensation greater than 50 times than that of the median wage in the organization. The greater the gap, the more likely it will lead to feelings of inequity. If the leader asserts his veto powers and his compensation is perceived as inequitable he will lose his ethical capital. Thus leader needs to be mindful of this aspect so that he may use compensation as symbol. If the leader is perceived to be ethical then forming a trusting relationship with employees may become easy. Exhibit 3 takes a look at the Indian scenario at some of the well-known Indian companies (http://www.livemint.com/Companies/LMSdocnyzGimu9lLcuctZP/Pay-gap-rule-India-ahead-of-US-only-in-timing-not-thorough.html). The exhibit clearly shows that apart from honorable exceptions like those of some of the Tata Group companies who are traditionally known to be highly ethical and are one of the most trusted brands in India (http://www.bbc.com/news/world-asia-india-37796748), most other organizations have very steep differences between the median salary of employees and their respective leaders. This has led to a leadership crisis which has engulfed companies across a spectrum of industry sectors from information technology to manufacturing (http://www.gadgetsnow.com/tech-news/Leadership-crisis-in-Indian-IT-Top-companies-opt-for-outsider-CEOs/articleshow/50480729.cms, http://www.firstpost.com/business/infosys-governance-issues-board-not-keen-on-tata-style-row-with-founders-3277596.html).

Demeanor and Mannerism

The leader may not be able to speak to each of his followers on an individual basis. Yet the followers recognize him as the leader and look up to him. In such a case where individual communication is not possible the mannerisms and style of speaking of the leader, allow the employees to get a glimpse of their leader. This fulfills to some extent the emotional need to connect with the leader. It also forms the basis for them to make an understanding of their leader. The larger social political environment of a country also has an impact on the expectation of the followers. In case of India the politico-social environment has seen as a lot churning with the coming of a right wing conservative party to center stage. The public discourse has shown inclination towards blunt, statement of fact approach rather than diplomatic and political correct statements. For an excerpt of media report read Exhibit 4 that points to this fact (http://www.business-standard.com/article/current-affairs/arnab-s-republic-hints-at-mainstreaming-right-wing-opinion-as-a-business-117012600235_1.html). The leader's mannerism needs to factor in these aspects as he/she may use sub- lingual cues to communicate with his/her followers. The leader may conduct themselves in a manner that is in sync with the macro environment of the organization. This may lead to a wider acceptance of their leadership style. If a leader's conduct is perceived in a positive light then he/she may be able to generate more trust with the followers. After having established the core symbols of leadership and how they are being used we shift our focus to Patanjali the firm and Baba Ramdev the leader.

Patanjali

There are many technology startups which have come in India in the last few years. Most of the startups which have made it big are in the business of online retail. Some of the big names are Flipkart, Snapdeal and Shopclues. These startups have scaled up rapidly. Most of these startups have been started by technocrats who have received education in the elite Indian Institute of Technology family of institutions.

The founders had good business exposure before they became entrepreneurs and they also received liberal venture capital funding. However one startup which has made big in this group is not a technology startup. Neither does it have promoters who have been educated and have had business exposure of working in corporate setup. This startup has come up in a sector where usually few startups come.

This is the area of fast moving consumer goods (FMCG), which includes toilet soaps, detergents, shampoos, toothpaste, shaving products, shoe polish, packaged foodstuff, and household accessories. These items are meant for daily and frequent consumption and often have a high return. This startup is Patanjali. The startup has been named after the legendary Indian monk who had written the most authoritative text on yoga. It is also intriguing to note that not only does Patanjali break the rules by coming up in a mature sector, which is dominated by big giants like Unilever and Proctor&Gamble but it did not receive any robust venture capitalist support which the other startups had received. To get an idea of the scale and extent of disruption and breaking of rules which has been caused by the birth of Patanjali we need to look at the Indian FMCG market. The Indian FMCG market is a success story because India is the second most populous country in the world. With such a sizeable population and disposable incomes the FMCG market in India is worth US$ 49 billion and is the fourth largest sector of the economy (http://economictimes.indiatimes.com/industry/cons-products/fmcg/indias-fmcg-sector-to-reach-104-bn-by-2020-study/articleshow/54697324.cms). Its projected to reach a whopping US$104 billion by 2020. With European and US markets maturing a lot of multinationals are shifting their focus to India to maintain their profitability and deal with intense competition. Well-established distribution networks, as well as intense competition between the organised and unorganised segments are the characteristics of this sector. The requirements of a wide distribution network, need for a powerful brand image, intense competition are steep barriers which make entry of new entrants difficult. Yet it is under these adverse circumstances that not only Patanjali has been able to gain a foothold in the competitive FMCG market but also make its presence felt. It is not often that the big Daddy of FMCG = Unilever acknowledges a new entrant but Patanjali has that to its credit as comments from Andrew Stephen, Head of investor relations at Unilever, who remarked that there are "a couple of great examples" in India in the herbal segment: "Patanjali, which everybody is looking forward to with lot of interest." (http://economictimes.indiatimes.com/industry/cons-products/fmcg/unilever-admits-to-new-competition-in-patanjali/articleshow/54926013.cms)

Patanjali has grown at a phenomenal compounded annual growth rate of 64.7% in the period 2012–2015 (Abneesh et al. 2015a).Growth is being driven by the company's largest selling product, cow's ghee(edible oil made from clarified butter) followed by Dant Kanti(a herbal toothpaste) and Kesh Kanti(hair oil) (Abneesh et al. 2015b). Patanjali also has a robust pipeline of new products, which will help achieve its target of becoming a US 1bn $ corporation by the year 2017. It has already achieved sales of Rs. 5000 Cr in 2016 and reaching Rs. 7000 Cr or a bit over US 1 bn $ in 2017 is easily achievable (http://economictimes.indiatimes.com/industry/cons-products/fmcg/patanjali-on-track-to-hit-1-billion-sales-in-fy17/

printarticle/51422878.cms). "Patanjali could become the fifth largest FMCG company in the country, after Hindustan Unilever ITC, Nestle India and Britannia Industries. This would bring it well ahead of traditional FMCG players like Dabur, Godrej Consumer Products and Marico." (http://economictimes.indiatimes.com/industry/cons-products/fmcg/patanjali-on-track-to-hit-1-billion-sales-in-fy17/printarticle/51422878.cms)

"…The company is focused on top line growth rather than profitability. Its business ideology is inspired by Swami Ramdev's ideologies to touch day to day lives of people through Patanjali products which will help the consumers and help Patanjali be present in all the segments where the consumers feel they can get a better product at a better price. The organization conducts its business on the following three main principles: (1) Providing world class products to consumers (making sure the company does not add any preservatives or uses natural preservatives as far as possible); (2) Producing products in the most cost effective manner so that the products are priced very reasonably; and (3) Whatever profits the company earns are ploughed back into business so that it can invest the same for launch of new products, cost effectiveness or further capacity expansion…" (Abneesh et al. 2015c) One of the factors helping the organization to scale new heights is the bold and dynamic leadership of its founder Baba Ramdev. In the next section we closely look at Baba Ramdev and his approach towards organizational issues.

Baba Ramdev

Baba Ramdev was born in a poor family of farmers to Ram Niwas Yadav and Gulabo Devi (http://www.divyayoga.com/trustees/swami-ramdev-ji/). There is little authentic source of information available about his early childhood. However our focus is on the perceptions which are widely shared and promoted by Baba Radev through his official websites. It is said that he was a sick child to begin with. In order to overcome his ailments he started practicing yoga regularly. Yoga is an ancient system of Indian exercise comprising of stretching postures, breathing practices and meditation. The health benefits of yoga have been extensively researched and widely accepted. After intensive practice of yoga Baba Ramdev was cured of his ailments. This sparked of his interest in Yoga and Ayurved: the ancient system of Indian living and healing through herbal medicine. He is said to have left his home and gone to Haridwar acity in the foothills of Himalayas to learn yoga. Little is known about the methods and process through which Ramdev learned and mastered the skills of yoga. There is no as certification from a government recognized agency for the practice and knowledge of Yoga which he has received. While learning yoga, Ramdev became a monk. As a Hindu monk, he left his family to live in a monastery, an austere and simple life. The monastery system in India is very widespread and is well organized. The monasteries have historically performed various functions apart from being religious centers. Some of these functions have been shelter places for travelers, helping civic authorities in time of natural crisis, and furthering research in Indian Ayurvedic system of medicine. These activities have been part of the spiritual ethos of social welfare and service to the needy. After being exposed to the monastery system Ramdev was motivated to use his knowledge of yoga and use it for health awareness. The monastery framework allowed him to start his yoga camps for devotees of the monastery. These small camps were the foundation on which future Yoga and related initiatives of Ramdev were built on. In later years Ramdev scaled up the size of his camps. However the turning point came in 2003 where he got the morning slot on a spiritual TV channel to teach yoga.

Ramdev simplified yoga postures and started teaching them through television. Some of his medical claims were unscientific but it was his communication style wherein he mixed religious scriptures, national pride, and common sense which struck a chord with the masses. In spite of several controversies he became increasingly popular. His typical yoga sessions included home/herbal remedies and yoga postures for specific diseases and disorders. In these yoga sessions he would bluntly target Multinational Corporations (MNCs) of exploiting Indian consumers with substandard products. He would extol virtues of Indian culture and cite that he is a monk and his only motivation was public welfare. This message from a monk found a lot of credibility and legitimacy in India, which was witnessing major revolution against corruption scandals at the time and increasing public disquiet about politician- business nexus. Ramdev would perform difficult yogic postures on stage which were cheered on by the crowds at his camps. Often he would randomly choose people in his camps to share their personal experiences of benefits they received from his system of yoga. With the live telecast of such camps Ramdev had become a household name. Soon Ramdev started to speak on national issues, specifically corruption and economic issues.

He started an enrollment exercise for a national movement against corruption and public welfare. Some of these volunteers became the future employees and distributors of Patanjali. With this backdrop Ramdev gave a call that he would be starting an organization which would free people of India from economic exploitation of MNCs. He declared that his organization would provide quality products at cheap prices using Indian Ayurvedic Medicine principles. This has become the core value propostion of Patanjali's advertising strategy and all their brands emphasize the benefits of these herbal formulations. Ramdev has declared that all the profits from Patanjali will be used for charity. He said that since he is a monk he would not take any salary or make any property and Patanjali would use all its profits for creating public goods. These messages had wide acceptance and appeal with the Indian public. Allegations were made that all the promises of Baba Ramdev are not being adhered to but they have not yet been able to change the positive perception that he enjoys. Infact he has claimed that he is being victimized for taking up public issues. He has tried to re-enforce and supplement his nationalistic image by associating himself with movie stars, sport stars, security agencies and politicians by inviting them to his yoga camps. Inspite of being the chief executive of Patanjali a big FMCG company, Ramdev is often seen in press discussing health and economic issues with policymakers. Ramdev has motivated his employees by extolling to them on same lines that they are working for a national cause. It is a usual site to find posters of national pride and heritage at Patanjali exclusive outlets. The application form for becoming a distributor at Pantajali is being appended in Exhibit 4.

The distinctive features of the form are as its appeals to its applicants like "…By the blessing of H.H[His Holiness] Param Pujya Swami Ramdev Ji Maharaj and the determination of Patanjali Ayurved Limited., cheap and best quality Swadeshi Product is to be made available to each and every household, I am a well-wisher and supporter of this movement and is committed to get rid of the foreign MNCs loot to make the country self-reliant and economic super power…" In this way it is enrolling its distributors for a national mission and a noble cause. Even though Patanjali is a commercial organization running on commercial principles the form states that "The Person who deals with the trade of Intoxication Business are not eligible to fill the form because our organisation is a Social and Spiritual Organisation". It is also interesting to note that the form also asks whether the applicant is already a member of the Patanjali family by being a volunteer in Baba Ramdev yoga camps. Thus the organization gives preference to its volunteers of yoga to become its distributors.

Baba Ramdev's attempts have borne fruit. A recent media report highlights that change is unfolding fast: "Patanjali is emerging as an 'Employer of Choice' as many professionals are independently coming forward to work with the company. During our visit and interactions we found there any many professionals who are managing different units and have past work experience in companies like Dabur, Shehnaz Hussain, SGH Labs, Alkem Laboratories, etc" (Abneesh et al. 2015d)These individuals have been inspired by the leadership style of Baba Ramdev. In its interactions with employees Baba Ramdev highlights the fact that he does not take any salary, live as frugal monk and works tirelessly. The massive sales growth, increasing employee strength, implementation of ERP indicates that his message has found support from his employees, distributors and consumers. There has been criticism that though Baba Ramdev doesnot take a salary and is a monk but he has a lavish lifestyle with all the comforts Ramdev lives in cottage named as Shant Kutir or Peace cottage in Haridwar. An excerpt of a media report who took his interview at the cottage is as follows "…Shant Kutir is a gated property spread over a couple of acres, and the cottage was built in 2009–10, modelled partly on Mahatma Gandhi's Sabarmati Ashram in Ahmedabad, Gujarat. The compound has no air of the frugality that Mohandas Karamchand Gandhi, India's independence hero, famously practiced. It is guarded 24 × 7 by the Central Reserve Police Force (CRPF), has a man-made water well and an artificial waterfall and watch towers. Neatly manicured lawns surround the main cottage. The cottage itself is air-conditioned, with Persian-design carpets and cushioned sofas in the room where Ramdev receives visitors. Ramdev, who is driven around in a white Range Rover Evoque…" (http://www.livemint.com/Companies/hLEBBx17cFY5rPjTjmIP9O/The-Patanjali-story.html) There are serious issues regarding corporate governance at Patanjali, which is not a listed company and it is difficult to get any verifiable data (http://brandequity.economictimes.indiatimes.com/news/advertising/baba-ramdev-in-trouble-again-25-patanjali-ads-violates-asci-code/53461109). One of the reasons for not being a listed company might be to avoid harsh scrutiny of these issues. Yet till now Baba Ramdev has been able to emerge as effective leader for his organization.

Leadership Issues

"…The media and analysts will agree that the top bosses of multinationals in India tend to be boring, strait-laced and politically correct. This is probably why Baba Ramdev, yoga guru, brand ambassador and maverick founder of Patanjali Ayurved, has been getting such rave reviews. He cheerfully does headstands while posing for press shoots, rants against MNCs for conspiring against him and 'looting' India, and puts forth revenue targets that are four times his last reported sales. The rise of Patanjali has inspired CLSA to write a wistful research note titled "Wish you were listed, Patanjali" heaping praise on the business model. Brand consultants have credited Patanjali with bringing about a "tectonic shift" in FMCG branding and there are stories a plenty about how Ramdev is set to oust the Unilevers and Nestles in India…" (http://www.thehindubusinessline.com/opinion/columns/a-reality-check-on-patanjali/article8710429.ece?css=print) Baba Ramdev and Patanjali are unique and have changed the rules of the game. Baba Ramdev's Leadership style has allowed Patanjali to become a very dynamic organization. It is relevant to note that few startups are attempted in the FMCG category. What is more surprising is that the leadership of this organization has come from a person who does not possess systematic business knowledge. It is this contrast the reader should ponder over in context of leadership.

Exhibit 1: Mr. Kumar Mangalam Birla's Profile

Mr. Kumar Mangalam Birla (49) is the Chairman of the US $41 billion multinational Aditya Birla Group, which operates in 36 countries across six continents. Over 50 per cent of its revenues flow from its operations outside India. Mr. Birla chairs the Boards of all of the Group's major companies in India and globally. Its clutch of global companies features Novelis, Columbian Chemicals, Aditya Birla Minerals, Aditya Birla Chemicals, Thai Carbon Black, Alexandria Carbon Black, Domsjö Fabriker and Terrace Bay Pulp Mill, among others. In India, he chairs the Boards of Hindalco, Grasim, Aditya Birla Nuvo, UltraTech and Idea. The Group's businesses are spread across a swath of industries. These include aluminium, copper, cement, textiles (pulp, fibre, yarn, fabric and branded apparel), carbon black, insulators, natural resources, power, agribusiness, telecommunications, financial services, retail and trading.

Beyond Business: Reaching Out to the Marginalised Sections of the Society

A firm practitioner of the trusteeship concept, Mr. Birla has institutionalised the concept of caring and giving at the Aditya Birla Group. With his mandate, the Group is involved in meaningful welfare driven activities that distinctively impact the quality of life of weaker sections of society, surrounding hundreds of villages that are among the poorest in India, Thailand, Indonesia, Philippines and Egypt. In India, the Aditya Birla Group is engaged in 5,000 villages, reaching out to 7.5 million people annually and making a difference to their lives through meticulously conceived projects focusing on health care, education, sustainable livelihood, infrastructure and social causes. For instance, the Group runs 42 schools which provide quality education to 45,000 children. Of these, over 18,000 children receive free education. Additionally, over a 100,000 youngsters benefit from bridge educational programmes and vocational training. Its 18 hospitals tend to more than a million villagers. In line with its commitment to sustainable development, the Group has partnered with the Columbia University in establishing the Columbia Global Centre's Earth Institute in Mumbai. To embed CSR as a way of life in organisations, the company has set up the FICCI – Aditya Birla CSR Centre for Excellence in Delhi.

Educational Background

A commerce graduate from Mumbai University, Mr. Birla is a Chartered Accountant. He earned an MBA from the London Business School.

Personal Details

Born June 14, 1967, in Kolkata, Mr. Birla was raised in Mumbai. Mr. Birla and his wife, Mrs. Neerja Birla, have three children, Ananyashree, Aryaman Vikram and Advaitesha.

Exhibit 2: The Earning Disparity in Indian Companies

EARNINGS DIVIDE

Among the top 20 companies in India, on an average, a chief executive earned 289.5 times the median salary of employees.

COMPANY	NAME	CEO/CMD salary (in cr)	RATIO OF CEO PAY TO MEDIAN SALARY	MEDIAN PAY OF EMPLOYEES (IN LAKHS)
Axis Bank	Shikha Sharma, MD	4.12	74	5.6
Bharti Airtel	Sunil Mittal, chairman	27.17	323.63	8.3
Cipla	Subhanu Saxena, MD and CEO	13.31	453	2.9
Dr Reddy's Laboratories	G.V. Prasad, CEO	12.93	363	3.5
HDFC Bank	Aditya Puri, MD	7.39	117	6.3
Hero MotoCorp	Pawan Munjal, chairman	44.62	631.11	7.07
Hindustan Unilever	Sanjiv Mehta, MD and CEO	14.17	93	15.2
Housing Development Finance Corp.	Keki Mistry, CEO	8.12	83	9.7
ICICI Bank	Chanda Kochhar, MD	5.1	97	5.2
Infosys	U.B. Pravin Rao, COO	6.08	124.15	4.8
ITC	Y.C. Deveshwar, chairman	15.28	439	3.5
Larsen and Toubro	A.M. Naik, group exec chairman	27.32	453.75	6.0
Lupin	Desh Bandhu Gupta, chairman	37.5	1168	3.2
Mahindra and Mahindra	Pawan Goenka, ED	10.38	157.21	6.60
Reliance Industries	Mukesh Ambani, chairman	15	205.71	7.29
Tata Consultancy Services	N. Chandrasekaran, CEO and MD	21.28	416.51	5.1
Tata Motors	Ravi Pisharody, ED	2.7	51.15	5.2
Tata Steel	T.V. Narendran, MD	6.47	77.64	7.8
Vedanta	Navin Agrawal, exec chairman	15.08	292.77	7.8
Wipro	T.K. Kurien, CEO	9.11	169.63	5.3

Source: 2015 annual reports

Exhibit 3: Right Wing National Discourse

"…Goswami's Republic indicates the mainstreaming of right-wing opinion as a business enterprise. Already, Swarajya and Open magazine – along with sundry portals like OpIndia and PGurus (not to speak of social media trolls) – are trying to carve a space for right-wing opinion-makers in the public sphere. Goswami at the head of a well-funded television network will undoubtedly lead the pack. In the United States, this has already happened and across media platforms – television, print, radio and digital. Fox News, like the Arnab-led Times Now earlier in India, leads CNN in ratings and has done so for a very long time…"

Exhibit 4: Application form for Patanjali's Distributorship

APPLICATION FORM TO BECAME DISTRIBUTOR OF PATANJALI AYURVED LIMITED

FOOD UNIT [ ]   COSMETIC UNIT [ ]

By the blessing of H.H Param Pujya Swami Ramdev Ji Maharaj and the determination of Patanjali Ayurved Limited., cheap and best quality Swadeshi Product is to be made available to each and every household, I am a well-wisher and supporter of this movement and is committed to get rid of the foreign MNCs loot to make the country self-reliant and economic super power.

Name Of the Applicant : _____

Name of the Company/Firm : _____

Address : _____

Email : _____ Phone No. [ ][ ][ ][ ][ ][ ][ ][ ][ ][ ]

1. Level at which you can become a distributor

   A. District Level [ ]   District _____ State _____

   B. Tehsil Level [ ]   Tehsil _____ District _____ State _____

   C. Mandi Level [ ]   Mandi _____ Tehsil _____ District _____ State _____

2. Do you Have Any experience of FMCG distribution / Wholesale distribution / Other distribution?

   Yes [ ]   No [ ]

   Brief History of the products of the distribution business you have done so far :
   _____
   _____

   If not then give detail of your present business :
   _____
   _____

3. Name of the company for whom you have already done the distribution

Name of the company	Duration
1. _____	Year _____ To _____
2. _____	Year _____ To _____
3. _____	Year _____ To _____

4. Last One Year Turnover : _____

5. Investment Capacity : _____

6. If you accept the above terms and conditions and is ready to give us all the information's metioned above then please attach your last year ITR (Income Tax Return) and balance sheets with this application form and send to Email ID. abhsydaivibhag@patanjaliayurved.org.

Note :

A. Patanjali Ayurved Limited Reserves the right to reject or accept any application without assigning any reason, however the information given in this form would not used anywhere and would be hightly confidential.

B. Are you alredy engage with patanjali pariwar? Yes [ ]   No [ ]   If yes then mention the cadre. (Karyakarta/Yog Teacher/Life /Patron/Founder/Corporate Member, Others_____

C. The Person who deals with the trade of Schnapps Business are not eligible to fill the form because our organisation is a Social and Spirtual Organisation.

Date: _____   SIGNATURE OF APPLICANT

Case Study Questions

1. How did Baba Ramdev emerge as a leader, even though he does not possess the symbols of leadership which are usually employed?
2. Are use of symbols important in framing leadership as applied to the case study? Why/why not?
3. Based on the material presented here and other publically available information, were the strategic choices exercised by Baba Ramdev in framing the Patanjali narrative effective?
4. Discuss the strategic choices exercised by Patanjali's leadership in dealing with the institutional environment?

References

Abneesh, R., Pooja, L., & Tanmay, S. (2015a). *PATANJALI AYURVED Waiting in the wings* (pp. 1–2). Edelweiss Securities Limited.

Abneesh, R., Pooja, L., & Tanmay, S. (2015b). *PATANJALI AYURVED Waiting in the wings* (pp. 3–4). Edelweiss Securities Limited.

Abneesh, R., Pooja, L., & Tanmay, S. (2015c). *PATANJALI AYURVED Waiting in the wings* (pp. 2–3). Edelweiss Securities Limited.

Abneesh, R., Pooja, L., & Tanmay, S. (2015d). *PATANJALI AYURVED Waiting in the wings* (pp. 11–12). Edelweiss Securities Limited.

Case 8: Recontextualizing Diversity: The German Case

Jasmin Mahadevan and Iuliana Ancuţa Ilie

Introduction

This chapter is based on the insight that today's organizations in many national and societal contexts face the challenge of managing an increasingly diverse workforce. This increase in workforce diversity is partly due to a changing business environment, but also due to new technologies and social media, increasing individual mobility, and profound socio-political and economic shifts (Urry 2007). Even though the need to manage a diverse workforce is shared across nations and societies, organizations nonetheless need to do so within specific frameworks. The latter are often country-specific and extend to the very meanings of diversity. For strategic international HRM, this is a relevant finding. It suggests that HR first needs to identify what diversity 'means' to those involved prior to being able to manage it or to assess the international and global scope of corporate diversity management campaigns. Based on this insight, this chapter highlights the meanings of diversity in the German context and provides the reader with the background knowledge for investigating the contextual dimension of diversity.

Key Aspects of Workplace Diversity

Diversity does not merely refer to matters of difference: In the end, all individuals are different from each other. Diversity at work considers those aspects of 'who individuals are' or as 'who they are perceived' which might advantage some groups over others (Prasad et al. 2006). For analyzing these effects, diversity studies focus on six diversity markers which contribute to our perceptions of ourselves and

---

J. Mahadevan (✉) · I. A. Ilie
Pforzheim University, Pforzheim, Germany
e-mail: jasmin.mahadevan@hs-pforzheim.de; iuliana.ilie@hs-pforzheim.de

© Springer Nature Singapore Pte Ltd. 2018
A. Malik (ed.), *Strategic Human Resource Management and Employment Relations*, Springer Texts in Business and Economics,
https://doi.org/10.1007/978-981-13-0399-9_22

others. These are gender, ethnicity (or: race), age, ability, religion (or: worldview/*Weltanschauung*), and sexual orientation (overview in Plummer 2003: 25; Bührmann 2015: 23–42). For considering diversity, two arguments are given in the literature, namely a business case: diversity increases performance, and the human case: individuals should have equal opportunities in life. In the words of Van Dijk et al. (2012: 73), the business case means "supporting diversity as a means to achieve, ultimately, organizational profit", whereas the human case "depart(s) from the perspective that power inequalities in societies exist in organizations too and that, as a consequence, organizations should pursue diversity in order to empower minority groups and transform these inequalities". In addition, the critical perspective not only advocates equal opportunities but also suggests favouring those groups who are historically or structurally disadvantaged or excluded, so called positive discrimination (Prasad et al. 2006).

Diversity is also linked to our 'social identity' (Tajfel and Turner 1986), that is: who we are in relation to others, and the social categories to which our self is related. Social identity is not an objective category, rather, it refers to how others perceive us (ascription), how we relate to our self (self-referencing), and to how we experience potential discrepancies between the two (Mahadevan 2017: 84). This reminds us that a self-identification also needs to be recognized by others in order to make a person feel that they 'belong' to a certain group (Hall 1990). Even a category such as 'race' is not a biological given, as it might seem. For instance, Barack Obama is often referred to as the 'first Afro-American president of the United States'. In reality, however, his background is both multi-racial and multi-ethnic. Still, if he fails to be recognized as 'Caucasian' or 'bi-racial', he might – voluntarily or in-voluntarily – self-identify as 'Afro-American'. As this example suggests, we tend to perceive social identities as more dichotomist than they might actually be. This is of particular importance when we consider those markers of diversity which are visible, in contrast to those which might be disclosed voluntarily or remain hidden.

Studies also suggest that hierarchies are attached to diversity markers and related social identities, and that this might have critical implications (e.g. Tretheway 1999; Ward and Winstanley 2003; Zanoni et al. 2010; Acker 2012; Levay 2014; Mahadevan and Kilian-Yasin 2016; Mik-Meyer 2016). For instance, in international management, it is the 'white, heterosexual, western, middle/upper class, able man' (Zanoni et al. 2010: 13) who constitutes the implicit point of reference for all, and this makes other social identities a 'minority' identity. Therefore, when analysing social identities, one not only needs to consider diversity markers objectively, but to reflect upon how some social identities are more 'normal' than others, as they are represented by the majority or those in power (Eriksen 2010). Furthermore, individuals tend to value their own group identity (social identity) over others, and this is called an 'in-group' bias (Tajfel and Turner 1986). The likelihood of in-group biases tends to increase if competition is felt towards members of another group or if another social identity seems to challenge or endanger own identities (e.g. Weichselbaumer 2016). It might then be that some individuals are discriminated against, excluded or marginalized at work, based on 'who they are' or as 'who they are perceived' (Prasad et al. 2006). For international HRM, this is problematic, for it thwarts the assumptions that workplaces should be merit-based and provide equal opportunities to all. A critical condition emerges if perceptions of negative difference are even institutionalized on the level of structures and practices, for instance, if members of a certain religion are not selected for employment (practice) or if national laws don't permit their employment (structures). To prevent explicit discrimination on the level of structures, most greater regional units, such as the European Union, or countries, such as Germany, have anti-discriminatory legal frameworks considering the Big 6 diversity markers (Bendl et al. 2012: 79). Often, however, discrimination is more subtle and does not show in formal structures (it is implicit), and it is this type of discrimination that is the hardest to be tackled by (international) HRM, for it is related to what we consider 'normal', how we have learned to perceive ourselves and others, and what we hold to be the most favourable social identity.

Diversity Recontextualization and International HRM

In multinational companies, HR managers need to design diversity management campaigns in a global context. For understanding how the meanings of diversity might differ across contexts, the concept of re-contextualization is helpful (Brannen 2004). This term was coined by Mary Yoko Brannen (2004) who investigated the success of Disneyland in Japan and its near failure in France. Her study showed that, in the case of Japan, the values and image of Disneyland was successfully translated into the local context, whereas, in the case of France, this did not happen. Brannen concluded that companies cannot be sure that intended meaning, for instance: what Disneyland 'represents', will automatically be interpreted the same way in another context. Rather, meaning will be subjected to an unforeseeable and dynamic process of recontextualization, and companies need to monitor this process and its success. When doing so, they should pay particular attention to the minimum "semantic fit" which is required for meaning to be successfully linked to a new context.

A recent study by Fiona Moore (2015) has applied this understanding to diversity management campaigns in multinational companies, specifically to the BMW/Mini plant at Cowley, United Kingdom (UK). She showed that, whereas 'diversity' in a UK setting tends to refer to diverse ethnicities and also includes a certain class element of the gender role, in Germany it concerns questions of how to increase gender equality (Moore 2015). A German multinational company such as BMW operating in the UK might therefore experience difficulties in transferring certain diversity management initiatives to its subsidiary, in this case: to the production facility at Crowley, UK. The intended 'global' message by German BMW headquarters – namely to promote women to executive positions – was not understood in the local UK context wherein the learned and already established understanding was that 'diversity' concerns equal opportunities for members of all ethnic groups. At the same time, the focus on the gender dimension of diversity at BMW does not consider ethnicity, race or other potential factors. This suggests that every diversity management initiative has certain 'blind-spots' which are beyond what diversity 'normally means' and which are not considered in HRM policies.

Based on the previous considerations, HR managers need to become and remain aware of how diversity is normally understood in the national, societal and organizational context wherein they operate. It also suggests that we, as individuals, have also learned certain context-specific meanings of diversity (a HR manager originating from the UK might instinctively promote ethnic diversity in a multinational company whereas an HR manager originating from Germany might focus on gender equality). This implies that individual HR managers also need to reflect upon themselves and what they consider the purposes and meanings of 'diversity management'.

Case Example: The Meanings of Diversity at Robert Bosch

Robert Bosch (short: Bosch) is one of the biggest German companies and located in the federal state of Baden-Württemberg (IHK 2016). It is headquartered in the Stuttgart region and known for its long tradition, innovation and excellent quality. Founded in 1886 as "Workshop for Precision Mechanics and Electrical Engineering", the Bosch Group is present in 150 countries across the world, it has no less than 440 subsidiaries and regional companies and at the end of 2015 it employed a total workforce of 374,800 (Bosch, Annual Report 2015). Bosch is one of the world's largest automotive supplier, drive and control technology supplier, power tools and accessories supplier and its activities are divided into four main business sectors: Mobility Solutions, Industrial Technology, Consumer Goods and Energy and Building Technology (Bosch, Annual Report 2015: 21–25). The Bosch Group's reported a sales revenue for 2015 of 70.6 billion euros and the earnings before interest and taxes (EBIT) rose to 4.6 billion euros, in comparison to the 3.0 billion euros generated in 2014 (Bosch, Annual Report 2015, p. 46). In the annual report of Bosch, diversity is presented as a core value of the group and a factor of success (Bosch, Annual Report 2015: 38): "we strongly believe that mixed teams of men and women, embracing different generations and lifestyles and from diverse backgrounds, promote excellence and increase our capacity to innovate".

Bosch also dedicated a section of its webspace to 'diversity'. In 2013 (Bosch 2013) the diversity webpage is further divided into "gender" and "intercultural competency". Diversity management goals were defined as follows (Bosch 2013): "Besides an equal representation of women and men in leadership positions, our most important goal is the involvement of different cultures in our worldwide work relations." This means that two diversity markers are explicitly mentioned, namely gender and cultural diversity. However, these are linked to different implications and requirements: Whereas gender equality should be reached and is mentioned as a definite goal, the considerations regarding 'cultural diversity' remain fuzzy and are not further specified (what does involvement mean and how can it be measured?).

Accordingly, "securing and promoting women" (Bosch 2013) is already institutionalized and implemented in the company on the level of practice and indicators. For instance, in 2013, the corporate webpage read (Bosch 2013): "We want to increase the number of women in executive positions. In the last ten years, we increased the proportion to almost ten percent. Our ambitious goal is to achieve 15 percent at the end of 2013." In 2017, the corporate webpage reads (Bosch 2017): "Until 2020, 20 percent of all executive positions worldwide shall be filled with women." What is notable is that the new webpage now explicitly mentions 'worldwide executive positions'. This suggests that, despite the fact that the total number of female executives being targeted has increased, it is not certain whether this increase will actually take place in Germany.

In 2017, the same webpage (Bosch 2017) is structured into "securing and promoting women", "(not) a question of age", "intercultural competency", "work and private life", "individuals with disabilities". The diversity management goals are presented as:

> *Besides an equal representation of women and men in leadership positions, it is also about valuing employees of different generations and nationalities. In addition, we continually work towards a flexible work culture and place value upon a good reconcilability of work and private life. This involves a change from a 'culture of presence' towards a 'culture of results', which does not put presence, but achieved results centre stage.*

This suggests that certain diversity markers, such as age and ability, have become more prominent, based on the national and EU-wide legislative requirements for anti-discrimination (see following section). At the same time, the underlying rationale for diversity is corporate success (Bosch 2017), which is a new aspect in comparison with the the 2013 webpage. Furthermore, we can see specific interpretations of "work-life-balance", which is the international diversity term used, namely 'reconcilability of work and private life". This can be linked to a specific German understanding of work, namely as work and private life being two separate spheres of living and as work requiring full-time presence (called 'culture of presence'). In the end, diversity is rationalized by a new 'culture of achievement and results' against which all groups need to measure themselves against.

In contrast, the goals on the subsection "intercultural competency" are fuzzy at best and have remained so, throughout the years. In 2013, the corporate webpage on "intercultural competency", stated:

> *multinational teams create openness, facilitate understanding and acceptance of the other culture and, this way, reduce obstacles to everyday interaction and working together. Due to the fact that working in international teams is a key aspect of our daily business, we develop the intercultural competencies of our employees continuously. Just in the past two years, we founded two intercultural forums, on the one hand, the Turkish Forum at Bosch (TFB), and on the other hand, the Cameroonian Forum. The goal of both is to promote intercultural understanding and to contribute to more equal opportunities via more educational, athletic and leisure time offers.*

The content of the 2017 Bosch webpage is more or less the same, however, the visitor is redirected to 'Internationality' of which its content is now a part. This suggests that intercultural competency is not understood as a diversity requirement at home, but rather as an additional aspect of 'international work'. The content of this item also implies that 'intercultural understanding' is somehow an outcome of voluntary activities and not a corporate obligation. It does not concern matters of ethnic or religious diversity of the German workforce.

Managing Diversity in Germany: The Wider Frameworks

The previous example shows how a specific German company interprets 'diversity management'. These meanings of diversity do not emerge in a corporate vacuum but rather are related to macro-environmental, meso-organizational and micro-individual levels; they involve structure, practices and individual action. For a more holistic diversity management, HR managers should investigate these effects, they should reflect upon current and past diversity trends, and they should uncover the underlying corporate rationale for managing diversity. We do so in the following for the case of Germany.

Structural Aspects and Wider Frameworks

Germany is a member-state of the European Union (EU) and EU legislation prohibits discrimination on grounds of gender, sexual orientation, ethnic or racial origin, disability, age and nationality (European Commission 2015a: 4). Additionally, most of the member states have adopted at national level other criteria in order to offer a wider protection against discrimination. The French legislation covers for example discrimination on grounds of health, political opinion, physical appearance, place of residence (European Commission 2016a). In Germany, discrimination on grounds of race, ethnic origin, religion or philosophical beliefs, gender, sexual identity and disability are addressed by the General Act on Equal Treatment (Allgemeines Gleichbehandlungsgesetz – AGG) which was adopted in 2006 (European Commission 2016b).

This suggests that explicit discrimination on structural level regarding the Big 6 diversity markers is prevented by anti-discrimination legislation in Germany. At the same time, actively promoting diversity is not a corporate requirement in Germany. The only legal requirement is non-discrimination, as specified in EU-law and the German AGG. For Germany, this implies that companies do not feel the need to move beyond demographic variables, which also Research suggests that the term 'diversity management' is not commonly institutionalized in German companies. For instance, in 2007, Süß and Kleiner found that "no generally accepted catalogue of diversity management actions [could] be found in the corresponding literature and no systematic empirical research findings existed for the German-speaking area" (p. 1941). They also found that 42.4 percept of the 160 German companies "do not know about diversity management at all" (Süß and Kleiner 2007: 1943). To close this gap, they suggest a set of 12 diversity management actions for German companies, such as flexible working time agreements, mixed teams, determining the requirement for diversity management, mentoring programmes, integrating diversity management into corporate culture, consulting services for diversity groups, works council agreements, communicating diversity management, diversity trainings, institutionalizing diversity management, diversity-oriented facilities, diversity-oriented design of human resource management, and evaluating diversity management.

Nonetheless, a so called "Charta der Vielfalt" (Diversity Charta) exists, which has been signed by numerous companies. In 2016, a study by Ernst & Young and the Diversity Charta Association that promotes the Diversity Charta in investigated the actual conditions of corporate diversity management. 349 German companies who had signed the diversity charta and 250 companies who had not participated in this survey (Ernst & Young and Charta der Vielfalt e.V., 2016). Across all companies, increasing the number of women in companies and the number of women in leadership positions, in particular, is viewed as the key diversity management focus (Ernst & Young and Charta der Vielfalt e.V., 2016: 15). At the same time, the study finds that "2/3 of the German companies did not implement any diversity management actions, and only 19% intend to do so in the future" [p. 17, *translated by the authors*]. 60 percent don't assume sexual orientation and gender identity to require any action, and 52% hold the same opinion for religion and worldview (p. 17). This brings about the question as to whether these topics might be taboo for some of the German companies. For instance, in the 2015 Eurobarometer on discrimination, 68% of the German respondents believe that it is being done enough to promote diversity in their workplace in terms of gender. Yet, only 35% and 46% of the respondents believe that enough is being done with regard to gender identity, respectively sexual orientation (European Commission 2015b: 86). The following section investigates the underlying reasons for why this specific diversity management focus on gender might have emerged.

Two Diversity Trends and the Business Case for Diversity

Historically and presently, Germany is a societal context which depicts two divergent diversity trends. These concern firstly the markers 'ethnicity' and 'religion', as linked to immigration, and secondly, the question of gender. For instance, it is reported that "about 20% of all German residents today have a background of immigration" (European Commission 2016b: 6). In this context, it can be stated that Germany has become a country of immigration, the accompanying discourse on pluralism/diversity shifting from the claim "Germany is not a country of immigration", to multiculturalism (Schwarz 2007; Ramm 2010) and to intended integration and labour market absorption of the immigrants (IMF 2016). From a social identity perspective, immigration in Germany is linked to questions of ethnicity and religion, Muslim minorities experiencing combined in-group biases (Forstenlechner and Al-Waqfi 2010), some of them also involving gender (Weichselbaumer 2016).

Diversity management in Germany seems to be driven less by the fairness perspective and more by a business case perspective. Süß and Kleiner (2007) suggest that the main driver for companies to implement diversity management is the expectation of gaining legitimacy: "Large, listed companies in particular strive for legitimacy for their actions. They have to comply with public expectations that discrimination of minorities in companies should be prevented..." (p. 1950–1951). Therefore, legitimacy in the eyes of the stakeholders and law compliance determine the adoption of diversity management in companies.

It is at this point, that public images and dominant in-group biases become relevant to diversity management: For instance, if one group, e.g. women at work, have a more positive image than another group, e.g. migrants, it is likely that a business-case oriented diversity management will focus on the more positive social identity, as stakeholders are more likely to accept such an initiative. Together, the previous considerations suggest that 'diversity' on the level of corporate strategy and practice is largely related to 'gender' in the German context. In the case of Bosch, we can see that gender is promoted and, instead of ethnicity, 'culture' is chosen as the fuzzy 'international' and presumably more positive alternative. We can also observe that Bosch interprets diversity within the business case argument, unless otherwise specified by legal frameworks (e.g. regarding disability or age).

The Gender Equality Meaning of Diversity

The actual diversity findings regarding gender are paradoxical for Germany and also suggest a recent trend. For instance, the principle of gender equal pay for equal work was enshrined in the Treaty of Rome in 1957. Nonetheless, Germany had in 2014 the third highest gender pay gap (the difference in average gross hourly wage between men and women in an economy) in the EU: 22.3% while the average gender pay gap in the EU in the same year was 16.7% (European Commission 2016c). The pension wage gap might be an even better indicator than the gender pay gap, as it contains "cumulated employment outcomes over the entire life course" (Allmendinger and von den Driesch 2015: 36). While women receive lower pensions in all member states of the EU, Germany had the highest gender gap in pensions: 45% in 2012 in comparison to the EU-28 average (38%) and this gap translates into higher poverty risk for German women in old age (European Institute for Gender Equality 2015: 20–21). This suggests that the promotion of gender equality via corporate action is a recent trend in Germany.

The mechanism chosen for promoting women at work in Germany is a quota for women in top positions. This is linked to a general, EU-wide debate on the discrepancy between the high number of well-qualified women, which even out-perform men in terms of educational attainment (European Commission 2015c: 1), and their underrepresentation in top-level positions. Due to a slow progress in the gender balance of corporate boards, the European Commission decided in 2012 to introduce a legislative measure: by 2020, 40% of the non-executive directors of listed companies ought to be female (European Commission 2015d). However, the member states were free in designing their national policies, "on condition that their approach delivers concrete results" (European Commission 2015d). The United Kingdom for example embarked on a voluntary-led business approach, with a voluntary target of 25% female directors to be achieved by 2015 by the 100 companies of the Financial

Time Stock Exchange (FTSE) Index. In 2011, France (which was therefore ahead of the directive of the European Commission) introduced a mandatory quota of 40 % (applicable to non-executive directors in listed and non-listed companies) to be achieved by 2017. In Germany, a mandatory quota of 30% was adopted and it became effective in January 2016.

Opinions diverge on the topic. Jutta von Falkenhausen, vice-president of the Initiative for More Women in Advisory Boards (FidAR) considers quotas a necessary instrument to implement change "We don't like quotas, we don't like coercion. But if we don't have mandatory rules, nothing will change" (Barrett 2014). The European Commission, though it also sustains voluntary measures in improving gender balance, argues in favour of binding legal regulation: "The figures show that it is the legislative measures that result in substantial progress, especially if they are accompanied by sanctions" (European Commission 2012: 13). Michel Ferrary considers quotas a temporary but necessary measure: "Quotas help to change unconscious barriers and allow companies to learn diversity. In a decade or two, when gender equality has been established, quotas can then be removed" (cf. Chan 2015).

Germany is among the few member states which registered a significant progress in the percentage of women on boards (+12.8%) between October 2010 and April 2015, reaching 25.4%. This is an advance of 4.2% in comparison to the EU-28 average (European Commission 2015d). The 2016 gender quota should accelerate the change, at least with regard to the numerical representation of women on German boards. However, in a special gender barometer of the European Commission, 6% totally agreed and 28% of the German respondents tended to agree with the statement: "Women are less willing than men to make a career for themselves" (European Commission 2015e). For those respondents believing that women are less assertive then men in pursuing a career, imposing a gender quota might have seem senseless and it might be indeed so, if the quota does not bring in the long run also a change in mentality. In the short run the quota should be able to change the existing representations of the working world at the top. Together, this suggests that, whereas the structural frameworks of gender inequality have been addressed by the quota in Germany, the implicit meanings of gender – namely women being the primary caretaker at home – has not changed.

Allmendinger (2010) identifies another paradox: while there was an ongoing debate on the existence of a shortage of skilled labour in Germany, the employers did not seem to consider the untapped potential of 5.6 million unemployed women (representing 28% of the women between 25 and 59 years old) of which only 1.8 million were officially registered as seeking for a job. Moreover, it has to be noted that there are no formal or legal requirement to increase the number of men in jobs which are traditionally dominated by women, for instance, childcare or nursing. From a critical diversity perspective, these jobs are also rather low-paid and unattractive compared to favourable industry jobs, and therefore this only reinforce findings on the gender pay or pension gap as well as traditional 'gender roles' also on the level of whole industries and professions. Also the finding that women between 25 and 59 do not officially register as seeking employment contributes to the insight that the meaning given to gender roles in Germany is still linked to traditional gender role differentiation. For instance, the Special Eurobarometer 428 "Gender Equality" also finds that 20% of the German respondents 'totally agree' and 32% 'tend to agree' with the statement "men are less competent than women at performing household tasks" (European Commission 2015e: 19). We can therefore identify a strong discrepancy between ideal (gender equality) and meaning (traditional gender roles) and need to doubt whether a structural diversity mechanism (quota) can actually change such meaning and prevent related in-group biases and implicit discrimination. In the case of Bosch, corporate diversity management also appears to focus on structural gender aspects (quota) which might result in a neglect of other diversity markers, such as ethnicity or religion. The paradoxical findings regarding gender equality in Germany suggest that gender roles in Germany might have remained traditional. This can be considered an additional blind-spot of the contextual dimension of German diversity management.

Suggested Case Study Questions

1. What are the specifics of the German context, both on corporate and wider levels, and how can they be differentiated into macro-, meso- and micro-levels?
2. How and to what extent are the policies of Robert Bosch representative of the wider frameworks wherein they emerge?
3. How and to what extent are the policies of Robert Bosch related to theoretical insights on diversity management – is this a 'good' policy from your perspective and why (not)?
4. Why could the Robert Bosch approach 'make sense' to the company?
5. Considering the previous question: It is always easy to judge HR limitations 'from the outside'. What are the meanings of diversity in your country of origin or societal and national contexts you are familiar with? Which corporate or organizational diversity management aspects have you encountered?
6. What are the challenges and opportunities, and strengths and weaknesses of the German approach to diversity? What are their blind-spots?
7. Why and how can corporate HRM never be 'context-free'? What HRM theories do you know that argue in favour of the 'embeddedness' of corporate HRM?
8. How can national laws and societal sentiments influence corporate diversity management to the better or to the worse?
9. What is re-contextualization and what are the HRM challenges associated with it?
10. Do HRM managers also need to 're-contextualize' themselves in their role as HR managers? If so: How should they achieve semantic fit with multiple contexts in a multinational company or an international HRM environment?
11. Regarding Robert Bosch: Please look into other countries wherein the company operates or compare this company with another company or national context you are familiar with: What aspects of the Bosch understanding of diversity management might be easy or difficult to recontextualize? Why? How would you achieve semantic fit, and is this even possible?

References

Acker, J. (2012). Gendered organizations and intersectionality: Problems and possibilities. *Equality, Diversity and Inclusion: An International Journal, 31*(3), 214–224.

Allmendinger, J. (2010). *Verschenkte Potenziale?* [Untapped Potential?] Frankfurt am Main: Campus Verlag.

Allmendinger, J., & von den Driesch, E. (2015). Der wahre Unterschied. Erst die Rente zeigt den ganzen Umfang der Geschlechterungleichheit. [The real difference. The pension is the genuine indicator of gender inequality]. Available at: https://www.wzb.eu/sites/default/files/publikationen/wzb_mitteilungen/s36-39ja-vdriesch.pdf. Accessed 22 Nov 2016.

Barrett, C. (2014). Gender quotas feel coercive but appear to work. *Financial times* (online). Available from: https://www.ft.com/content/aef9d9c4-d521-11e3-9187-00144feabdc0. Accessed 29 Nov 2016.

Bendl, R., Eberherr, H., & Mensi-Klarbach, H. (2012). Vertiefende Betrachtung zu ausgewählten Diversitätsdimensionen [in-depth view on selected dimensions of diversity]. In: R. Bendl, E. Hanappi-Egger, and R. Hofmann (Eds.), *Diversität und diversity management* [Diversity and diversity management] (pp. 79–135). Wien: UTB-Facultas.

Bosch (2013). http://www.bosch.com/de/com/sustainability/issues/associates_young_talent/managementsystems_2/managementsystems_3.php. Accessed 1 Apr 2013.

Bosch. (2015). *Bosch annual report*. Available from: http://annual-report.bosch.com/fileadmin/user_upload/Group_management_report.pdf. Accessed 20 Feb 2017.

Bosch. (2017). http://www.bosch.com/de/com/sustainability/associates/diversity/diversity.php. Accessed 1 Feb 2017.

Brannen, M. Y. (2004). When "Mickey" loses face: Recontextualization, semantic fit and the semiotics of foreignness. *Academy of Management Review, 29*(4), 593–616.

Bührmann, A. (2015). Gender – A central dimension of diversity. In S. Vertovec (Ed.), *Routledge international handbook of diversity studies* (pp. 23–42). London/New York: Taylor and Francis.

Chan, W. (2015). Are gender quotas needed? *Financial times* (online). Available from: https://www.ft.com/content/d65795f2-0de6-11e5-9a65-00144feabdc0. Accessed 30 Nov 2016.

Eriksen, T. H. (2010). *Small places, large issues* (1st edn, 1995). London: Pluto Press.

European Commission. (2012). *Women in economic decision-making in the EU: Progress report*. Available from: http://ec.europa.eu/information_society/newsroom/image/document/2016-49/women-on-boards_en_40298.pdf. Accessed 19 Sept 2016.

European Commission. (2015a). *Know your rights. Protection from discrimination*. Available at: http://bookshop.europa.eu/en/know-your-rights-pbDS0415271/?CatalogCategoryID=cOwKABstC3oAAAEjeJEY4e5L. Accessed 17 Nov 2016.

European Commission. (2015b). *Special Eurobarometer 437. Discrimination in the EU in 2015*. Available at: http://ec.europa.eu/COMMFrontOffice/publicopinion/index.cfm/Survey/getSurveyDetail/instruments/SPECIAL/surveyKy/2077. Accessed 17 Nov 2016.

European Commission. (2015c). *Labour market participation of women*. Available at: http://ec.europa.eu/europe2020/pdf/themes/2015/labour_market_participation_women_20151126.pdf. Accessed 22 Nov 2016.

European Commission. (2015d). *Gender balance on corporate boards. Europe is cracking the glass ceiling*. Available http://ec.europa.eu/justice/gender-equality/files/womenonboards/factsheet_women_on_boards_web_2015-10_en.pdf. Accessed 19 Sept 2016.

European Commission. (2015e). *Special Eurobarometer 428. Gender equality*. Available from: http://ec.europa.eu/justice/gender-equality/files/documents/eurobarometer_report_2015_en.pdf. Accessed 29 Nov 2016.

European Commission. (2016a). *Country report. Non-discrimination*. France 2016. Available at: http://www.equalitylaw.eu/downloads/3707-2016-fr-country-report-nd. Accessed 18 Nov 2016.

European Commission. (2016b). *Country report. Non-discrimination*. Germany 2016. Available at: http://www.equalitylaw.eu/downloads/3706-2016-de-country-report-nd. Accessed 18 Nov 2016.

European Commission. (2016c). *The gender pay gap in Germany*. Available from: http://ec.europa.eu/justice/gender-equality/files/gender_pay_gap/2016/gpg_country_factsheet_de_2016_en.pdf. Accessed 20 Feb 2017.

European Institute for Gender Equality. (2015). *Gender gap in pensions in the EU*. Available from: http://eige.europa.eu/sites/default/files/documents/MH0415087ENN_Web.pdf. Accessed 22 Nov 2016.

Forstenlechner, I., & Al-Waqfi, M. A. (2010). A job interview for Mo, but none for Mohammed. *Personnel Review, 39*(6), 767–784.

Hall, S. (1990). Cultural identity and diaspora. In J. Rutherford (Ed.), *Identity, community, culture, difference* (pp. 222–237). London: Lawrence and Wishart.

IHK. (2016). *Die größten Unternehmen in Baden-Württemberg* [The biggest companies in Baden-Württemberg]. Available from: http://www.bw.ihk.de/_Resources/Persistent/2492457c004c62 6cbc0af60dea61d310bab4ad5c/Brosch%C3%BCre%20Die%20gr%C3%B6%C3%9Ften%20 Unternehmen%20in%20Baden-W%C3%BCrttemberg%202016.pdf. Accessed 20 Feb 2017.

International Monetary Fund. (2016). *The refugee surge in Europe: Economic challenges*. Available at: https://www.imf.org/external/pubs/ft/sdn/2016/sdn1602.pdf. Accessed 21 Nov 2016.

Levay, C. (2014). Obesity in organizational context. *Human Relations, 67*(5), 565–585.

Mahadevan, J. (2017). *A very short, fairly interesting and reasonably cheap book about cross-cultural management*. London: Sage.

Mahadevan, J., & Kilian-Yasin, K. (2016). Dominant discourse, orientalism and the need for reflexive HRM: Skilled Muslim migrants in the German context. *International Journal of Human Resource Management*, 1–23. https://doi.org/10.1080/09585192.2016.1166786.

Mik-Meyer, N.. (2016). Othering, ableism and disability: A discursive analysis of co-workers' construction of colleagues with visible impairments. *Human Relations*, 1–23. https://doi.org/10.1177/0018726715618454.

Moore, F. (2015). An unsuitable job for a woman: A 'native category approach to gender, diversity and cross-cultural management. *International Journal of Human Resource Management, 26*(2), 216–230.

Plummer, D. L. (2003). Overview of the field of diversity management. In D. L. Plummer (Ed.), *Handbook of diversity management – Beyond awareness to competency based learning*. Lanham/New York/Oxford: University Press of America.

Prasad, P., Pringle, J. K., & Konrad, A. M. (2006). Examining the contours of workplace diversity. In A. M. Konrad, P. Prasad, & J. K. Pringle (Eds.), *Handbook of workplace diversity* (pp. 1–22). London: Sage.

Ramm, C. (2010). The Muslim makers. How Germany 'Islamizes' Turkish immigrants. *Interventions, 12*(2), 183–197.

Schwarz, A. (2007). Strategic uses of multiculturalism in Germany and Australia. In A. Schwarz & R. West-Pavlov (Eds.), *Polyculturalism and discourse*. Amsterdam: Rodopi.

Süß, S., & Kleiner, M. (2007). Diversity management in Germany: Dissemination and design of the concept. *International Journal of Human Resource Management, 18*(11), 1934–1953.

Tajfel, H., & Turner, J. C. (1986). The social identity theory of intergroup behavior. In S. Worchel & W. G. Austin (Eds.), *Psychology of intergroup relations* (pp. 7–24). Chicago: Nelson-Hall.

Tretheway, A. (1999). Disciplined bodies: Women's embodied identities at work. *Organization Studies, 20*(3), 423–450.

Urry, J. (2007). *Sociology beyond societies – mobilities for the twenty-first century*. London: Routledge.

Van Dijk, H., van Engen, M., & Paauwe, J. (2012). Reframing the business case for diversity: A values and virtues perspective. *Journal of Business Ethics, 11*(1), 73–84.

Ward, J., & Winstanley, D. (2003). The absent presence: Negative space within discourse and the construction of minority sexual identity in the workplace. *Human Relations, 56*(10), 1255–1280.

Weichselbaumer, D. (2016). Discrimination against female migrants wearing headscarves. IZA Discussion Paper No. 10217. Available from: http://ftp.iza.org/dp10217.pdf. Accessed 12 Dec 2016.

Zanoni, P., Janssens, M., Benschop, Y., & Nkomo, S. (2010). Guest editorial: Unpacking diversity, grasping inequality: Rethinking difference through critical perspectives. *Organization, 17*(1), 9–29.

Case 9: Stressed and Demotivated Public Servants… Looking for a (Motivational) Miracle at Paywell Agency

S. De Simone, L. Giustiniano, and R. Pinna

Introduction

Ms. Wolf is the Director of a large Agency, a branch of a national public administration dealing with formal compliance and respect of the law. Her "military branch" is made of civil servants working as inspectors. Ms. Wolf has recently noted a growing level of absenteeism, conflicts at work and rising employee turnover. Not being an expert in the field, she has started reading a book on people management but what she reads does not look totally convincing to her. She read: "Happy employees → happy customers → happy employees".

Such an employee-customer-employee sequence is the underlying behavioral mantra for many for-profit firms, especially in the service sectors or, more in generally in the front-end customer contact activities. This applies both to profit-oriented organizations, in which higher customer satisfaction could mean higher prices, therefore higher affluence and eventually the possibility to compensate the productive/effective employees via monetary rewards. The same applies also to non-profit organizations – such as public hospitals or volunteering associations – in which the satisfaction of the patients or those being served may be the ultimate trigger and act

---

Fictional name

S. De Simone (✉)
Department of Pedagogy, Psychology, Philosophy, University of Cagliari, Cagliari, Italy
e-mail: desimone@unica.it

L. Giustiniano
Department of Business and Management, LUISS Guido Carli University, Rome, Italy
e-mail: lgiusti@luiss.it

R. Pinna
Department of Economics and Management, University of Cagliari, Cagliari, Italy
e-mail: pinnar@unica.it

© Springer Nature Singapore Pte Ltd. 2018
A. Malik (ed.), *Strategic Human Resource Management and Employment Relations*, Springer Texts in Business and Economics,
https://doi.org/10.1007/978-981-13-0399-9_23

as a powerful implicit incentive for the employees. Unfortunately, for the enthusiasts of the happy-customer-happy-employee supporters, there are institutional and organizational barriers which prevent this from happening. This is especially the case of employees working for organizations whose mission serves a higher, overarching aim and clashes with the "satisfaction" of the very "customers" they interact with –the public audience or citizens. This case focuses on the judicial police officers of inspectors. Such jobs, compared to private employees, are generally performed by public servants, often presenting high levels of dissatisfaction with their job (Baldwin and Farley 2001; Rainey 1989; Steel and Warner 1990). These jobs also offer consideration of great(er) level of bureaucracy and they have to deal with the limited opportunity to realize their professional satisfaction (i.e. because of the lack of measurability of their actual performance, limited career opportunities, public awareness and recognition and so on). In fact, relative to other types of organizations, these public administrations appear to be problematic in terms of work engagement, job satisfaction, and work-related stress (WRS) (De Simone et al. 2016b). Notwithstanding, such employees appear to be infused with an institutional mission they wish to pursue. A mission that often relies upon altruistic or higher order needs, characterizing the so-called "public servant motivation". When the possibility to offer "traditional" external incentive is limited, and the likelihood to leverage upon implicit incentive (i.e. customer satisfaction) is practically impossible, can organizations such as these still aim at enhancing the employee motivation? This very question that is perturbing Ms. Wolf's mind.

Public Servants and Public Service Motivation

Some jobs seem to be more stressful than others. Prolonged or intense stress has been proved to have a negative impact on individuals' health (Cooper et al. 2001). In particular, work-related stress (WRS) is taking the center-stage as one of the major health and safety problems in affecting the EU (EU-OSHA 2014) and the US (AIS 2013). WRS affects both employees' psycho and social conditions, adversely impacts productivity, increases absenteeism and employee turnover. Furthermore, all these phenomena affect job satisfaction in a negative way, not just in terms of mere productivity but also in terms of absenteeism and turnover (Spector 1997). To this extent, being a judicial police officer of the inspectors puts the employess performing in such a job in a challenge of "chasing" citizens that had some issues with the judicial system and make them aware of the situation. As a matter of fact, inspectors cannot expect the individuals they interact with to be happy and expect happiness from them in return of their services.

Despite the stressors and the uneasy conditions in which they perform their jobs, public servants are motivated by a particular and specific type of motivation–Public Service Motivation (PSM). Following Perry and Wise (1990), such forms of motivation are substantiated by altruistic intentions to serve in the public interest. Hence, individuals operating in public organizations should be expected to achieve a significantly high levels of job satisfaction, performance, and commitment when

Table 1 Study 1: constructs and scales used in the questionnaire

Dimension	Definition	Scales
Work-related stress	The work stressors represent a set of occupational difficulties that affect well-being and organizational performance teaching (De Simone et al. 2016a)	HSE Management Standards Indicator Tool (Kerr et al. 2009): *Demands, control, supervisors' support, colleagues' support, relationships, role and change*
Public service motivation	Altruistic motivation to delivering services to people with a purpose to do good for others and society (Perry and Wise 1990; Perry and Hondeghem 2008)	PSM (Alonso and Lewis, 2001)
Work engagement	a positive state of mind, related to work and characterized by vigor, dedication, and absorption (Schaufeli et al. 2002)	Utrecht Work Engagement Scale (Schaufeli et al. 2002; Balducci et al. 2010)
Job satisfaction	Overall feeling about the job	Brief Overall Job satisfaction measure II (Judge et al. 1998; De Simone et al. 2014)
Life satisfaction	Overall feeling about the life	Life Satisfaction (Lance et al. 1989)

boasting high levels of PSM –or at the very least have higher levels of motivation, compared with individuals with lower PSM.

According to Alonso and Lewis (2001), *Public Service Motivation* (PSM) can be captured by the following five statements:

1. *Meaningful public service is very important to me.*
2. *I am not afraid to go to bat for the rights of others even if it means I will be ridiculed.*
3. *Making a difference in society means more to me than personal achievements.*
4. *I am prepared to make enormous sacrifices for the good of society.*
5. *I am often reminded by daily events about how dependent we are on one another.*

An individual experiences different situations at work that have an impact upon his/her personal and professional life. Any public administration aiming at enhancing the work engagement has to balance PSM with work-related stress and job satisfaction activities (see Table 1).

The Paywell Agency that Ms. Wolf is leading in a South Italian branch of the Italian Public Administration, takes care of the formal compliance in work-related activities. Among other categories of employees, the Agency employs a large number of "inspectors" and knowledge workers who are in-charge of verifying companies and firms that comply with the national laws. Such inspections might take place in three possible work settings: externally (i.e., at the firm headquarters), internally with direct contact with the public (i.e. at the front office of the firm's representatives showing up at Paywell Agency's windows) and internally without any contact with public (i.e. through back-office work wherein inspectors simply interact with their colleagues).

Following a grant received by the agency's management, these employees have been studied by a group of consultants with the aim of unveiling how PSM and WRS were affecting their professional and personal life. The analysis included two complementary studies: one based on an anonymous online questionnaire and the second study focused on conducting five focus groups involving members of the inspection service to unveil the specific stressors related to their jobs.

The first study was able to identify the main sources of stress at work and their relationships with PSM, job satisfaction, work engagement, and life satisfaction in a specific profession, that of inspectors (see Exhibit 1).

Exhibit 1

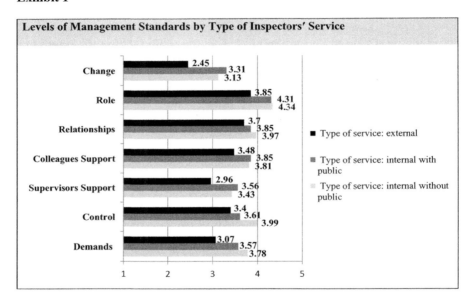

The results show the work setting seems to affect the individual perceptions of work-related features (e.g. stressors or management instruments). The three groupings were: internal inspectors in contact with the public working within the facilities of the Agency, providing assistance to citizens; inspectors in internal service without public contact working within the offices of the agency but interact only in contact with colleagues; and the inspectors who perform external service by carrying out unannounced inspections in local firms. Furthermore, the analysis of the data showed that the group of inspectors in external service had different levels of engagement, job satisfaction, and PSM, which were lower than that of the other groups. A more direct interaction with the inspectors, in the second study, allowed the consultants to investigate the specificity of stressors that characterize the work of judicial police officers of the inspectors. The inspectors took part to the focus groups on a voluntary basis. The group sessions focused on the topic of "stressors at work". Here some quotes:

> *I'd love my job more if I could do it—actually and mostly—in favor of citizens, getting rid of the rush for figures.* [Here she refers to the "number of sanctions" as a parameter for performance evaluation.] (Mary, 56 years old (y.o.), female)

> *Rather than punish the companies we should inform them and give them the opportunity to remedy the deficiencies instead of issue penalties which are so severe that they have to stop the business and fire personnel.* (Allison, 38 y.o., female)

> *To educate companies to be inspected in order to inform them of the risks related to penalties.* (Bill, 52 y.o., female)

> *It's not surprising that the inspection activity is seen as unpleasant to a part of the [companies'] owner's culture, being resistant to any form of control. Controls on respect of rules exercised by the inspectors are seen as a major threat, something to tackle. What is unacceptable is that the management displays indifference and annoyance in the face of violence, threats, and retorts to which inspectors are exposed every day during their job.* (Donald, 56 y.o., male)

> *The tension in doing our job is perceived mostly when we are outside [at companies]. You do not feel either protected or supported by anybody. You feel at the mercy of the mood of the others [visited companies].* (Katie, 44 y.o., female)

> *We need to be trained for coping with the aggressions we suffer from the subjects we control.* (Samantha, 41 y.o., female)

> *"The State we serve sees us as mere collection agents, leaving us alone without a lead ... with no guidelines, also physically, considering that also the police forces do not rescue us in case of aggression."* (Chuck, 40 y.o., male)

> *The external perception of the role of the inspector is highly disappointing. Only a few people appreciate my job, while most of them disregard it.* (Michael, 38 y.o., male)

> *I feel unmotivated and I'm almost convinced my job is socially useless. Maybe we should have more credibility.* (Nick, 62 y.o., male)

> *We are not educated and trained properly. That generates high stress, since we are called to confront very updated subjects [companies' personnel].* (Violet, 39 y.o., female)

> *More than the job itself, the legislative changes create stress.* (Felix, 56 y.o., male)

> *The main problem is often represented by the colleagues we work with. Not all of them are able to control their temper. Some of them are not well mannered or tend to boast about their job title (as it would mean anything, per se!). Some statements can often be misunderstood and generate conflicts with the users under their control.* (Philip, 58 y.o., male)

> *I believe that having available colleagues and in line with your way of thinking is important for doing your job well ... here it does not happen though.* (Arianna, 39 y.o., female)

> *I consider my job a service to the state and for the workers that refer to us, and I want to do it at the best. So even if we have plenty of duties and worries, I don't care as they are part of my job.* (Leslie, 51 y.o., female)

> *Despite the common sense around public employees, I'm very proud of being one a 'state employee' working for the general interest.* (Xavier, 57 y.o., male)

I love my job. I do it with attention, dedication, satisfaction, and professionalism. (Eloise, 60 y.o., female)

Overall, I'm satisfied by my job. (Todd, 47 y.o., male)

My job is stimulating. (Lilly, 52 y.o., female)

The data analysis showed five principal themes, which explain the work stressors of inspectors interviewed: job impoverishment, aggressions and protections, social recognition, need for training, and relationships with colleagues. After having read the first preliminary results of the studies, Ms. Wolf started to jot down another set of question to ask to the consultants:

Questions

1. Does the work setting of the Agency (external, internal with/without the public) affect the perception of stress? Why/why not? Would it be possible to mitigate its effects in any possible way?
2. What is the relationship between work related stress and job satisfaction? And between job satisfaction and engagement?
3. Is it possible to identify some typologies of inspectors? For example, considering the quotes, to analyse any gender- or age-related themes in relation to work stressors?
4. If the organization can offer a good quality of working life, can managers rely on that? Would that be enough to mitigate the work-related stress and trigger employee engagement in a sustainable way?

References

AIS – American Institute of Stress. (2013). *Workplace stress causes and consequences.* Available at: http://www.stress.org/workplace-stress-causes-and-consequences/. Accessed 4 Aug 2015.

Alonso, P., & Lewis, G. B. (2001). Public service motivation and job performance evidence from the federal sector. *The American Review of Public Administration, 31*(4), 363–380.

Balducci, C., Fraccaroli, F., & Schaufeli, W. B. (2010). Psychometric properties of the Italian version of the Utrecht work engagement scale (UWES-9). *European Journal of Psychological Assessment, 26*(2), 143–149.

Baldwin, J. N., & Farley, Q. A. (2001). Comparing the public and private sectors in the United States: A review of the empirical research. *Public Administration and Public Policy, 94*, 119–130.

Brewer, G. A., & Selden, S. C. (1998). Whistle blowers in the federal civil service: New evidence of the public service ethic. *Journal of Public Administration Research and Theory, 8*(3), 413–440.

Brief, A. P. (1998). *Attitudes in and around organizations.* Thousand Oaks: Sage.

Cooper, C. L., Dewe, P. J., & O'Driscoll, M. P. (2001). *Organizational stress: A review and critique of theory, research, and applications.* Thousand Oaks: Sage.

Cooper, C. L., & Marshall, J. (1976). Occupational sources of stress: A review of the literature relating to coronary heart disease and mental ill health. *Journal of Occupational Psychology, 49*(1), 11–28.

De Simone, S., Lampis, J., Lasio, D., Serri, F., Cicotto, G., & Putzu, D. (2014). Influences of work-family interface on job and life satisfaction. *Applied Research in Quality of Life, 9*(4), 831–861.

De Simone, S., Cicotto, G., & Lampis, J. (2016a). Occupational stress, job satisfaction and physical health in teachers. *Revue Européenne de Psychologie Appliquée/European Review of Applied Psychology, 66*(2), 65–77.

De Simone, S., Cicotto, G., Pinna, R., & Giustiniano, L. (2016b). Engaging public servants: Public service motivation, work engagement and work-related stress. *Management Decision, 54*(7), 1569–1594.

EU-OSHA – European Agency for Safety and Health at Work. (2014). *Calculating the cost of work-related stress and psychosocial risks*. Available at: https://osha.europa.eu/en/highlights/calculating-the-cost-of-work-relatedstress. Accessed 4 Aug 2015.

Goffee, R., & Jones, G. (1996). What holds the modern company together? *Harvard Business Review, 74*(6), 133.

Herzberg, F. (1959). *The motivation to work*. New York: Wiley.

Johnson, S., Cooper, C., Cartwright, S., Donald, I., Taylor, P., & Millet, C. (2005). The experience of work-related stress across occupations. *Journal of Managerial Psychology, 20*(2), 178–187.

Judge, T. A., Locke, E. A., Durham, C. C., & Kluger, A. N. (1998). Dispositional effects on job and life satisfaction: The role of core evaluations. *Journal of Applied Psychology, 83*(1), 17–34.

Kerr, R., McHugh, M., & McCrory, M. (2009). HSE management standards and stress-related work outcomes. *Occupational Medicine, 59*(8), 574–579.

Lance, C. E., Lautenschlager, G. J., Sloan, C. E., & Varca, P. E. (1989). A comparison between bottom-up, topdown, and bidirectional models of relationships between global and life facet satisfaction. *Journal of Personality, 57*, 601–624.

Locke, E. A. (1969). What is job satisfaction? *Organizational Behavior and Human Performance, 4*(4), 309–336.

Perry, J. L., & Hondeghem, A. (Eds.). (2008). *Motivation in public management: The call of public service*. Oxford: Oxford University Press.

Perry, J. L., & Wise, L. R. (1990). The motivational bases of public service. *Public Administration Review, 50*(3), 367–373.

Rainey, H. G. (1989). Public management: Recent research on the political context and managerial roles, structures, and behaviors. *Journal of Management, 15*(2), 229–250.

Rainey, H. G., & Steinbauer, P. (1999). Galloping elephants: Developing elements of a theory of effective government organizations. *Journal of Public Administration Research and Theory, 9*(1), 1–32.

Schaufeli, W. B., & Bakker, A. B. (2001). Werk en welbevinden: naar een positieve benadering in de Arbeids- en Gezondheidspsychologie [Work and well-being: Towards a positive occupational health psychology]. *Gedrag and Organisatie, 14*, 229–253.

Schaufeli, W. B., Salanova, M., González-Romá, V., & Bakker, A. B. (2002). The measurement of engagement and burnout: A two sample confirmatory factor analytic approach. *Journal of Happiness Studies, 3*(1), 71–92.

Schaufeli, W. B., & Bakker, A. B. (2004). Job demands, job resources, and their relationship with burnout and engagement: A multi-sample study. *Journal of Organizational Behavior, 25*(3), 293–315.

Spector, P. E. (1997). *Job satisfaction: Application, assessment, causes, and consequences*. Thousand Oaks: Sage.

Steel, B. S., & Warner, R. L. (1990). Job satisfaction among early labor force participants: Unexpected outcomes in public and private sector comparisons. *Review of Public Personnel Administration, 10*(3), 4–22.

Case 10: Managing Change and Employee Well-being in an Italian School: Psychosocial Training Intervention as a Possible Solution

S. De Simone, R. Pinna, and L. Giustiniano

Introduction

Over the last 20 years the Italian education system has lived an intense and tormented epoch of reforms and radical changes culminated in the introduction of school autonomy and decentralisation. Such institutional pressures have created, in the Italian school system, contradictory effects at an individual and organizational levels leading to employee resistance or indifference on one hand, and investment in training for developing coping strategies, on the other. The Italian school system comprises of teachers–the largest professional group of workers within public schools, who are also viewed as individual participants of change. Managing professionals and their professions is increasingly gaining momentum as organisations realize the importance of attracting and retaining key talent and human capital. Managing change in a professional setting such as in the case of school teachers, can be difficult as the nature of their profession affords them high autonomy, paradoxically, at the same time, there is a low level of observed cohesiveness amongst the teachers.

S. De Simone (✉)
Department of Pedagogy, Psychology, Philosophy, University of Cagliari, Cagliari, Italy

R. Pinna
Department of Economics and Management, University of Cagliari, Cagliari, Italy
e-mail: pinnar@unica.it

L. Giustiniano
Department of Business and Management, LUISS Guido Carli University, Rome, Italy
e-mail: lgiusti@luiss.it

© Springer Nature Singapore Pte Ltd. 2018
A. Malik (ed.), *Strategic Human Resource Management and Employment Relations*, Springer Texts in Business and Economics,
https://doi.org/10.1007/978-981-13-0399-9_24

The Italian Educational System

The education system in Italy is organised as follows:

- pre-primary school for children between 3 and 6 years of age;
- first cycle of education lasting 8 years, comprise of: primary education (six-10 years) and lower secondary school for children between 11 and 14 years
- second cycle of education offering two different pathways: State upper secondary school, for students from 14 to 19 years of age; three and four-year vocational training courses organized by the Regions; and higher education

The principal institutional bodies governing the Italian education system are: at national level, The Ministry of Education, University and Research (MIUR, Ministero dell'Istruzione, dell'Università e della ricerca) at regional level, the Regional School Authorities and the Regions; at local level, the Provinces, Municipalities and schools. In Italy, the responsibility of educational system general administration is the Ministry of Education, University and Research (MIUR). The MIUR is organised into three Departments:

- Department for the Education and Training System, responsible for the general organisation of the school system;
- Department for the Planning and Management of Human, Financial and Capital Resources, responsible for financial policy, procurement, administrative human resources in schools, and managing information systems;
- Department for Higher Education and Research, responsible for higher Education.

School education is organised at a decentralised level through the Regional School Offices, which operate at provincial level in Local Offices and support and advise schools on matters such as administrative and accounting procedures and the planning and innovation of the educational offers. The Local Offices, which operate at provincial level, are an internal division of the Regional School Office and have no autonomy. The Regions are responsible for the planning, management and provision of vocational education and training through recognised institutions. Through the State/Regions Conference, the Regions work closely with the Ministry of Education and the Ministry of Labour, which define the minimum national standards for the education system and the vocational education and training system. Local administration includes Provinces and municipalities have responsibilities in different areas and at different levels of the education system. Provinces are assigned specific functions for upper secondary education only. Municipalities, often representing small residential communities and restricted areas, are distributed throughout Italy and have their own or regionally or provincially delegated responsibilities for functions and services relating to pre-primary, primary and lower secondary schools.

Reforms in the Italian School's Institutional Environment

Since the year 2000, the Italian education system was significantly reformed with the aim to establish a new institutional structure opening new spaces of autonomy for educational institutes (Law n. 59/1997). They can now plan and implement interventions in education, training and instruction, adapting them to different contexts in line with the objectives of the National Education System. Each school draws up its own Educational Offer Plan (POF, Piano Offerta Formativa) which is the basic document setting out the cultural and planning identity of the school. It must be consistent with the general and educational objectives of the various kinds of study and specialisms set at national level and, at the same time, it must reflect cultural, social and economic requirements at local level. Schools are allowed to adopt flexi-hour timetables and activate personalized courses, create training programmes to answers the special needs of the territory, choose methods and instruments in line with the training/teaching opportunities on offer. Secondly, schools were strongly encouraged to build partnerships with other public and private stakeholders, in order to pursue their educational mission. Partnerships were explicitly identified as a potential channel through which to gain public or private extraresources and enrich the educational provision. In this perspective, the "School Autonomy Regulations" (Legislative Decree No. 275/99) strongly stressed the possibility for schools to constitute networks with other schools and public or private actors in order to pursue their educational aims. In order to create greater flexibility and customisation of training from 1 September 2010 a reform of the upper secondary schools was launched (DPR 81/2009; DPR 89/2009; MoU MPO-MIUR 2012). The spirit of the reform was in line with a search for greater clarity, and the aim of facilitating the choice of the course of study and to better address university education and the world of work. Among the strengths of the "new secondary education", there is definitely a closer link with universities and higher education, with the world of work (i.e., internships and project works) and with the territory (e.g., with the presence in technical and scientific committees, representatives of the business community in the area). Within this general framework, primary education plays a crucial role since learning is becoming increasingly more tied to the way the new generations learn through practical experience and cutting-edge practices and techniques with an enhanced use of laboratories, which make the school a centre of permanent innovation.

Schools are administered and managed by the school manager who is also the legal representative of the institution and responsible for its overall management, and the school manager acts autonomously in discharging his/her duties of direction, coordination, and deployment of human resources, in order to organize school activities efficiently and effectively. In carrying out the management and administrative duties, the school manager can delegate specific tasks to Teachers' Council. It formulates the educational offer plan (POF) in accordance with the general management and administration guidelines issued by the School. The Council submits proposals to the School Manager on the organization of class groups, teaching timetable and allocation of teachers to individual classes. The Council is also tasked with evaluating the general development of teaching staff and verify its effectiveness in line with the planned objectives and proposes, and wherever necessary, take appropriate measures to improve the educational activities by making decisions on teaching methods. Finally, the Council selects textbooks, after consulting the Inter-class Council and the Class Council, as well as teaching materials within the financial limits laid down by the District/School Council.

The Reform of the Educational System in Italy and the New Skills of Teachers

The Italian public schools have been asked to play a role much more complex than what they did in the past, as they are now called to help young people to design a way of life, with a sense of contributing to the training of future citizens. The reform of education systems is essential to achieving higher productivity and the supply of highly skilled workers. In this context, the Ministry has defined the knowledge and competences that all students are expected to have acquire on completion of their compulsory education. New curricula are now defined in National Guidelines that suggests the specific learning objectives, knowledge and skills that students are expected to acquire as the basis for building their competencies. The teachers need to help students to not only acquire *"the skills that are easiest to teach and easiest to test"* but more importantly, *ways of thinking (creativity, critical thinking, problem-solving, decision-making and learning); ways of working (communication and collaboration); tools for working (including information and communications technologies); and skills around citizenship, life and career and personal and social responsibility for success in modern democracies"* (OECD 2011).

The roles of teachers is changing, and so are the expectations from them. Teachers are now asked to teach in an increasingly multicultural classroom, integrate with students with special needs, implement use of ICT in effectively teaching students, engage in evaluation and accountability processes, and involve parents in school meetings. These changes have implied a critical redefinition of the teaching profession and the identification of new competences needed by teachers. A competence is described as 'a complex combination of knowledge, skills, understanding, values, attitudes and desire which lead to effective, embodied human action in the world, in a particular domain' (Deakin Crick 2008). The concept of competencies, in teaching, include having a combination of tacit and explicit knowledge, cognitive and practical skills, as well as dispositions such as motivation, beliefs, value orientations and emotions (Rychen and Salganik 2003). The new approach enables teachers to meet complex demands, by mobilising psychosocial resources in context, deploying them in a coherent way and it empowers the teachers to act professionally and appropriately in a given situation (Koster and Dengerink 2008). It also helps ensure teachers' undertaking of tasks effectively (achieving the desired outcome) and efficiently (optimizing resources and efforts).

The knowledge, skills and commitment of teachers, as well as the quality of school leadership, are of most important factors in achieving the high quality of educational outcomes. For this reason, it is essential for selecting and preparing teachers to fulfil their tasks.

General Changes

The changes in institutional setting and the definition of tasks and roles within the school context has been redesigned due to the profound changes that have involved the figure of the teacher. The advent of the computer age and the increasing demand for more important socio-educational, psychological, relational and management skills, for which the teacher has rarely received proper training and often remain confined to his or her initiative and its personal capacity, have certainly disturbed teachers' awareness of their professional skills. In addition, in many developed countries, the school environment has become increasingly multiethnic and multicultural. Furthermore, the numerous cultural exchanges enacted by globalisation, new policies for disability which have led to the inclusion of disabled pupils in the classes, the presence of an increasing number of single-parent families, and the constantly growing number of women being introduced into the workforce, have burdened teachers with more responsibility for the education of students. Finally, the relatively low salary, the lack of career opportunities, and the – often – difficult relationship with colleagues, school manager, students and their parents, are factors that seem to justify a situation of general dissatisfaction for the Italian school teachers (Ichino and Tabellini 2014).

Nature and Extent of Impacts

The radical changes that have affected the Italian school system in recent times have focused on creating a more flexible way of organising the work of teachers and the management of human resources in schools, thus, making it more individual and more result-oriented. Together with this, the efforts were addressed towards the achievement of positive effects on health issues in the workplace or, more generally, on well-being at work. For several years, psychology and occupational medicine have been dealing with diseases that may arise in the workplace and that may depend on the relationships between people. In particular, despite the large number of European documents dealing with the issue of the risks from work-related stress, the Italian legislation has delayed this matter and made it the subject of regulation as late as 2008, with the Legislative Decree No. 81/2008 – "The Code on Health and Safety Protection of Employees in the Workplace". More specifically, the Art. 28 reads: "The risk assessment should include […] all the risks to health and safety […] including those related to work related stress, according to the contents of the Europe Agreement of 8 October 2004, and those relating to workers in pregnant […] as well as those related to gender, age, origin from other countries […]" (Legislative Decree No. 81/2008, Art. 28).

The fact that the European and Italian national legislations have focused more and more on psychosocial factors is related to the clinical risks that medicine and psychology scholars have emphasised during the last decade. Accordingly, a higher level of social awareness has also pervaded the job design in all areas. Stress itself is not considered a disease, instead, it is a functional adaptation of organisms to their environment and its stressors. One of the most common definitions of stress speaks of adaptation syndrome for relatively nonspecific stressors of the stimuli (Selye 1956). The adaptive response to stimuli can to become dysfunctional – or what is commonly noted as distress or negative stress – because of the particular intensity of the stimuli, its duration, or the individual's personal dispositions. People, in fact, can withstand intense stress situations very well, provided such stress is reduced over time. Among the employment sectors most affected by work-related stress, education is identified in the literature as a sector that is increasingly becoming prone to high risk.

Different researches (Austin et al. 2005; Johnson et al. 2005; Pithers and Fogarty 1995) have found that the teaching profession is exposed to numerous stressors. A recent study has identified workload, perception of work environment, teachers' perceptions of the head teacher's and attitude towards change as typical work stressors in Italian teaching (De Simone et al. 2016). In Italy, as a result of the Legislative Decree No. 81/2008, all employers should have a specific policy on work-stress issues for the management of the health of their workers. Work stress can be managed effectively by applying risk management assessment tools, which could enlighten the possible risks that the work environment might generate, and the specific hazards it might to cause to employees.

The Case of Margherita School

The case presented here is that of an Italian school committed to managing change processes invoked by the Italian education system. These changes have led to school autonomy. Margherita primary school is a southern Italian typical school, headed by a School Manager, a young man, who graduated in science and this is his first experience as a school manager, responsible for managing human, financial and instrumental resources. The Teachers' Council is composed of eight members supporting the School Manager in some specific tasks, while the Teachers' College is composed of all teachers in service in the school and is responsible for the didactic-educational goals.

The Margherita school takes 126 teachers, predominantly women, and 500 students, about 6 to 10 years, divided into 32 classes (between first, second, third, fourth and fifth levels) in different sections. According to Legislative Decree No. 81/2008 that obliges all Italian employers to assess work-stress risk and to manage health risks of their workers, the School Manager turned to an external professional to measure the teachers' work-related stress risk. A medium-low level of risk was found and the School Manager decided to implement training intervention, as indicated in the Art. 36 of Legislative Decree 81, and to organise a lesson about work-related stress risk conducted by an external trainer and addressed to all school' teachers. At the end of the lesson, the Assessment

Questionnaire was given to the teachers in order to identify the specific training needs and subsequently design training. From data emerged that teachers complain about relational and communicative problems linked to ongoing change processes (see Exhibit 1).

Exhibit 1: Description of Process

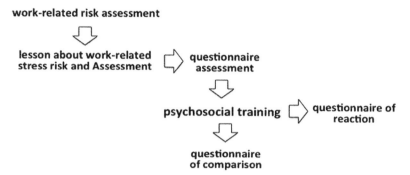

Based on the expressed needs, and taking into account the work-related stress theme, an intervention of psychosocial training was planned, performed and subsequently its effectiveness was evaluated through the administration of a Questionnaire of Reaction and a Questionnaire of Comparison. The training lasted 4 months and involved 92 volunteer teachers. Questionnaire of Reaction was administrated to all participants in the training at the end of each training module in order to measure the affective reactions and the utility judgments. The efficacy of the training was tested by a Questionnaire of Comparison, that was administered before the training program (test) and 2 months after the end of the training (re-test) also to a control group, composed of school teachers who did not attend the training (see Exhibit 2).

Exhibit 2: Assessment' Tools

Tools	Objects	When	Who
Questionnaire of assessment	Training needs	At the end of the lesson	All school teachers
Questionnaire of reaction	Reactions of training participants	At the end of each training module	Only training participants
Questionnaire of comparison	Subject dimensions: *Interpersonal strain* (ISW Scale, Borgogni et al. 2007, 2012) *Job satisfaction* (Brief Overall Job satisfaction measure II, Judge et al. 1998; De Simone et al. 2014) *Self-efficacy* (Bandura 1994, 2006)	Before the training (test) and after the end of the training (re-test)	All school teachers (*training group* and *control group*)

The Intervention

The intervention presented follows the model of psychosocial training, focused on social processes and based on practical activities and on experience useful to "help" the teachers to manage the change processes. According to a sociological learning approach, the psychosocial training is effective in producing change, when it responds to the training' needs and it focuses on social processes. According to this approach, learning is the process whereby knowledge is created through the transformation of experience (Kolb 1984). Learning is based on practical activities and on experience: learning occurs through the interaction with others and learners acquire new skills and knowledge when they see these as relevant to what they do in practice.

The psychosocial training intervention consisted of four training sessions, one behind the other, of 3 h each, involving on a voluntary basis the school' 92 teachers divided into groups of 20 participants. The training program addressed the following topics: work-related stress and coping strategies, group dynamics, effective communication, problem solving, and decision making. The sessions with the teachers were highly interactive, with open discussion, role playing, teamwork and case study (Cicotto et al. 2014; Kolb 1984; Putnam and Borko 2000; Wilson and Beard 2003) to involve the learners. The tests were administered to make teachers aware about coping strategies, communication style, ability to work in a team, and problem-solving ability (see Exhibit 3).

Exhibit 3: Psychosocial Training Program

Training sessions	Goals	Contents/ activities	Methods	Times	Assessment
Start up	To share the training program	Presentation of the training program and definition of objectives Administration of the questionnaire	Interactive lesson open discussion	Three hours	Questionnaire of comparison
Face the stress	To understand the stress and make the participants aware of their coping strategies	Definition of stress, antecedents, consequences Administration of two questionnaires, one on coping style and the other on problem solving	Interactive lesson tests administration open discussion teamwork	Three hours	Questionnaire of reaction

(continued)

Training sessions	Goals	Contents/activities	Methods	Times	Assessment
Communicate in group	To experience the communicative styles in group settings	The characteristics of the groups and the communicative styles Administration of two questionnaires, one on ability To teamwork and the other on communicative styles	Interactive lesson tests administration open discussion teamwork	Three hours	Questionnaire of reaction
Tackle the critical issues	Learn to analyse critical cases of school life and make appropriate decisions with the help of colleagues	The critical issues at school The decision-making process	Case study role playing teamwork	Three hours	Questionnaire of reaction

92 teachers, all women, participated in the training. The mean age was 45 years (SD = 7.3), the average tenure was 6.7 years (SD = 7.4) and the average employment seniority in teaching was 17 years (SD = 8.7). The absence of male teachers is not a surprise, since in Italy the majority of teachers are women (OECD 2012). An external trainer was chosen, a psychologist with experience in organizational training, in fact the psychosocial training programs require a psychological expertise. The trainer was well received by the teachers who participated with the involvement and motivation for the activities proposed, probably because in line with their needs. The teachers' feedback and his monitoring of the data (Questionnaire of Reaction) suggested a high degree of appreciation, a signal that the contents and methodologies have satisfied the participants' expectations. The participants' evaluation of what they learned was very positive, and this denotes that the goal to make the teachers aware of themselves and of their actions was achieved. The trainer said that during the course, the class group climate was collaborative and enthusiastic. The excellent interaction between teacher and class group favoured the learning process. These results underscore the utility, in the design phase, to include the needs expressed by the recipients of the training. The results of the Questionnaire of Comparison showed a decrease, slight but significant, in Interpersonal Strain, and an increase, slight but significant, in Self Efficacy, as expected, while there has been no change in job satisfaction, dimension not subject to training.

Exhibit 4: Effectiveness of Psychosocial Training

Psychological dimension measured	Definition	Outcomes of training
Self-efficacy	Beliefs relative to various activities and challenges at work	*Increased*
Job satisfaction	Overall feeling about the job	*Unchanged*
Interpersonal strain	Mental and emotional distance from others at work	*Decreased*

The case presented suggests the effectiveness of psychosocial training program as enabler of change management (see Exhibit 4). Teaching profession is exposed to numerous stressors and the teachers interviewed expressed a need to train on how to handle stress at school and what strategies to adopt to deal with difficulties. The teachers claim to have learned something useful for their working life evaluating positively the psychosocial training intervention. Teachers have expressed substantially high beliefs of human agency that regards acts performed intentionally to achieve particular results (Bandura 2001). The training has implemented self-efficacy beliefs and reduced interpersonal strain. Furthermore, teachers said they are more aware of their coping strategies, communicative styles in group settings and decision-making styles, skills that can be used to prevent stress and improve results in teaching with students.

Case Study Questions

Q1. Describe the nature of institutional changes in the Italian schooling system. How did these have an impact on the school in question?
Q2. Explain the importance of teacher' competences for the achievement of educational goals. What are the principal competences that the teachers of the school in question should possess to keep the pace with the ongoing changes?
Q3. Students may first discuss the nature of the stressors and then identify from a list the principal stressors for the teacher of the school in question.
Q4. Evaluate the effectiveness of the training intervention. Did it work? Why/why not?
Q5. Would you have done anything differently? Provide a rationale for your choices.

References

Austin, V., Shah, S., & Muncer, S. (2005). Teacher stress and coping strategies used to reduce stress. *Occupational Therapy International, 12*(2), 63–80.
Bandura, A. (1994). *Self efficacy*. Hoboken: John Wiley.
Bandura, A. (2001). Sociocognitive theory: An agentic perspective. *Annual Review of Psychology, 52*, 1–26.

Bandura, A. (2006). Guide for constructing self-efficacy scales. In F. Pajares & T. Urdan (Eds.), *Self-efficacy beliefs of adolescents* (pp. 307–337). Greenwich: Information Age Publishing.

Borgogni, L., Armandi, F., Amaducci, M., & Consiglio, C. (2007). Integrazione alla misura del job burnout: la scala di sovraccarico relazionale. *Giornale italiano di psicologia, 34*(3), 699–714.

Borgogni, L., Consiglio, C., Alessandri, G., & Schaufeli, W. B. (2012). "Don't throw the baby out with the bathwater!" Interpersonal strain at work and burnout. *European Journal of Work and Organizational Psychology, 21*(6), 875–898.

Cicotto, G., De Simone, S., Giustiniano, L., & Pinna, R. (2014). Psychosocial training: A case of self-efficacy improvement in an Italian school. *Journal of Change Management, 14*(4), 475–499.

Deakin Crick, R. (2008). Pedagogy for citizenship. In F. Oser & W. Veugelers (Eds.), *Getting involved: Global citizenship development and sources of moral values* (pp. 31–55). Rotterdam: Sense Publishers.

De Simone, S., Cicotto, G., & Lampis, J. (2016). Occupational stress, job satisfaction and physical health in teachers. *Revue Européenne de Psychologie Appliquée/European Review of Applied Psychology, 66*(2), 65–77.

De Simone, S., Lampis, J., Lasio, D., Serri, F., Cicotto, G., & Putzu, D. (2014). Influences of work-family interface on job and life satisfaction. *Applied Research in Quality of Life, 9*(4), 831–861.

Ichino, A., & Tabellini, G. (2014). Freeing the Italian school system, *Labour Economics*. Retreived June 1, 2014, from http://www.sciencedirect.com/science/article/pii/S0927537114000736, https://doi.org/https://doi.org/10.1016/j.labeco.2014.05.009

Johnson, S., Cooper, C., Cartwright, S., Donald, I., Taylor, P., & Millet, C. (2005). The experience of work related stress across occupations. *Journal of Managerial Psychology, 20*(2), 178–187.

Judge, T. A., Locke, E. A., Durham, C. C., & Kluger, A. N. (1998). Dispositional effects on job and life satisfaction: The role of core evaluations. *Journal of Applied Psychology, 83*, 17–34.

Kolb, G. A. (1984). *Experiental learning*. New Jersey: Prentice Hall.

Koster, B., & Dengerink, J. J. (2008). Professional standards for teacher educators: How to deal with complexity, ownership and function. Experiences from the Netherlands. *European Journal of Teacher Education, 31*(2), 135–149.

MoU MPO-MIUR. (2012). – *Memorandum of Understanding* – Ministero per le Pari Opportunità (Ministry for the Equal Opportunities)-Ministero dell'Istruzione e delle Ricerca (MIUR: Ministry of Education, University and Research): http://www.ricercainternazionale.miur.it/media/2977/protocollo-miur-dpo_eng.pdf

OECD. (2011). *Preparing teachers and developing school leaders for 21st century – lessons from around the world* (Background Report for the International Summit on the Teaching Profession)

OECD. (2012). *Education at a glance 2012: OECD indicators*. Paris: OECD Publishing. https://doi.org/10.1787/eag-2012-en.

Pithers, R. T., & Fogarty, G. J. (1995). Occupational stress among vocational teachers. *British Journal of Educational Psychology, 65*(1), 3–14.

Putnam, R. T., & Borko, H. (2000). What do new views of knowledge and thinking have to say about research on teacher learning? *Educational Researcher, 29*, 4–15.

Rychen, D. S., & Salganik, L. H. (2003). *Key competencies for a successful life and a well-functioning society*. Göttingen: Hogrefe & Huber.

Selye, H. (1956). *The stress of life*. New York: McGraw-Hill.

Wilson, J. P., & Beard, C. (2003). The learning combination lock: An experiential approach to learning design. *Journal of European Industrial Training, 27*, 88–97.

Case 11: Gender Inclusive Leadership for Innovation and Change: An HR Head's Reflections

Payyazhi Jayashree, Therese Sevaldsen, and Valerie Lindsay

Introduction

Therese Sevaldsen was the Head of Human Resources at Philips Middle East and Turkey, based in the regional headquarters in Dubai, UAE. Throughout her years at Philips, she had led major HR transformation projects. Her passion, dedication and expertise had placed her as an influential role model at Philips. She was known to be business oriented, passionate about people, and a strong advocate for women in leadership. She adopted a leadership style which was inclusive and based on trust. In addition, she tried to be an inspirational leader, providing clear direction, encouraging her team to challenge the status quo, and leading them to implement new innovative HR solutions that better served internal and external customers. Prior to her role at Phillips, Therese was the Head of HR for Schneider Electric in Dubai, a fortune 500 Company with 2000 employees across 14 countries, and 1 billion EUR revenue. Before this she had a number of business partner roles in Schneider Electric and other companies in the lighting and high tech industry. Therese was a mother of two school-aged boys. She enjoyed balancing her personal life with a very successful career. Activities like building Lego structures with her boys, and family Sci-Fi movie evenings gave her immense pleasure. She had just returned from a Best Practices session, held this morning at the Dubai Business Women's Council, as

---

P. Jayashree (✉)
University of Wollongong in Dubai, Dubai, UAE
e-mail: payyazhijayashree@uowdubai.ac.ae

T. Sevaldsen
Philips, Middle East and Turkey, Dubai, UAE
e-mail: therese.sevaldsen@philips.com

V. Lindsay
American University of Sharjah, Sharjah, UAE
e-mail: Vlindsay@aus.edu

© Springer Nature Singapore Pte Ltd. 2018
A. Malik (ed.), *Strategic Human Resource Management and Employment Relations*, Springer Texts in Business and Economics,
https://doi.org/10.1007/978-981-13-0399-9_25

part of the International Women's Day celebrationsfor 2017, in which her CEO had spoken about the various steps Philips was taking to ensure gender equality. It was only 2 days before, that Therese and her team at Philips MET had received news that they had won an award for being among the best places to work within the UAE. This accolade was further validation for the key value espoused by Philips, which had people at its core (Exhibit 1). Further, as the Performance highlights in 2015 indicated, 1.7 billion lives had been improved by Phillips Green Products alone, 0.88 billion lives by Phillips Care Products and 0.3 billion by Phillips wellbeing products (Philips Annual Report 2015, and Exhibit 2).

Exhibit 1: Phillips Company – Our People
We attract, inspire and develop exceptional people who share our passion to improve people's lives through meaningful innovation. They demonstrate this by being eager to win, taking ownership, and teaming up to excel – while always acting with integrity. Our people reflect our customers and markets. We develop our people to become outstanding leaders, to drive operational excellence, and to provide world-class competencies in our priority areas.

Exhibit 2: Philips Group – Lives Improved in Billions

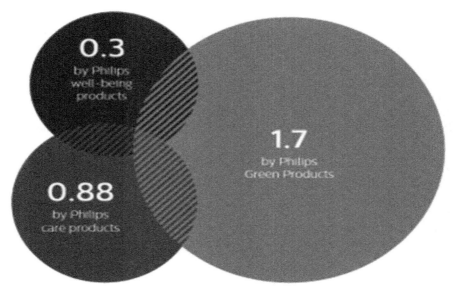

Source: Performance Highlights in 2015, Available url https://2015.annualreport.philips.com/#!/performance-highlights, Accessed 24-05-2017

About Philips Global

2017 was a milestone year for Phillips, which had completed 125 years in business, with a steadfast commitment to its core value of improving people's lives through innovation. Since its origins in 1891, Phillips had been a trailblazer in making lives easier, with its frame-breaking efforts towards producing a continuous flow of innovative products, from radio and television, to electric shavers. With this commitment to innovation and sustainability continuing into the twenty-first century, Philips had an array of technological break-throughs in diverse areas, such as sound and vision, women's health care and household accessories. Their fundamental focus on improving lives was driven by the core assumption that, through challenging the status quo and taking solution-centred, collaborative and innovative approaches, any problem could be resolved to improve and impact lives of the people.

A Strategic Approach to Creating Value

A holistic approach formed the hallmark of Philips' value creation process. Specifically, its mission **'to improve people's lives through meaningful innovation'** and the vision **'to make the world healthier and more sustainable through innovation'** was driven by identifying and understanding the specific challenges faced by the people (Exhibit 3). An integrated Philips Business System, comprising four key strategic elements then helped to deliver on the insights gained (Exhibit 4). Specifically, the Phillips Business System, developed to deliver sustained value, was driven by a clearly defined Group Strategy and resource allocation processes, to further facilitate strategy execution. Finally, the Core Capabilities, Assets and Positions (CAPs) which included the People, technological innovation, insights gained from customers over the years and the Brand value, were then leveraged and invested in, to foster Excellence and Sustainable Value for Customers.

Exhibit 3: Philips Company: How We Create Value Understanding and Meeting People's Needs

At Philips, our starting point is always to understand the specific challenges local people face – whether they be a hospital director, a nurse, a patient, a consumer, etc.

Having gained these deep insights, we then apply our outstanding innovation capabilities, strong brand, global footprint and talented and engaged people – often in value-adding partnerships – to deliver solutions that meet these needs and make the world healthier and more sustainable.

We measure the impact our solutions are having around the world with our independently verified Lives Improved model. We take a two-dimensional approach – social and ecological – to improving people's lives. Products and solutions that directly support the curative (care) or preventive (well-being) side of people's health, determine the contribution to the social dimension. The contribution to the ecological dimension is determined by means of our Green Product portfolio.

Our Business System.

To ensure that success is repeatable, i.e. that we create value for our stakeholder's time and time again and deliver on our mission and vision, we have adopted the Philips Business System. Having a single business system reduces complexity, increases speed and, crucially, allows us to spend more time with customers and driving improvement across the company.

Our Mission

To improve people's lives through meaningful innovation.

Our Vision

At Philips, we strive to make the world healthier and more sustainable through innovation. Our goal is to improve the lives of three billion people a year by 2025. We will be the best place to work for people who share our passion. Together we will deliver superior value for our customers and shareholders. Source: Available http://www.philips.com/a-w/about/company/our-strategy/how-we-create-value.html, Accessed 20-05-2017.

Exhibit 4: Philips Business System

Group Strategy
We manage our portfolio with clearly defined strategies and allocate resources to maximize value creation.
CAPs
We strengthen and leverage our core Capabilities, Assets and Positions as they create differential value: deep customer insight, technology innovation, our brand, global footprint, and our people.
Excellence
We are a learning organisation that applies common operating principles and practices to deliver to our customers with excellence.
Path to Value
We define and execute business plans that deliver sustainable results along a credible Path to Value.

Philips Middle East, Turkey and Africa

Philips Middle East, Turkey and Africa (Philips MET)has its Head Office located in Dubai, through which, all the activities in the Middle-East are coordinated. The core team of talented and diverse members were drawn from within the region and deployed across key portfolios of Health and Wellbeing, Lighting, Consumer Life-style and Sustainability. In alignment with Philips' focus on building strategic alliances to drive innovation, several key partnerships were formed within the region, one of which included a recent MOU signed with Dubai Municipality. This is to provide sustainable and innovative solutions to the city, in alignment with UAE's 2021 vision to be among the top countries in the world on the Global Innovation Index,[1] and in alignment with Phillips mission to 'improve people's lives with meaningful innovations' (Exhibit 3). Therese was conscious that one of the key contributors of Innovation was an organisational culture that celebrated diversity and inclusion. Phillips, with its rich legacy and commitment to improving people's lives, was in a much better position to achieve its goals of innovation, through building an organisational culture that fostered innovation.

People Strategy Aligned with Business Strategy

The Phillips Business System, which formed the core of the Philips value creation processes, is driven by six key capital inputs, these being human, intellectual, financial, manufacturing, natural and social (Exhibit 5). These are strategically aligned to drive innovation and value creation, in the short, medium and long term. Specifically, the People Strategy at Philips, is aligned with the Business Strategy, with a commitment to build six core competencies for driving innovation and transformation. It is worth noting that, with regard to human capital, the learning and development investments that were made in 2015 alone, amounted to EUR 50 million, with an employee engagement index of 71%. Philips' commitment to building a performance and innovation driven culture (where talent and inclusiveness are nurtured) was further strengthened with the introduction of the **Accelerate Roadmap** (Exhibit 6). This roadmap focussed on three key strategic action points, these being: first, to execute the Philips Business System and transforming the organisational culture to address underperformance, through a combined focus on top down economic interventions and bottom up organisational developmental approaches; second, 'expansion of global leadership positions'; and third, 'initiating new growth engines' through investments in new regions and geographies, while continuing to strengthen core businesses.

---

[1] Available http://www.mea.philips.com/a-w/about/news/archive/standard/news/2016/20160212_Philips_MoU_release.html, accessed 10th May, 2016.

Exhibit 5: Creating Value for Our Stakeholders

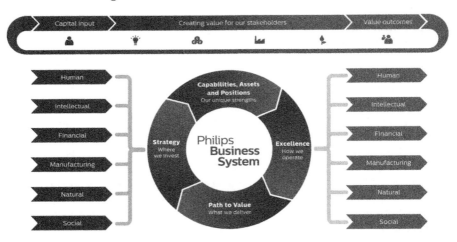

Exhibit 6: Accelerate Roadmap

Source: Phillips Annual Report, 2015, p.13. Available, https://2015.annualreport.philips.com/downloads/pdf/en/PhilipsFullAnnualReport2015_English.pdf, Accessed 30-05-2016

The Best Practices Session that Therese had attended this morning at the Dubai Business Women's Council had showcased success stories related to gender inclusive leadership for women, within corporates within the AME region. The insightful discussions at the session had made Therese increasingly conscious that Philips MET was operating in a unique environment as compared to the rest of the AME region, with more than 70% of the women within the region having completed tertiary education. Therese had listened intently when Global Gender Gap Report (2016) data was shared by the facilitator at the Forum; these data included the following: that United Arab Emirates (UAE) was ranked 32nd out of 144 countries (among the top Arab Middle East countries) with regard to investments in education of women, in alignment with UAE's goal to become among the top 25 countries in the world for gender equality by 2021. There had also been significant discussions in the session on the business case for having a diversity and inclusion strategy for fostering innovation. Since the core business of Philips was focussed on providing innovative solutions, it was imperative that diversity and inclusion was fostered. Therese reflected on her experiences at Philips, both as a woman leader and as an HR Director. From the available figures, 35% of Phillips employees (out of the 104,204 employees worldwide) were females. Therese's review of the workforce demographics at Philips MET revealed findings that exceeded the global average, with 43% of core MET members being female and 36% of the extended MET members being females in the UAE office. Even in the Kingdom of Saudi Arabia (KSA), with a country average of 4% females in employment, Philips had 6% female employees. Further, there were 55 nationalities in the MET, mainly in UAE and KSA, with Turkey employing predominantly local talent.

Reflecting on the current workforce, Therese knew how hard she had worked with her team to help the organisation get this far in terms of creating the pipeline, but she also knew there was always more that could be done to foster the core value of a people-centred approach. There was enough evidence that it was not so much about the numbers as it was about challenging psychosocial assumptions that could still tend to operate from a binary space (the blue and pink, or male and female binaries), if there were no mechanisms in place to challenge it. She thought about her conversation with her team just the previous week concerning performance management practices. She was advised to "tone down her communication style a little", as she was being perceived by some men not to display the warmth that is expected of the Head of HR. She wondered if this was a subconscious bias about how men and women are expected to behave. She reflected on this and felt that, if her view was correct, and if such bias could be experienced at her level, then she should be concerned about how her younger female colleagues would fare. In Therese's view, these women might not have the confidence or assertiveness to bring any perceived bias to the organisation's attention. She was committed to the core values at Philips and knew her responsibility as Head of HR involved ensuring that every voice was heard, and she thought of ways in which she could institutionalise processes to ensure that this happened. As she pondered on this, she called to mind her own childhood and early socialisation experiences that had helped her to build independence and confidence as a young girl.

Growing Up in Denmark and Gendered Scripts

Therese cast her mind back to her early years in Denmark, a society where, in school, she was never conscious about different roles and expectations of men and women. She grew up believing that societies were equal. She remembered a specific incident when she was running against the boys during a school athletics event. She was very good at running 100 meters, and when boys and girls were all racing against each other, she generally finished in second or third place. Just competing at her best and running towards the finishing line was what motivated her. And this, she sees now, removed the whole gender discussion. It was only about, 'do your best and get out there and compete'. In school, the children were all expected to participate, explore, criticize, ask questions, and share and openly discuss problems. It was always about, 'let's solve this issue together, and let the best ideas get to the table.' Therese learned, of course, that people had different strengths, but these did not come from gendered (pink and blue) scripts; rather they reflected people's individual uniqueness. She knew that her school system was the essence of who she was.

The Glass Ceiling

Over time, as Therese embarked on, and developed, her career, she saw the notorious glass ceiling in action. She also observed other women around her having the same experiences, and knew that not every woman was equipped to break through it. As she saw things, the glass ceiling consisted of the male network, the male club - a club that women often did not find the door to. Her own observations had shown her that men and women were different in the way they interacted and dealt with issues in the workplace. For example, she observed that when men were together, they generally kept things light and not emotional, and tended to take a more task-oriented approach to issues. She saw the women, on the other hand, as being more connected emotionally, and often thought about what might be influencing the issue; and before considering potential solutions, women usually assessed their implications for those who might be impacted.

Therese thought, that perhaps the different approach that women took came from the constant mental and emotional multi-tasking that many working women took for granted – in other words, the tendencyto always consider things from every angle, as well as their impacts on others. For example, women could seldom completely lose sight of their wide range of responsibilities, including as a mother, wife, daughter, sister, and friend in need, so often associated with their female roles in society. These roles were most apparent in the Arab Middle East context, where many women came from largely patriarchal societies, with strong family traditions setting clear expectations for girls and women. While Therese could definitely see these influences playing out among some of her female colleagues, she was also noticing that women in this region were becoming far less constrained by these factors, and were exercising a lot more independence. Her own organisation had made great strides in recognising the challenges faced by its women employees, but the potential for gender role stereotyping was still an overarching issue in Therese's mind.

Part of the glass ceiling problem, she thought, was that women did not have time to spend on networking, especially when it happened after work-hours. Networking led to visibility and, hence, to opportunities. She didn't think that men were being deliberately exclusive; it was not that they didn't want women in their club. Rather, it was more an outcome of a natural socialization that was happening on the golf course, or at the boating club, where women were just not present. Therese experienced this first-hand, at a previous employer, when she was the only woman from her management team invited to a boating trip. She remembered the conversation where the men in the management team had said, 'Ah, Therese, we are going out boating in the weekend. Do you want to come?' And I said, 'Uh, am I the only woman there? Because I'm not sure.' And they said, 'Yeah, because you're one of the boys.'

Given her upbringing, she would normally have just tried to fit in, regardless of whether these people were men or women. But, she didn't feel right about having that opportunity and the other two women from the management team being excluded. Both women were extremely competent, but they were not being given the chance to interact and share their insights, albeit in an informal setting. They simply were not perceived to fit into that particular male-dominated environment. This incident suggested to Therese that maybe this was the real problem and a key reason why women were prevented from reaching the upper echelons in organisations, especially where men dominated these positions.

Therese knew from her personal experience that women had to fight more to be heard. Whereas, for the men who had already bonded, it was easier for them to get their ideas through - they had to argue less in order to be heard. If a women had a different perspective, she would need to provide stronger, and more convincing arguments. Therese believed that this was a big and real issue encountered by women in the workplace every day. According to her own values and as per the core values at Philips, diversity in a team was to be encouraged and decisions should be taken on the basis of their merits. Gender should have nothing to do with the legitimacy of the arguments or decisions. She wondered again what needed to be done to create an environment where everyone had a fair chance. She went back to her reflection on her motivation to join Philips, and recalled that she was greatly influenced and encouraged by this organisation's focus on creativity and innovation through inclusive teamwork and collaboration.

Alignment with Core Values

Therese thought about how she had created room for herself in the Senior Management Team at Philips, in what was then a very masculine space. In her view, it had a lot to do with the alignment of her own and the organisation's core values. Therese knew that Phillips was in a space conducive to fostering values of gender parity and inclusiveness, because these values were at the core of its identity. First, Philips is in the business of selling products that were female friendly, including baby bottles and pacifiers, and innovative products such as the Philips Avent uGrow digital platform, an app to support new parents track their baby's developmental needs. Second, Philips was in the core business of health-care, which is about saving lives and making people healthier and longer-lived. Thus, the core value of the company was about 'caring' – a value that women could readily relate to, and which motivated many of the women in Philips to join the organisation. The organisation's clarity in its core values helped in recruiting people who shared the passion to improve people's lives.

Philips had for many years worked consciously at Headquarters to establish systems and processes in alignment with the Phillips vision and mission, making it possible for them to underpin everything the company did. Senior management was aware that companies that had more women in executive positions generally had a better bottom line. With a clear supporting business logic, the company had, over many years, worked hard to ensure that its recruitment mechanisms actively attracted women. Furthermore, Phillips was able to create leverage from the 50% of its customers who were women, by tapping into this customer voice inside the company. And that, Therese knew, had actually made a difference to the product range and marketing messages created for the female consumer group.

Since taking on the position of Head of HR (Middle East & Turkey), Therese had developed a number of initiatives to further promote opportunities for women in the organisation. She started by putting diversity and inclusion at top of all the agendas, with a particular focus on the recruitment and succession planning processes. Therese was supported by a global data-based approach to succession planning, which was created to identify the career stages to which female employees had progressed, and the female representation in the various positions in the company. With top management agreement, she campaigned for some measures – for example, an agreement was put in place for one of the three core businesses in the Middle East division to be led by women, aligning with the global practice in the organisation. The general mandate was that, out of every director that Phillips sourced for every position they had, where they were recruiting globally, one of the three final candidates had to be a woman. Therese was conscious that, while it was not always possible to get the right candidate, just having a mindset that was open to recruiting women was an important step in the right direction, and would lead to long-term benefits for the organisation.

Leadership Capacity Development to Address a Leaking Pipeline

Therese was only too aware that creating a pipeline of women for senior management roles was just one step. Real change happened when the organisational culture became fully inclusive – but cultural change takes time. She also realised that changing attitudes of both men and women were part of the cultural shift needed. At the same time, men in the organisation could make a difference by being aware of the need to give women an equal chance – in some cases, potentially contrary to their culturally embedded beliefs. It became evident to Therese quite quickly that, in this regional setting, both organisational culture and individual mindsets influenced by national culture and tradition were at play in shaping the environment. Changes at both levels were needed. While Philips was making very positive progress with such changes, as evidenced by the increased recruitment of women into management roles, and with increased retention, Therese was acutely aware as HR manager, that many of the women who were successful at the middle management level were not progressing to more senior levels, resulting in the women's pipeline becoming thinner at the senior levels. Global statistics showed that not all women step into the next level roles because of various constraints, including familial responsibilities; hence, the pyramid becomes unevenly thin at the top, while fatter at the bottom. Therese had not investigated the local trends, but assumed that they may be similar to those at the global level.

In order to investigate this issue further and to arrive at steps moving forward, a women's leadership committee was set up inside Phillips to investigate reasons preventing women from seeking roles at the senior managerial level. It was discovered that a key challenge was a lack of female networks, as Therese herself had noted earlier, and other key issues related to career management. This investigation had led to a request to the Phillips University to create a program for women in mid-level management positions to help them further their careers into senior leadership roles; this program was called Next Gen Women (Exhibit 7).

Exhibit 7: Next Gen Women Program at Philips MET
Program overview

Increasing the diversity of the workforce has been identified as a strategic priority for Philips to support our growth agenda. To that end, Philips has committed to increasing our share of women in Senior Management positions and above all, to strengthen the talent pipeline, as well as to creating a more inclusive workplace to fully leverage their diversity.

Our approach to achieving that ambition is two-fold:

We have a strong focus on building a more inclusive culture to make sure that everyone has equal opportunities to progress in Philips and feels valued, respected and able to contribute in full. This includes, for example, revising some of our processes to ensure that they support our ambitions and do not create unintended barriers to inclusion.

At the same time, we are taking action to support the development of our female talents through a leadership program specifically for women in Manager and Senior Manager positions. The idea for such a program came out of the focus groups conducted around the world by the Women's Leadership Council in 2013 – and it is closely aligned with external best practices.

The new NextGen Women Leaders Program addresses the most important challenges that women tend to encounter at this critical stage of their career: getting clarity on professional ambitions, understanding and leveraging personal strengths, building a persuasive personal brand and negotiating effectively.

The new leadership program is a 3-month learning journey for groups of 8–12 participants that begins with a one-hour kick-off call and is built around three classroom modules of 3 h each. Between modules, candidates are required to complete additional assignments and to support one other in "buddy groups".

A key focus of the program was on enabling the participants to understand their core motivations and key strengths, and, importantly, to develop a career plan.

Therese had been surprised to find that not a single woman out of the 30 who attended the program had created a plan for her career, either formally or informally. In fact, many of them did not know who to go to for guidance, and had no mentors or network of female colleagues. Few had analysed their main strengths, or figured out how to position themselves in the organisation. The participants learned to develop something called 'the elevator pitch', whereby a female colleague could give a confident review of own performance in just a few sentences. The women were asked to map out strengths, ambitions, purpose in life, passions and major achievements. This program enabled them to build an elevator speech, so that, at any point in time, they could make their achievements more visible and not be self-conscious about what they initially felt was bragging. Another feature that Therese thought was quite unique to the region was that there was a reticence on the part of women to not take credit individually, but to assign credit in collective terms, such as, 'We worked on that' and 'We did this'. The next step then was to create organisational awareness of the contributions that its' female employees made, and to ensure that they had sufficient visibility to be considered for the senior positions within the corporate hierarchy, next to themselves raising the hand when an opportunity came up.

Changes in Individual Career Strategy

A key learning from the Next Gen Women program was the awareness that many women needed to change their individual workplace strategies. Therese had heard her CEO saying this morning at the Best Practices Session that when men entered a new position, they were busy looking out for the next one; when women entered a new position, on the other hand, they were more focused on putting their head down and getting on with the new job and working to the best of their ability. How true, Therese thought, as she was invariably suggesting to women that, in addition to focussing on the things they were solving right now, they also must spend some time on planning towards the future, making their pitch, talking about their achievements, promoting themselves, and actively seeking those projects where they would get broader visibility. She smiled to herself as she recalled that the Program, the first of its kind in the region, was so impactful that men in the company also sought to be part of it.

While Therese had always demanded parity in pay in her own career (and always succeeded), one area where some disparity had remained was in job titles. Despite taking on some very senior positions, there had always been some resistance towards giving her position titles commensurate with the responsibilities. She had also noted that no such reticence occurred when male colleagues took on the same or similar roles. Her salary had never been inequitable, but this was because she had always negotiated strongly, going into the negotiation table, knowing that it could backfire – though she was prepared to take the risk. But she stuck to her steadfast approach to salary negotiation, because she strongly believed in fairness, and was driven by her fundamental philosophy of life, that we are all equal. Therese and her team subsequently set up training programs for women in negotiation techniques. In her own department, Therese had recruited very strong women, who had the confidence to be assertive when necessary. She coached her female colleagues to be familiar with market research on salaries, in order to build credibility around their own sense of worth to the organisation.

Therese strongly believed that the changes she was seeking for women in the workplace were the dual responsibility of their organization and the women themselves. The companies could create an environment enabling women to progress along a career path, and the women could respond by asserting their value to the company. Something that had worked at Phillips was identifying where employees were in the salary ranges and positions. Were they female or male, and what was their level of experience? How quickly did they reach that position and why? Were they relatively early in their career? Did they achieve rapid advancement, or was it more incremental? With this kind of information, it was possible for the HR Department to recommend the correct position and level for each person, thus ensuring that the company was better equipped to retain its valuable talent.

Organisational measures were one thing, but Therese knew that women must become more aware of their roles in the change process. She encouraged them to take steps towards greater self-promotion, making themselves visible and creating awareness around themselves in the work environment. They had to consciously ask questions of themselves, like: Where is it that I want to go? When do I want to go there? Do I have the support of my spouse, of my family? Is my network in order? And do I feel comfortable? What's my leadership style, and how can I use it to benefit the organisation?

Therese reflected on her own leadership style. Leading people came naturally to her and was very much a part of who she was. Throughout her childhood she was called "Bestyrerinden"(The Manager) and was seen as someone who would be comfortable taking charge. She remembered being told that, at 5 years of age, she was asked what she wanted to be when she grew up; she replied that she wanted to be the Managing Director. Therese had always enjoyed taking decisions, and liked giving directions and guidance when people sought her opinion. She also liked including everyone, listening to their needs and contributions, and then making decisions collectively. She was the first to acknowledge when she made wrong decisions, but she did not dwell on these, as she believed it was more important to keep moving forward. Having to balance work and family later in life had also taught her to work 'smartly' and efficiently, and these were characteristics that she carried through in her leadership roles as she counselled others to do the same.

The Double-Bind

Therese had also tried to create an open and inclusive spirit around her team by keeping things light-hearted and fun. Just yesterday morning she had asked her assistant to, 'please send someone to Starbucks – 'we all need coffee and cakes to celebrate a great week at work'. Celebration of small successes is something that she believed differentiated her from others. Her own supervisor positively acknowledged her authentic approach to leadership. She also was comfortable with showing her emotions, which had not always been appreciated among her senior male colleagues,. She remembered being told on a few occasions by her male colleagues 'to calm down', with the implication that this was not conducive to being "a good leader". Therese did not like that, she was expected to be assertive - but not too assertive; soft - but not too soft, when she believed in showing her authenticity. This was a 'double-bind' situation, where the expectations of her were contradictory and felt not respectful of the person she was. From these experiences, Therese realised that many women might frequently face the 'double-bind' situation at work, and had little support to help them deal with it.

But Therese had also had some profound and enlightening conversations with some of her male superiors over the course of her career. She remembered her most recent conversation with her boss, who had told her, 'you know what, don't change…. because it's authentic'. This reminded her of another conversation, one that she had with a professional coach in one of her first jobs, and which had opened her eyes as to what it meant to be a leader. Her coach helped her realise that it was essentially about being free of expectations that were limiting - such as, 'you are not supposed to do that.' She recalled him telling her to challenge others' expectations, as well as her own self-limiting assumptions, through asking - 'Why? Who said that? Who said, I'm not supposed to do that, or say that, or act like that?' She was so grateful for these conversations with her coach, her current supervisor and others who had influenced her so positively. As a result of these conversations Therese believed that a leader was someone who was able to remain authentic, while enabling those around them to find the best in themselves, without attempting to mould them into a template written by others. But organisational realities, as she realised herself, were not always so simple.

Balancing Work and Family

Therese knew that a key reason why many women had chosen to abandon their careers was due to the pressure of balancing work and family. Therese reflected upon her career and how she often found that men had a wife who supported the husband's career and managed the house, kids and friends in a way that would allow the man to focus on his career. She found that when women would dedicate a large amount of time on their career that it was not perceived as well by the society. Therese acknowledged that she could not have achieved this level of career growth, if she had not had a husband who was behind her and supporting her with the children and with all the chores that comes with running a household. Often her husband would ensure that she and the children had a social life by being the one arranging dinner parties, playdates etc. These sort of tasks were often associated with the women's tasks. Therese was very grateful for the support she had in her husband and the fact that he saw this as a team effort and challenged the society's belief why it is only the women who can do that, when men can also do that, next to their own career.

One of the reasons why Therese had joined Philips was because she was offered flexibility to balance work, with bringing up her young children. As further evidence of Phillip's commitment to providing a supportive work environment for women to balance work and family responsibilities, Philip's launched a nation-wide UAE initiative in December 2016 for its mother and childcare brand, Avent. This intitative enabled breast-feeding mothers to return to work by providing breast-pumping facilities at work. "At Philips AVENT, we believe that mothers, newborn babies and children represent the well-being of a society and its potential for the future. We are committed to supporting returning mothers and helping them to give their babies the best start in life. By launching the 'Mommy's Expressing Lounge' initiative we address challenges women face with breastfeeding, specifically fitting it in around work commitments. With research showing that 69% of women do not feel they have adequate or even existent breastfeeding facilities at work, the issue is a pressing one," said Vincenzo Ventricelli, Vice President Personal Health Philips Middle East & Turkey.[2] Therese had also taken ownership to create workplace flexibility herself. She was required to meet her goals, but had to learn to say 'no,' and, 'yes,' and delegate as much as possible. In this way, she was able to meet the dual demands of work and home. Even now, Therese was conscious that, because perceptions of productivity were still largely built on being visible at the workplace, her non- availability at work after 5 pm had the potential to impact her career growth, although this had not, in fact, happened. Given her own success in setting up a flexible work environment, she went on to actively encourage the adoption of flexi-time for parents in the organisation. Recently she encouraged one of her team members, who was struggling with balancing work and her family, to work 4 days a week and leave by 4 pm. Together, they agreed that, if she could still deliver what she had been delivering in a five-day work-week, then it did not matter how or where she accomplished this. Therese remained an advocate for flexibility around on-site working hours, and believed that senior leadership had an important role to play in communicating and embodying the importance of work-life balance for employee welfare, as well as sustained productivity.

Creating an Inclusive Culture – Next Steps

As she thought about next steps, Therese acknowledged that, while she had been fortunate in recognising and, for the most part, successfully challenging, the barriers to her own career development, not every woman had the same confidence or opportunity – especially in organisations that did not yet practice and celebrate equality for women. Therese felt proud of belonging to her current organisation, Philips, which

---

[2] Source: Available, http://www.mea.philips.com/aw/about/news/archive/standard/news/2016/20161207-philips-avent-launches-uae-initiative-to-support-breast-pumping-facilities-in-the-workplace.html, accessed 15th May, 2017.

had taken some significant steps to attract female talent and achieve parity in many of the levels of management. Therese now saw that it was time to take gender inclusiveness to the next level, and to try to bring about change systemically within the region and in alignment with Philip's existing Business Strategy. She knew this would require a major shift in mind-set among women (particularly with regard to any self-limiting assumptions), within organisations (where gender-biased practices are replaced by gender-sensitive opportunities), and among men (with respect to inclusiveness towards women). There was now substantial evidence that companies with more women in senior management positions outperformed companies with fewer women in such positions; therefore, Therese knew that recruitment and retention of women in senior roles must be a strategic imperative for organisations. As Therese stepped out of office for her next meeting, she thought about how she might chart out a strategy for institutionalising an organisational culture focused on the value of gender diversity and inclusiveness. Diversity and Inclusion was a key driver for Innovation and Philips had continued to increase its investments over the years, both in Green Innovation and other Innovation in their path towards excellence and value creation (Exhibit 8). Therese believed that Philips, with a strong scoreboard of equity achievements so far, would be a good place to initiate her ideas, since the company could go even further in embracing a cultural shift, and achieving its goals of improving people's lives in sustainable ways.

Exhibit 8: Research and Development Expenses 2011–2015

Philips Group
Research and development expenses in millions of EUR
2011 - 2015

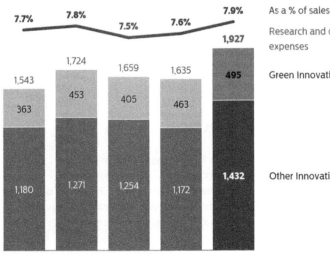

Case Study Questions

1. Research provides evidence that organisations that invest in Diversity and Inclusion are more innovative in the long run and outperform organisations that do not.
   - Critically evaluate the significance of Diversity and Inclusion (D&I) as a strategic imperative, with specific reference to the relevance of strategic alignment to achieve D& I goals at Philips.
   - What would be the key elements of this D&I Strategy?
2. Stereotype threat, "arises when one is in a situation or doing something for which a negative stereotype about one's group applies" (Steele 1997:614) and has the potential to lower the motivation and performance of the person who identifies with the group being stereotyped.
   - Critically evaluate, using relevant literature, the conditions that foster stereotype threat.
   - Discuss the strengths of the HR interventions that are already introduced by Phillips to build a gender-inclusive culture. Provide a clear direction for the specific talent-management strategies that Phillips can develop, to ensure that a pipeline is created, to strengthen gender diversity at multiple levels of the organisational hierarchy.
3. As stated in the case, Therese strongly believes that the changes she was seeking for women in the workplace, were the dual responsibility of organizations and women themselves.
   - Critically evaluate the significance of Leadership Capacity Development and proactively taking ownership for one's career, for women at the workplace, with specific reference to relevant literature and to the facts presented in the case.
4. The Social Justice case for D&I has been argued in strategic human resource management literature as having longer term impact in building an inclusive culture, as opposed to the Business Case, focussed on legislative compliance, which is considered to be short-term. Critically evaluate the above statement and discuss (in the context of the above case and relevant scholarly literature), the specific steps that can be taken by the Leadership team, to foster an inclusive culture focused on workplace diversity.

Acknowledgements The case study is written as part of a larger research project, led by Principal Investigator, Payyazhi Jayashree, University of Wollongong in Dubai (UOWD), in collaboration with Co-investigator, Valerie Lindsay, funded by United Arab Emirates National Research Foundation (NRF), University-Industry Research Collaboration Award (2015), and the key Industry partner, **Dubai Business Women Council (DBWC),** which 'established in 2002, under the umbrella of the Dubai Chamber of Commerce and Industry, is the official representative organization for business women, both professionals and entrepreneurs, in the Emirate of Dubai' (available, http://www.dbwc.ae/). The research focusses on examining workplace engagement and leadership among women in the UAE and the authors gratefully acknowledge the contribution of both DBWC and NRF towards this research.